Praise for *American Imam*

"Captivating and poignant, *American Imam* traces the formative influences and wildly shifting fortunes of esteemed Black American convert Taymullah Abdur-Rahman. From his encounters mentoring men who are 'warehoused like cattle' in American prisons to his stories of Harvard students navigating their ideological differences in the midst of wider American culture wars, Abdur-Rahman offers readers honest and perceptive commentary on the social issues of our time. This lively memoir is a welcome addition to the growing shelf of literature on Muslims in the United States. The book will be a provocative addition to the reading lists of interfaith book clubs, will hold appeal for students of religion who are weary of dredging through more stodgy texts, and will be a valuable resource for American Muslim community leaders across generations."

—**Celene Ibrahim**, PhD, author of *Women and Gender in the Qur'an*

"*American Imam: From Pop Stardom to Prison Abolition* promises to tell one story, that of the metamorphosis of Tyrone Sutton to Taymullah Abdur-Rahman. But Taymullah does so much more than that! In the telling of his story he invites his readers to take a long, hard look at their own lives, to go naked to the mirror and spend time in honest conversation with the person they see there; to ask difficult questions and stay there for the answers. Taymullah does this and, in so doing, models for us what is possible. And why is this necessary? Because we were not placed on this planet to live solitary lives. We were made to be in healthy relationship with others, especially those others who are less able to fend for themselves. Yes, this is one man's story, but it is also a call to action! Read, enjoy, get involved!"

—**Dr. Terrence J. Roberts**, one of the Little Rock Nine and author of *Lessons from Little Rock*

"Imam Taymullah Abdur-Rahman has managed to bridge the gap between hip-hop and faith in such a unique way that it is easy to digest. His life and experience exemplify the power in hip-hop culture beyond just music, using its influence for social justice and religion. This is a must-read for anyone who wants a peek into the birth of '80s/'90s street culture and the personalities it produced."

—**Clinton Sparks**, Grammy-nominated, multi-platinum music producer and songwriter

"What a blessing it is to read the stories, wisdom, love, and activism that emanate from this book. This text by Imam Taymullah 'Tay' Abdur-Rahman should be read by leaders in all social, political, educational, and religious sectors. And I'm not leaving out corporate and foundation leaders either. Why? We all have a stake in the future of our country, as well as of humanity. This book provides guidance and inspiration on how we must work together to ensure that *all* of us are thriving in support of one another."

—**Irvin L. Scott**, EdD, Harvard Graduate School of Education

"Imam Taymullah Abdur-Rahman's life journey has explored peaks and valleys most of us never see. Deeply rooted now in Islam, he has lived to reflect not only with great thinkers of the Islamic tradition but also with great writers of the civil rights movement. Abdur-Rahman's compelling stories, his engaging scholarship, and his rebounding life keep the reader hooked. He and these scholars invite us all to participate in keeping young people out of prison and in welcoming those leaving prison into loving, fruitful communities."

—**Eileen M. Daily**, JD, PhD, retired director of the Doctor
of Ministry in Transformational Leadership program,
Boston University School of Theology

"Imam Taymullah Abdur-Rahman has written a long-overdue call to action for Muslims living in the West. This memoir is an ode to the much-overlooked pioneering generation of Black Muslims who helped establish the Islamic norm in America. As a former prison chaplain myself, I thoroughly appreciate Abdur-Rahman's representation of system-affected Muslims and the social/emotional/economic struggles they face on a daily basis. Imam Taymullah's stories, descriptions, and references to sacred texts are some of the most profound missing pieces to the Islamic narrative in America. This is a must-read for anyone looking to raise their critical conscience."

—**Imam Abdul-Latif Sackor**, Masjid Al Kareem

American Imam

TAYMULLAH ABDUR-RAHMAN

AMERICAN IMAM

FROM POP STARDOM TO PRISON ABOLITION

Broadleaf Books
Minneapolis

AMERICAN IMAM
From Pop Stardom to Prison Abolition

Library of Congress Cataloging-in-Publication Data

Names: Abdur-Rahman, Taymullah, author.
Title: American imam : from pop stardom to prison abolition / Taymullah
    Abdur-Rahman.
Description: Minneapolis : Broadleaf Books, 2024.
Identifiers: LCCN 2023017277 (print) | LCCN 2023017278 (ebook) |
    ISBN 9781506489285 (hardcover) | ISBN 9781506489292 (ebook)
Subjects: LCSH: Abdur-Rahman, Taymullah. | Black Muslims--Biography. |
    African Americans--Biography.
Classification: LCC BP223.Z8 A63 2024 (print) | LCC BP223.Z8 (ebook) |
    DDC 297.8/7092 [B]--dc23/eng/20230509
LC record available at https://lccn.loc.gov/2023017277
LC ebook record available at https://lccn.loc.gov/2023017278

Cover design: Jarrhette Burke

Print ISBN: 978-1-5064-8928-5
eBook ISBN: 978-1-5064-8929-2

For the brothers at MCI–Shirley, Allah opens doors . . .

CONTENTS

ACKNOWLEDGMENTS

ALL MY PRAISE, gratitude, and worship are directed to Allah, who guided me out of the darkness of disbelief and then gave me many blessed opportunities to share my experiences, one of which is the book you hold in your hands today.

I pledge my loyalty and devotion to the Prophet Muhammad bin Abdullah, who sacrificed his life to deliver the message of Islam to the world and gave me an example of the ideal male identity to strive for.

As to what follows: I started writing this book in 2008. I didn't quite know why I felt compelled to put my life on paper because there wasn't anything extraordinary in my career or worship life up to that point.

However, in the succeeding decade extraordinary things did start to happen in my life from a faith-based perspective. I began to meet a variety of incredible people who held very different worldviews than mine. As a result, my intellectual positions began to shift. This succession of encounters lent me purpose and perspective.

Subsequently, I found myself writing about the illuminating moments I've spent with some of these individuals, and the lessons I've learned from our interactions. This volume is the result of those writings.

Allah saw fit to delay this book until I was able to begin the terrifying process of confronting my own childhood trauma and coming to terms with my social and religious blind spots. I'm truly grateful for that delay.

As a result, I want to thank all the wonderful people who've contributed to the content of my life and ultimately provided me with the basis for the subject matter of my book.

At Broadleaf Books: Adrienne Ingrum, thank you for giving me the opportunity to finally push my thoughts into the world. I'm grateful for your maverick spirit and willingness to take a chance on my story. Jarrod Harrison, you were my first point of contact. I knocked on so many other publishing doors, but they didn't know what to do with my story. Your initial commitment to help me is proof that when Black people are the gatekeepers, other unique voices have a shot at the spotlight. Your down-to-earth advice and editorial expertise on how to shape each chapter to convey a certain message was nothing short of brilliant. Thank you for literally understanding where I was coming from.

To my mother, Linda Ferriabough: The ethical framework you gave me as a child allowed me to stand up for myself and others as an adult. The ethos of this book comes from the spirit of courage you instilled in me. Thank you.

To my children and stepchildren—Khalil, Zorah, Tyrone, Atiyyah, Muhammad, Yahya, Azzaam, Musa, Zakariyya, Layla, and Hassan: Thank you for being so patient with all the days and nights that my work kept me away from you, on weekends or special occasions that I've missed. I hope you read this book and know how much it was subsidized by every one of you. To my adult children: I thank you for every piece of advice and encouragement you have offered me and for the emotional support you continue to give me concerning the choices I've made. To the young ones—Musa, Zak, Patayda, and Hassan: Thank you for running into my arms with unconditional love after a long difficult day in the world. This book is for you to read and learn everything you need to know about Islam and about your father. I couldn't have written it without the innocent love I draw on from the bond we have.

To my household: The sacrifices you've made so that I could seek Allah's pleasure through learning and teaching Islam and serving system-affected Muslims is more than I could ever ask. You put your life on hold so that I could spread the *Deen*. And you have always given me unfiltered advice about my mistakes even when it stung my ego. I am deeply grateful for all the late nights you stayed up with me encouraging me to keep pushing when I felt discouraged and out of hope. I pray my effort has been pleasing to you and you can forgive my shortcomings along the way. This book is the result of your wisdom and experience as much as it is mine. Thank you.

To my siblings—Wanda, Ali, Veronica, Ginene, and Tina: Thank you for loving on me and always lifting me up when I stumbled as a young man. This book is a culmination of the childhood we shared.

To my incarcerated brothers who are serious about becoming Restorative Muslims—Zakariya Ibrahim-Bush, Jaffar Silva, Ali Laporte, Abdul Malik Noel, Bilal Vasquez, Kuluwm Asar, Qadeer Carnes, Umar Delgado, Mikael Brawner, Dawood Miller, Abdul Qawi Hernandez, Abdullahi Huggins, and Abdul Haqq Richardson: Thank you for sharing your stories of tragedy and hope and for allowing me into your Islamic brotherhood. This book wouldn't have been possible without your advice, wisdom, and sacred contributions to my life and career.

To the Muslim leaders who have guided and/or supported me along the way—Imam Abdullah Faaruuq and Umm Sufia Hassan, Imam Taalib Mahdi, Imam Abdul Latif Sackor, Imam Samir Soulaiman, Imam Steven Shakir, Imam Omar Bassma, Imam Isa Najjar, Imam Ismail AbdurRashid, Sheikh Suheil Laher, Professor Ousmane Kane, Sheikh Abdul Badi Musawwir, Imam Suhaib Webb, Sheikh Hatem al-Haj, Umm Charlene Witherspoon, Ustaadh Mazin Abdel-Rahman, Dr. Alyaa Mohemad, Nezam Khan, Sheikh Hassan Dahir and Umm Sadiyo Farah, Demetrius "Abdul Latif" Dunston, Hanif Anwar, Larry "Ibrahim" Myers, Anthony "Ahmed" Thompson, Dr. Celene Ibrahim, Professor Kecia Ali, Salma Kazmi, Ahmed Bari, Nihad Nasim and Bushra Haque, Sheikh Issam Al Tawari, Abdul Alim Jami, Sheikh Taha Abdul Basser, Professor Daren Graves and Autumn Allen, Captain Haseeb Hosein, Malik Seals, Ernest Yasin "Bang," Munir Hassan and Farah Hassan,

Abdul Jalil Danfodio, Yusuf Bramble, Yusuff Hajara and Professor Leslie Grinner, Shahid Nawaz, Zahid Nawaz, Tyrone Malik Sutton Jr., Ustaadha Khalidah Bilal, Abadur Rahman, Shakir Abdullah, Tariq Ali, Dru "Akil" Akins, Ustaadha Najiba Akbar, Mohemad Khafif, Yusufi Vali, Sheikh Muhammad Ali-Salaam, Yusuf Red, Professor Ali Asani, Jordan "Neff" Romain, Ali Sutton Jr., Salahudin Ali-Salaam, Sheikh Abu Sufyan Zahid, Imam Yasir Fahmi, Imam Abdul Azeez Manning, Sheikh Muhammad ibn Abdul Muhsin Al-Tuwaijiri, Mufti Yusuf Mullan, Humayun Kabir, Professor Nouman Ashraf, Abrigal Forrester, Hamza Celso, Yusuf Akbar, Malik Horsley, Abdul Malik Bartelle, Rafi Kazi, Ustaadha Hala El Shamy, Ustaadh Ubaydullah Evans, Zaynab Blinker, the Islamic Center of Burlington, Aunty Judith Muhammad, and Dr. Ilyasah Shabazz: Your collective influence over my education, career, and life is what allowed me to gather enough sacred content to complete this book. Thank you.

To the gracious leaders who've never hesitated to assist me in my journey of growth and development—Deacon Bruce Nickerson, Dr. Robert Macy, Dr. Jennifer Howe Peace, Rabbi Or Rose, Reverend John Finley, Professor Eileen Daily, Brother Wilbur Brown, Brother Courtney Grey, Charlene Zuffante, Michelle Botus, Melanie Schanche, Dr. Terrence Roberts, Dr. Kermit Crawford, Dr. Natalie Cort, Rob Kirwin, Joel Olicker, Douglass "Red" Stevens, Lauren Moccia, Sam Ronson, Rabbi Arthur Green, Rabbi Sharon Cohen Anisfeld, Rabbi Allan Lehmann, Gordon Spencer, Rabbi Dan Judson, Reverend Elyse Nelson Winger, Peggy Stevens, Jimmy McNeil, Reverend Alexander Kern, Deacon "Tom" Anthony Thomas, Amy Belger, Marvette Neal, Dr. Daniel Osborn, Professor Harvey Cox, Fran Colletti, Jeremy Burton, Nahma "Nommi" Nadich, Jennifer Jones Clark, Dr. Peter Levine, Patti Keenan, Sheldon "Ty" Morgan, Mark Salafia, Jan Darsa, Princess Johnson, Marc Skvirsky, Dimitry Anselme, Jocelyn Stanton, Sunny Pai, Liz Vogel, Jody Snider, Elizabeth "Lizzy" Carroll, Kelly Horan, Bruce Gellerman, Anthony Brooks, Marshall W. Carter, Judi Bohn, Alan Epstein, Professor Irvin Scott, Alexia Prichard, Reverend Wayne

S. Daley, Jeremy Nesoff, Adam Strom, Milton Reynolds, Pastor Grant Magness, Reverend Nancy Taylor, Jaimie Roberts, Kathleen Patron, Shayok Chakraborty, Sherrice Lewis Thompson, Wanci Nana, Trevon Woodson, Big Chuck, Beverly Williams, Paris Alston, Clinton Sparks, Donnie Wahlberg, Stephen Goldstein, Bunny Rose, Jamie Thompson, Professor Irvin Scott, Corey Blakely, Maurice Starr, Stephen Starr, Maurice Starr Jr., Bobby Hill, Albie Montgomery and the Montgomery family, Larry Thomas, Richard McClain, Kay Standifer, Marlon Bouyer, Paschal Cockrill, Mika McNeil and the McNeil family, Deirdre Clayter, Dr. Debbie Brubaker, and the neighborhood of Roxbury, MA: I have come to each of you at different moments for different things. This book is an ode to our friendship. Thank you.

INTRODUCTION

Concord Prison

IT WAS A windy day in October of 2006, my first as Muslim chaplain for the Massachusetts Department of Correction. As I took the first exit off the rotary that connects Route 2 to Concord State Prison, the huge stone wall and barbed wire were all that separated 1,400 convicted felons from the rest of society. I parked my small, rusty blue Chevy in the factory-sized parking lot adjacent to the facility and peered through my windshield at the soaring watchtower. I had just finished a week of new employee training and I knew that inside the tower was a guard with binoculars and a rifle. His orders were to shoot any man trying to breech the stone fortress.

This was the place I would call work for the next six years. I had volunteered the previous year as a chaplain in other minimum-security prisons, but this was the real deal. I'd be expected to behave professionally while interacting with the inmate population, all while keeping myself safe. It was a large task for a rookie chaplain trying to gain the confidence of prison guards and inmates, some of whom I had known from my days running wild on the streets.

Concord Prison is an incongruous neighbor in an otherwise bucolic corner of Massachusetts, where the first cannon fire of the American Revolutionary War rang out in the Battles of Lexington and Concord. Evidence of war had long been swept away, supplanted now by sprawling trees and rolling green meadows, cozy middle-class homes—and opulent ones, too—and generic shopping plazas. Did the locals think about their proximity to murderers, thieves, and rapists? I did. I was very aware, and a bit cautious.

I was all too familiar with the criminal element. I was raised in Roxbury, a small ghetto section of Boston where drugs and violence had left all of us deeply affected during the 1980s and 1990s. I could've easily been on the other side of that foreboding concrete wall had it not been for a brief, albeit storied, career as a teen idol. I had been plucked out of a local rap talent show to lead a trio of preteen pop singers. By the time I was thirteen years old, my singing group, The Perfect Gentlemen, had a top ten pop hit on the Billboard Hot 100, "Ooh La La." I was touring the nation performing in stadiums by the time I turned fourteen, and by fifteen, I had appeared on the *Oprah Winfrey Show*—and run through tens of thousands of dollars, the kind of money I could never have imagined back home.

I was the youngest of six siblings. My father left when I was five years old, after my mom divorced him. We lived in an old, worn-down house that my mother inherited from her father, a postal worker who suffered a heart attack and died on his last day at work before his retirement, at fifty-nine. Thrust into the spotlight, taken on a whirlwind around the globe, by age sixteen, I was back in Roxbury broke, dejected, and delinquent. Life became a hurricane of trouble—fighting, drug dealing, and single fatherhood—after that.

Just as I had not seen fleeting stardom on the horizon, so I didn't see the spiritual awakening that I now realize was inevitable. Lost, at bottom, I accepted Islam in 1999, after almost ten years at loose ends. In short order, I married, had children, and settled down. On that day, my first day as a prison chaplain in 2006, I'd find myself chest to chest with some of my old buddies from Roxbury. I didn't know what would happen.

As I gathered my bag and double-checked my pockets, making sure they didn't contain anything the prison would consider to be contraband—a cell phone or something similar—I slammed my car door. I wore a long flowing Islamic shirt called a thobe. It reached just past my knees. The bottom of my pants didn't quite reach my ankles out of observance of an ascetic tradition of Islamic humility. I adjusted the kufi cap on my head, which signaled my status as a religious Muslim, and began the long walk down the trail that led to the prison entrance. The walk to that door had been a long time in the making.

Fifteen years prior, I held a gun out the window of my black BMW 325, aiming at one of my childhood friends, Jimmy Bleu. I'd grown up with Jimmy, a loudmouth who ran with the same guys I did before I left on my brief, meteoric music career. We'd fight, reconcile, fight again. I had seen Jimmy stab a friend of ours in the face with pencils, sending him to the hospital, when we were kids. His offense against me was nothing so violent, but I had vowed revenge.

One day, as I slowed my car to say hello to that old gang, Jimmy took out a supersoaker water gun and drenched my car, wetting me and my date just slightly through the window. I took my street credentials seriously then, and I was furious. I had to handle it, but not with my girl in the car. A few hours later, there I was, my .22 pointed straight at Jimmy. A bullet for water. I intended to blow him off his ten-speed bike. I was seventeen, and in my mind, he'd provoked it and he deserved what he got.

I aimed my gun at him and . . . "Click" "Click" "Click." My Derringer had jammed on me. Jimmy saw the determination on my face and heard those clicks. He flinched so hard he nearly fell off his bike. I was trying to shoot him right out of his seat. When I realized the gun wasn't going to shoot, I smiled and played it like a joke—"You're just a punk. You thought it was over for you. It's not even loaded." He gave a half-laugh and his boys laughed too. I drove off feeling better but not satisfied. I was going to have to settle it later.

Unfortunately for Jimmy, later would never come. He was stabbed to death a few weeks after that incident. He was only seventeen years old. I decided to pay my respects and attend his funeral. I looked at his baby face in the casket and felt bad that I tried to shoot him. The irony of it all came crashing down on me. I stared at his folded hands for a long time and noticed that his nails and cuticles were bitten and nibbled on. It reminded me that he was just a kid. I could've been the one who put him in that box. I said my so-longs and left feeling relieved that I had nothing to do with his death. From that moment on I knew that any decision I made would be permanent. I could always change my mind, but I couldn't change what I did. His death affected me deeply.

Who could've known that the young kid with the broken gun would today be walking into a prison, hired as a moral and spiritual authority? As I made my way past the beautifully groomed flower-lined pathway and into the prison entrance, the energy instantly changed from sunny and pleasant to cold and sterile.

"How can I help you?" the female officer said to me from the other side of the thick, dirty glass partition.

"Good morning, my name is Taymullah Abdur-Rahman and I'm the new Muslim chaplain." I must've had a big smile on my face. I was eager to get in there and change people's lives, or so I thought.

The officer was expecting me. She typed something into the computer, handed me a bronze chit with my name engraved on it and spelled wrong, and a set of prison keys I would use to open a very short list of chapel doors once inside the institution. In exchange I gave her my new state-issued prison ID to hold while I worked inside. The guards had to keep a strict tab on any "civilian" employees like me who were working behind the walls of the prison in case there was an emergency or hostage situation, so they would know exactly who to account for. As she placed my ID on a shelf with two dozen others, she pushed a big green button. Just then, the sound of giant, rusty chains mixed with old, corroded machinery began to ring loud in the prison lobby. The button she pushed was opening the first of ten cell doors to let me into the belly of Concord prison. If hell had a sound on earth, it seems to me it would be that unforgettable grind of rust, metal, and concrete rubbing together, struggling to let me in. I never got used to that sound.

When I entered the door there was a stern-faced officer with an army buzz cut. He wore an impeccably groomed blue uniform. He slipped on thin black gloves to search my possessions. As he instructed me to place my bag on the table, the old prison door coughed its way closed from behind me. After looking through the loose contents in my bag—a Qur'an, a few paperback books, and my lunch—he told me I was the "search of the day." In the prison system they don't perform a thorough body search of every single civilian employee. Evidently, they have a numbers system that alerts them when they must meet the quota of "search of the day." Later I would realize the "search of the day" fell on me about four times a week. That was fine. I knew my identity was disruptive and I also knew what I signed up for. State prisons are paramilitary organizations. Many of the guards were active-duty military veterans who'd been on numerous tours of Afghanistan and Iraq. They were battle-hardened and suspicious before they were friendly. It would take me years before I was able to make any real connections with any of them.

The guard politely asked me to step inside another smaller room. He said as professionally as he could, "Do you mind removing your shoes, your dress, and your belt?" I'm thinking, "Wait . . . my dress?" I was fresh from my travels in Saudi Arabia and had only been back in the States for a short while. I didn't think about how much I would stand out with my Islamic garb in this security-driven environment. I understood that the officer didn't have the language to recognize my religious attire as more than a dress. I obliged. He tipped my shoes upside down, asked me to show the bottoms of my feet, then opened my mouth with a popsicle stick and requested that I wiggle my tongue in case I was hiding a weapon or drugs underneath. As ridiculous as that may sound, I'd come to know how real it was for the many convicts I would soon be familiar with.

I gathered my things and walked out of the room and waited for the next gate of hell to slowly crack itself open. I would count ten full electronic doors before I was standing in the prison, boots-on-the-ground. When the last door opened, it was like walking into the twilight zone. The first thought that came to my mind was,

"So this is where all the strong Black men are!" Swarms of men of all ages, with white T-shirts and green state-issued pants, filed by me in small packs. I could've been in another dimension. The amount of clean, strong, healthy-looking men I saw stroll pass me by the dozens was dizzying. I pulled back my religious skullcap, scratched my head, and stood in awe, taking in the sight of this remarkable specimen of men being warehoused like cattle. It was like entering the savannah for the first time and seeing herds of beautiful buffalo, zebra, and elephants wander the land—breathtaking.

I must've looked out of place because just as I was gaining my composure, an Irish convict strolled by me and looked me up and down. With my Islamic thobe and my high-water pants, I must've been a sight for him. He stopped and yelled to his friend, commenting on my highwaters, "Hey Bobby, look at these downtown knickers!" He shook his head in amusement as they both laughed and kept walking. It was funny.

I had spent time in Saudi Arabia only for a short spell while completing my final exams for a distance-learning course I had been enrolled in, but during that period I had become enamored with the dress, the language, and the practice of my Arab brethren. For days and days, I sat in a large hotel conference room filled with American Muslims studying Islam from sunrise to midnight. We were visited by some of the greatest scholars in the Islamic world. It was there, in the holy cities of Mecca and Medina, that I began to appreciate the intricacies of the Islamic sciences which, for the most part, have been grossly misunderstood by the West and by Muslims themselves.

As guests of the state, we were given a very exclusive tour of the control center of the Masjid al-Haram, as well as access to the Kaabah and its machinations. We heard lectures by the Grand Mufti of Saudi Arabia, Sheikh Abdul-Aziz Al-Asheikh, as well as other great scholars. Toward the end of our exam period, our professors gave us three pieces of advice that have been the prime focus of my life from then until today.

The first item that was unanimously emphasized was to be relentless in seeking knowledge. Sheikh Wasiullah Abbass, a professor at Umm Al-Qura University and lecturer in the sacred mosque in Mecca said, "Knowledge cannot be gained by resting." And many of the others accentuated that the lifestyle of a seeker of divine knowledge is different from that of anyone else. He or she must be upright in his or her personal affairs at home as well as in public. He or she must always act with the best manners and character. He or she must dress in a dignified way and speak with magnanimity and articulation. And most of all, he or she must adopt a life of learning by using time wisely and not participating in too much food, drink, and play.

The second point that was underscored by all the scholars who visited us was moderation. Contrary to what many non-Muslims might assume about Islamic scholars, they highlighted that there should be gentleness and patience with all people, Muslim and non-Muslim. Sheikh Muhammad ibn Subayyal, one of the imams who led prayers at Masjid al-Haram, and a member of the Senior Council of Scholars, advised us, "Upon returning to America, you should adopt the humility of Muhammad who entered Mecca with his head low while riding a donkey."

The final virtue they encouraged was honesty to God. Every last one of them began their lessons by mentioning sincerity to the Lord. They admonished us that without sincerity all our worship and work for Islam and humanity would be without merit. This I had known, but hearing it from the mouths of such men drilled its significance into my chest. It has, indeed, been a struggle to remain honest to God and a task that I have failed miserably at many times. My journey has led me to this volume.

1

THE NEW PROPHETS

How Islam Became Hip-Hop's Religion

IN 1985, I was Tyrone Sutton, a ten-year-old, straight-A student at Agassiz Elementary School in Boston. There were six of us children being raised by a single mom in the heart of Roxbury. I was under the influence of my older brother Mel, who was eight years my senior. I was living the life of an Honor Roll elementary student by day and a rebel-rousing adult by night.

One of Mel's friends, Mizzy J, lived around the corner from us and he would throw huge basement parties for everyone in the neighborhood. Thugs from rival housing projects would show up to line the walls looking for trouble. There'd be dozens of girls from every shade of the brown rainbow, wearing tight Jordache jeans, colorful plastic jelly sandals, and giant 10k gold door-knocker earrings. The huge black industrial speakers sat in every corner of the basement, as tall as I was. The DJ blasted "La Di Da Di" by Doug E. Fresh or "Roxanne Roxanne" by UTFO, while yelling into a cheap hollow microphone, encouraging the crowd to scream, and say, "Hooooe!"

The party wouldn't even start until nine or ten on a Friday night. Nevertheless, my mother would entrust me to my brother and sisters, and we would walk two blocks to Mizzy J's basement.

Inside, the lights would be cut off and a strobe light illuminated the concrete floor with bright colors. By now I was used to the smell of marijuana, and it clouded the air heavily. The older teens in the party would hand me twelve-ounce glass bottles of Miller High Life beer, one after the other, and I guzzled them down. The taste wasn't appealing, but being a little guy in the center of a cloud of pot smoke, chugging down beers, brought me the attention I craved.

I would drink until I was in the middle of the floor drunk, dancing like a wild man with the crowd cheering me on, "Go Ty! Go Ty!" I loved it. My siblings would join in. They thought it was cute too. Then, after one too many beers, my oldest sister, Wanda, would take the bottle from me and laugh, "That's enough now." By the time we got home at two o'clock in the morning, my mother would be fast asleep. She had no idea what had gone on.

And this was the beginning of my undoing.

Once I became aware that I could live an alternate life without my mom having a clue, my life changed. Those moments of adolescence wherein my heart became indifferent to lying directly to her face; those were the times that I had indeed begun to curse myself, my life, and my well-being in general.

They say a worm who hasn't seen a human in many years thinks he's a dragon. Without a constant, positive father figure living in our house, this was me. This was my siblings. In fact, this was almost every kid in my neighborhood. We were worms pretending to be dragons because most of us didn't have access to an authentic masculine presence.

Islam teaches that, from birth to seven years of age, a male child needs the love and nurturing of his mother to develop a sense of compassion and to be emotionally present in relationships of all kinds. After that, from the age of seven to fourteen, the child should spend more time with his father, so that he can learn the ways of the world and the ethical framework for manhood. After fourteen, the father evolves into a disciplinarian and eventually lands at advisor by the time the boy reaches the age of maturity. If there were twelve of us in my childhood crew, nine didn't have fathers. We had Big Daddy Kane, Slick Rick, Public Enemy, and a host of ghetto superstars who filled a void of guidance for millions of Black and Brown youth in the 1980s.

Our fathers were strung out on crack, raging alcoholics, or in prison. We're far too familiar with how those blighted existences formed a sinister trifecta that obliterated the image of Black and Brown men all over the world, but what we don't appreciate enough is what that trifecta did to their children.

Studies link the adverse effect that parental incarceration has on children, highlighting that boys are more likely to exhibit externalized behavior problems (aggression, defiance, disobedience), while girls are more likely to display internalizing problems (depression, anxiety, withdrawal).

In one case a twelve-year-old girl, Davida, recalls watching her father beaten and arrested by the police and subsequently receiving prison time. She says, "I was upset by that. I started hanging out more, started drinking. I wasn't going to school. I was, like, 'Forget school.' In sixth grade I dropped out of school completely, I didn't want to go no more."

And why would Davida want to go to school? What once seemed like hope at the turn of the twentieth century had turned into disposability by the 1970s. Writer and activist Jonathan Kozol describes a visit to an inner-city school in 1988 that sounds all too familiar to me and my own personal experience with public school.

Beyond the inner doors a guard is seated. The lobby is long and narrow. The ceiling low. There are no windows. All the teachers that I see at first are middle-aged white women. The principal, who is also a white woman, tells me that the school's capacity is 900 but that there are 1,300 children there . . . I ask the principal where her children go to school. They are enrolled in private school, she says. Textbooks are scarce and children have to share their social studies books. . . . To make up for the building's lack of windows and the crowded feeling that results, the staff puts plants and fish tanks in the corridors. On the second floor I visit four classes taking place within another undivided space. The room has a low ceiling. File cabinets and movable blackboards give a small degree of isolation to each class. Again, there are no windows.

> *The library is a tiny, windowless and claustrophobic room. I
> count approximately 700 books. Seeing no reference books,
> I ask the teacher if encyclopedias and other reference books
> are kept in classrooms. "We don't have encyclopedias in
> classrooms," she replies. "That is for the suburbs."*

This was the reality I came of age in. My father was a deadbeat
dad and alcoholic. My mom was loving and nurturing, but she couldn't
possibly keep tabs on all six of her children. My middle school felt like
a state prison prep facility. It was always dark because the lighting in
the long narrow hallways was dingy yellow. The classrooms were dusty,
brown, and old. We had no cafeteria and the school had become a
bastion for gang recruitment where local thugs would sneak in through
the basement door to rob and assault students at will. All my teachers
were white women except for two Black females. Ironically, I never
had a Black male teacher in my entire public school tenure from first
through twelfth grade.

My neighborhood was just a wider space with the same issues. I
recall the first time I recognized the dangerous environment I lived in.
When I was eight, I went with Mel, who was just sixteen, to get some
Chinese food five minutes from our house. While we were waiting
for the food, three white men in jeans and baseball hats burst into the
takeout restaurant with their guns drawn, pointed specifically at my
brother. Everyone moved out of the way as the three men identified
themselves as Boston police officers.

They shouted for us to get up against the wall, spread our legs,
spread our arms, and lay the palms of our hands flat against the wall.
They had their guns pointed at my brother's ribs while I tried my best
to comply with their shouts. I doubt they were even addressing me, but
I was too afraid to do anything but obey.

They were searching my brother's pockets aggressively when
someone over their radios signaled that the suspect they were looking
for had been caught elsewhere. They thought my brother was a robbery

suspect because someone said it was a Black man with a black coat on and my brother had on a black jacket. The officers lowered their guns and said to one another, "Wrong guy," and left.

They didn't apologize. They didn't acknowledge that we were young kids, nor did they even look either of us in the eye to reassure us; to acknowledge our fear or our humanity. We were objects to them. Just little brown board-game pieces that they could move around, drag, shuffle, and even throw off the board if necessary. They shattered our lives that day in 1983. After that incident, whenever I heard a knock on the door at night I would hide behind my mother. I didn't think it was a burglar—I thought it was the police coming to kill me.

Plain-clothes detectives ran the streets of the ghetto like a gang in the 1980s and 1990s. We called them Blondies. Those white men with their blue jeans, big black guns, badges hanging on their necks like gold chains, glaring radios, cold blue-eyed glares, Irish clover tattoos on their forearms, and Red Sox baseball caps became me and my friends' worst fear. They were known to pull up on any street corner, jump out five-deep with guns drawn and rough young kids up. They'd make them sit on the sidewalk for an hour while they checked the bushes and behind buildings for guns and drugs.

We feared being "kidnapped" by them, which meant they would put you in the back of another unmarked vehicle and take you down to the police station to do whatever they chose. I know too many boys who were "kidnapped" in that manner who were totally good kids, but later took to the streets after traumatic episodes like that. By the age of twelve or so, you say "F-it, if it's my time to die then it's my time, but I'm not going to allow anyone to bully me anymore without a fight."

Hip-hop music and culture began under these strenuous circumstances for Black and Brown boys all over the country. Hip-hop wasn't just rap, it was a conduit for youth to use poetry, graffiti, and breakdancing to express the angst of being Black and powerless: powerless in the local Chinese food shop where they're accosted by Blondies; powerless when walking to the grocery store to get milk for their mom and they're stopped, slammed to the ground, and frisked for no apparent reason; powerless as they watch all their household amenities slowly disappear—lights, heat, and then groceries—because their single mothers work ten-hour shifts but still can't manage to make ends meet. All these scenarios have happened to me or to beloved friends and family and made a perfect storm for hip-hop.

So, when hip-hop produced superheroes like LL Cool J and Run DMC, they became mythical figures not unlike Achilles, Hector, and the warriors of the *Iliad* for young Black and Brown people. We'd all sit around on the steps in 1987, bouncing the basketball, and someone would say something like, "I heard LL Cool J beat Run (from Run DMC) in a rap battle but then DMC heard about it and came to jump in and crushed LL!" They were folklore personalities to us, truly larger than life.

With their black leather jackets, godfather hats, Fila, Troop, and Adidas sweat suits, and big four-finger rings and rope chains, they seemed to be above the law. Beyond public policy. They were from the same type of ghettos as us, but they seemed otherworldly. When they mentioned Queens, the Bronx, and Brooklyn in their songs, they might as well have lived in Godric's Hollow or Middle Earth. We had no idea what those places were like. Only the local drug dealers, who would take the four-hour drive to New York in the fall to buy sheepskin and goosedown coats, knew what those places were like back then. They would come back and tell us about seeing Doug E. Fresh on Delancey Street or shaking hands with Chuck D in Harlem. We were in total and complete awe of rap celebrities.

Before the likes of Run DMC and their Adidas trend, LL and his Kangol gear, we ordered our sneakers from the Sears and Roebuck catalog that came once a year and was as thick as the public phone books that were delivered to your doorstep back then. Almost overnight in 1985, the entire neighborhood went from wearing standard canvass Chuck Taylor Converse from the Sears catalog, to rocking shell-top Adidas, Stan Smiths, Suede Pumas with the fat laces, Levi's jeans with the jacket to match, Cazal glasses, Kangol hats, and gold chains. We adopted their style because hip-hop empowered us. It accomplished in the span of a few months what the civil rights movement had not managed to do in the fifteen years since the murder of King; it got us talking about being self-possessed, independent, and God-conscious.

Paul Tillich, the twentieth-century Lutheran philosopher wrote that "Faith as ultimate concern is an act of the total personality. It happens in the center of the personal life and includes all its elements." Tillich argues that all faith is the same, it just takes different forms. What these young celebrities were doing was instilling hope in us. They were allowing us a version of faith that could be integrated into our whole lives, and not isolated to a cold, sterile theology preached at us on Sunday mornings.

For many in Generation X, and those after, Christianity is somewhat suspect because it has become infamous and even antagonistic to the Black narrative. From the time the first slaves entered the shores of Portugal, America, Jamaica, and other lands, their experience with Christianity has been chalked by tumult and struggle. For many of them, it was a religion of submissiveness, tolerance of the slave master's cruelty, and patience for otherworldly salvation while living in the midst of an earthly hell.

Marie Augusta Neal writes:

> *Religious exhortation of people to raise their minds and*
> *hearts above the bread-and-butter concerns and to focus*
> *on the aspirations of the soul and on promises of salvation*
> *beyond the frustrations of human finitude and the promotion*
> *of a purely spiritual salvation—such emphasis should be*
> *recognized as the class-conditioned values of the affluent for*
> *whom the physical subsistence was no longer problematic.*

Black slaves were being taught to ignore their social condition and focus on heaven. But even back then many Black American slaves began to utilize early versions of what has come to be known as Black Liberation Theology.

John Boles gives detail to this phenomenon:

> *Black slaves found hope in gathering secretly in the woods, baptizing one another, licensing their own black ministers, referring to one another as brother and sister, praying for freedom, interpreting the Bible through song and being in community.*

Wash Wilson, a former slave, gives this description of their clandestine rendezvous:

> *When de niggers go round singin' "Steal Away to Jesus," dat mean dere gwine be a 'ligious meetin' dat night. De masters . . . didn't like dem 'ligious meetin's so us natcherly slips off at night, down in de bottoms or somewhere. Sometimes us sing and pray all night.*

Through this eye-witness testimony, what emerges is the idea that early Blacks believed that they could liberate themselves, if not physically, then certainly ideologically through belief in God and with the use of song, and by reinterpreting Scripture to suit their own social condition, and not the whims of white slave owners.

Hundreds of years after bondage, and still with no proof of heaven's existence beyond the stale hope of our grandparents, there was a gradual loss of hope triggered by decades of structural bigotry stemming from the remnants of colonialism. Thousands of Black children like me experienced those remnants in the dozens of burning rubber tires that littered abandoned lots in ghettos across the country. They saw those remnants in the boarded-up buildings that lined every block of their neighborhood. They felt them in their stomachs via the hunger pangs that a single mother's weekly pay couldn't satiate. By the 1980s, hope was gone, except for the raggedy churches situated in low-income neighborhoods across the country that no longer represented success, but *failure*.

Hip-hop established a renewed and different kind of Black liberation theological paradigm, albeit without the overt references to God. After the assassinations of Medgar, John and later Robert Kennedy, Malcolm, and Martin in the 1960s, the extrajudicial murders of the Black Panther Party by Oakland Police in the 1970s, Reaganomics' social effect on afterschool programs and welfare benefits in the early 1980s, these young Black rappers were giving us faith again. And that was enough of a catalyst to get us to say, do, or believe almost anything they promoted.

The rappers of the 1980s were not only revolutionaries, but they were also prophets and preachers to us. They rose from the dead as the voice of wild men in the wilderness, delivered a powerful message and gave life to our hearts. Sure, the form was different, but the content was the same: self-determination, anti-establishment, Black power, and hyper-masculinity.

They were a fresh dose of adrenaline to us children deeply wounded by Republican policies and police brutality. These hip-hop personalities defined the terms of success, failure, and what our collective priorities should be. It didn't matter that they didn't mention piety, righteousness, or even God directly, this genre had become our statement to the world about God, life, death, success, and failure, and these young men were our messengers.

So, when Big Daddy Kane rapped: "Take him and mold and make him, hold up the peace sign, As Salaamu Alaikum," in 1988, Islam became hip-hop's religion and Black and Brown youth all over the country began to identify with Islamic culture.

We knew the Islamic greeting of *As-Salaamu alaikum* meant, "Peace be upon you," because the men from the Nation of Islam who sold our mothers bean pies and *Final Call* newspapers in the streets greeted us with it almost every day. Ironically, hip-hop culture and music in general is frowned upon by Black conservative religious clergy and adherents, many of whom are old-school civil rights advocates who "marched with King," or "attended Malcolm's speeches" and view hip-hop as a bastardized art form born from derelict, immoral youth.

But what they fail to understand is that movements shift. And youth lead that shift regardless of what the sober-minded adults from the former movement think.

The youthful rappers of New York City had witnessed the birth of the Nation of Islam in the 1960s and 1970s; a militant, somewhat distorted version of orthodox Islam but nevertheless one that took the form and social context of the people into consideration.

The Nation of Islam was founded by Elijah Muhammad in Chicago in 1935. He was a Black nationalist separatist who used young fiery ministers like Malcolm X to preach an Islam branded as the natural religion for the Black man. Elijah's version of Islam included spaceships, an ancient scientist who crafted white people as his most diabolical creation six thousand years ago, and God's total annihilation of America for its mistreatment of the Black race. It was effective not because the theology was correct (because it was not) but because the strategies they implemented for drug addiction, prostitution intervention, and independent Black economic growth worked. Their social efforts reinforced their erroneous theology and made it easy for struggling Black people to accept, because they were being cured of substance abuse and seeing the fruits of Black wealth literacy.

Not much later, Clarence 13X, who was a former member of the Nation of Islam, defected and started his own group, the Five Percenters. Clarence 13X was a street intellectual and much more in touch with the lower-class community than the Nation of Islam had once been. His Five Percenter offshoot espoused that 85 percent of the world was deaf, dumb, and blind, 10 percent knew the truth but used it to manipulate the masses, and 5 percent were woke and enlightened. The Five Percenters had no orthodox Islamic theology, but instead took the vocabulary of Islam from the mosques to the street corners of the East Coast, addressing gang leaders, drug pushers, and pimps directly. Clarence 13X insisted that gambling, marijuana, and alcohol in moderation were permissible because, as Black men, they were "gods of their own cipher" and not to be controlled by any outside entity.

The white establishment had been privy to the influence that Clarence began to have on wayward youth who were homeless, looking for guidance, directionless. After initially embracing him as a youth intervention specialist, the establishment had him committed to a mental institute. It was too late. Their attempt to stigmatize him as mentally deranged only affirmed to Black and Brown youth that Clarence 13X was in fact preaching truth. It wasn't long before his influence showed up in hip-hop in the 1980s and 1990s, with groups like Brand Nubian, Leaders of the New School, and Wu Tang Clan praising him and his teachings. They, in turn, made it cool to believe in "Allah."

Even though those iterations were a molested version of mainstream Islam, they were accessible. In Nation of Islam theology, Allah was made to be a Black man who secretly came to the ghetto to save us from the devilish white man. In the Five-Percent version, all Black people were individual demi-gods: little Allahs.

For young people trapped in a cycle of racial bureaucracy and the web of a corrupt criminal justice system, witnessing their mothers being exploited by white employers and their fathers imprisoned, if this wasn't authentic revelation, it was close enough to our reality to hold sway over our value system.

We no longer had to be held hostage in church, staring at creepy paintings of a white depiction of Jesus. We no longer had to submit to the construct of a frail, stringy-haired, mostly naked Caucasian man dangling from those ominous, scary bronze statues we were traumatized by in our youth.

Now Big Daddy Kane believed in God. And God's name was Allah. And Allah loved Black and Brown people and specifically embraced Black and Brown youth. And Allah gave Black and Brown youth hip-hop as a vehicle for self-expression and wealth acquisition. And best of all, Allah loved style and flash.

Big Daddy Kane wore fly silk suits and had a high-top fade. He looked like us. When Chuck D rapped about being a "follower of Farrakhan" and praising the Fruit of Islam, the Nation of Islam's self-defense branch, we were open to the idea that Islam could possibly improve our condition, because Christianity in the Black community had become an old, saggy, hunched over, grouchy thing that grandma and old aunties and uncles did on the weekend.

Ironically, in these same formative years, I was a beneficiary of the social gospel through the Martin Family: three young, Black, Christian brothers from a strong local Christian family, who took a dozen of us young Black boys under their wing in the summer of 1988 and saved our lives.

The Martin family lived in a makeshift church at the top of the street I grew up on in the heart of Roxbury. The Martins' parents were both pastors and they held church service almost every day of the week. The Martin brothers, inspired by their faith and witnessing the poverty and violence in our neighborhood, founded Elite Cleaning Service in 1988. They obtained a contract with Fenway Park to clean the VIP booths the week after Red Sox games.

The brothers hired what seemed to be the entire neighborhood of us boys, aged twelve to sixteen, to clean the VIP booths in Fenway. I distinctly remember sweeping bleachers, picking up trash, and dumping tons of food into trash bins for several hours a day. I was paid $125.00 a week. At the age of twelve, it was the largest amount of money I had ever seen, and an inspiration to keep me distracted from the streets.

I only worked one summer for the Martins, but I never forgot the feeling of comradery, service, and accomplishment that I felt when the Martins would take all us boys out to dinner after work. They were true students of the social gospel and, up to this day, some of the most transformative leaders I have ever encountered.

Although apparently based on financial independence, I would call their transformational leadership style Public Love. Based on their intervention with twelve young Black boys, they managed to create an environment where it was okay to lift one another up, to complement each other, to embrace one another and smile. The Martins' leadership style gave us license to joke together, work side by side, and learn life lessons that would guide us through tough times to come. It was the embodiment of the social gospel in an urban context. And I imagine they had hoped to bring some of us to their faith. However, their effort, as noble as it was, couldn't compete with the tidal wave of hip-hop that had cast a spell on all of us that summer.

By 1990, to say you were Muslim or a Five Percenter was to announce that you were cool, rebellious, smart, and faithful all at once. Although it had been Dr. Martin Luther King Jr. and the Southern Christian Leadership Conference that pushed Black and Brown equality into the late twentieth century using their blood sweat and tears, and although it was the local Elliot church in Roxbury that took us unruly boys under their mentorship through afterschool programs and basketball camps in the 1980s, it was the Christian Right who controlled the public narrative, which was often utilized as a way to dehumanize people of color and reinforce scary stereotypes.

In an indirect response to this type of faith-based manipulation, Howard Thurman observed, "Too often the price exacted by society for security and respectability is that the Christian movement in its formal expression must be on the side of the strong against the weak."

For us hip-hop heads, Christianity had become too normalized. It was *the* religion of America. And, for us, America was a colonizing, supremacist regime made up of evil white men bent on destroying the Black family. As for the Black Church and what it came to represent, Islam had the better marketing and branding in the 'hood by then. The Black Church had become a refuge for "old heads" and middle-class Black folk.

Islam had Eric B. and Rakim, arguably the most important rap group in the canon of hip-hop. Their debut in 1986 came like a firestorm. They were intelligent gangsters from Long Island, New York, who ran with a strong Brooklyn crew. When we learned that the rapper of the duo, Rakim, chose *Allah* as his last name after being influenced by the Five Percenters, our respect for him increased tenfold. He refused to use profanity in his lyrics and insisted that he didn't eat pork but instead preferred fish. For people like us, living in what are now known as "food deserts," and with no information about healthy diet, these concepts were revolutionary to us. He was our first true scholar of rap.

Then came Brand Nubian, who were also Five Percenters. Their entire 1993 debut album, *In God We Trust*, was an homage to their faith, with song titles such as "Allah U Akbar," "The Meaning of 5%," and "Allah and Justice."

The Native Tongues were a rap collective that debuted in the late 1980s/early 1990s. The unit consisted of Afrcocentric/Islamic rappers such as the Jungle Brothers, A Tribe Called Quest, Queen Latifah, and De La Soul. They weren't all Muslim, but they certainly weren't Christian.

The first hip-hop group to embrace an almost entirely African/Islamic image was X Clan. They were extremely Afrocentric and you didn't know if they were Muslims, Five Percenters, or even Christian because they often quoted the Qur'an and the Bible. But when their lead rapper Brother J rapped, "Abracadabra, Allah baby, professor, All hail Funkin' Lesson," in 1990, their entire portrayal became a shining endorsement for Islam.

Nore, the famous Drink Champs podcast host, then known as Noreaga, was part of the street group Capone and Noreaga. He made one of the most iconic endorsements for Islam when, in 1997, he rapped, "You ain't ready yet, slow down and recollect, Stay in the car, Astaghfiru'lah bodyset, Yo, Allahu Akbar, look pa, now I'm set."

Who knows what he meant by this lyrically enigmatic verse? I certainly didn't. But it didn't matter. I heard him say *astaghfiru'lah*, which I knew meant "God forgive me," because my middle school art teacher, Ms. Bilal, who was Muslim, taught us children some Arabic sayings. This one line influenced me and my friends tremendously. Noreaga was from New York. He was the same age as me and my friends. The New York swagger of loosely tied Timberland boots, army jackets, and gold teeth were all the rage for us young men in the 'hood in the early 1990s. He single-handedly helped me embrace Islam as a legitimate path to faith.

Through groups like X Clan, and Boogie Down Productions who promoted Black nationalism, and Public Enemy who rapped about identity politics, that fragile generation of hip-hoppers became enlightened to the fact that an important component of social salvation is knowing who the enemy is, as well as one's true place in the social hierarchy, despite the fruits of a social illusion.

In 1949, Howard Thurman was beginning to address the loss of that critical objectivity that should be at the nexus of Christianity. He uses the Jews living in a pre-Messianic Rome as a euphemism for Blacks in America. "In essence Rome was the enemy. . . . No Jewish person of the period could deal with the question of his practical life, his vocation, his place in society until first he had settled deep within himself, this critical issue. This is the position of the disinherited of every age. What must be the attitude toward the rulers, the controllers of political, social, and economic life?"

Why did the Black Church thrive in the eighteenth and nineteenth centuries? Partly because it made accommodations for white supremacy. In 1895, AME bishop Henry McNeal Turner told his congregation at the National Baptists Convention's first gathering that "I worship a Negro God. I believe God is a Negro. Negroes should worship a God that is Negro." It didn't fly at all. Blacks of the day were too steeped in an ideology that included a white Jesus. This was before the Nation of Islam and the Five Percenters gave hip-hop its religious identity. He was trying to give us a religious narrative outside of white supremacy. Islam came along almost one hundred years later and did just that.

Today, there are still dozens of Islamic references in hip-hop.

Yasiin Bey begins every album with the Arabic phrase "Bismil-laah Ar-Rahman Ar-Raheem" (In the Name of God, the Beneficent the Merciful).

Kendrick Lamar raps, "I paid my way through, praying to Allah, you played your way through."

Kid Cudi raps, "Aiming high, passed the idea of slanging, praise Allah for keepin me away man."

Even Kanye, a Christian, has rapped, "I guess we just pray like the minister say, Allahu Akbar throw in some hot cars."

Drake raps "Mirror mirror on the ceiling of the suite in the royal palace, the TV playin Al Jazeera, Inshallah, I hope the mission keeps on getting clearer."

Jay-Z raps, "Made in the image of God, that's a selfie. Pray five times a day, so many felonies."

In addition, over the past thirty years, Islamic theology in hip-hop has been corrected thanks to orthodox Muslims like Lupe Fiasco, Freeway, Beanie Sigel, Yasiin Bey, Ali Shaheed Muhammad, French Montana, and Akon, to name a few.

Islam in hip-hop is no longer simply erroneous Nation of Islam and Five Percenter references. Rather the above-named rappers have given proper context to the correct theology that Allah is the name of the one Creator and he is not a man; he doesn't favor one race over the other; he does not dwell inside of us; he has no exclusive vendetta against America; he can't be found in spaceships; the Prophet Muhammad of seventh-century Arabia is Allah's final prophet not Elijah Muhammad from twentieth-century America; and white people are not manufactured devils.

BROKEN GODSENDS

The Harm of Being Guided by Broken Men with Good Intentions

"BACK UP FOR a second!" I yelled at the person on the other side of the door. He was standing too close and I wasn't opening it until his entire upper body was in full view. He was squinting at the peephole on the other side as if he was trying to see me also. When he heard me yell, he stepped back so I could get a better view. Once I had a good enough look at the junkie on the other side, I cracked the door and used my body as a doorstop. I didn't see the gun in his hand. He was holding it flush against his side with his arm straight down. I froze for a split second until my brain processed the situation and I understood what he wanted. Fortunately for me, armed robbery was the last thing on his mind. "Just give me five for it," he slurred as clear fluid oozed out of his nose and he tried in vain to sniff it back in.

He cuffed the pistol in the palm of his big dirty hands, which were ashen and stiff from wandering the streets in the frigid night. It was a black .38 revolver with a missing firing pin. He had just strong-armed someone for it moments before. Now he wanted me to give him five "bumps," equivalent to fifty dollars' worth of crack-rock for the old piece of steel. But I didn't need a broken gun, I needed money.

I sucked my teeth and frowned, "What am I gonna do with a broken gun that doesn't work?" I stepped back and let Fizz take my place as the human doorstop. Fizz was happy to purchase a gun minus the firing pin for the meager price of five pieces of crack.

"I know how to get one of those pins easy," he remarked as he dug in his pocket and pulled out a giant plastic bag. In it were little dingy yellowish balls separated into tightly twisted plastic wrappers. Each was worth ten dollars. He reached into the bag like there was candy inside. "One, two, three, four, five," he counted as he dropped them into the junkie's open palm. Fizz thrived in this environment. He yanked the gun from the junkie's hand and shut the door in his face without another word said. "The next one's mine since I gave you that one," I sneered, still disappointed at the missed opportunity for cash.

Fizz and Paul would take jars of pennies, food stamps, and sometimes oral sex. But I wasn't your ideal hustler. I had just started selling heavy a few weeks earlier, and I had a long way to go before I understood that profit was profit. Sometimes it was a few one-dollar bills and the rest quarters, dimes, and nickels. And for some guys occasionally satisfying their personal lusts through sexual favors from strung out women was payment enough.

It was January 1995 and I learned quite fast that this life was nothing like the privileged one I had left just two years prior. No chauffeured limousines, no cameras flashing, no girls waiting for me when I left the building. This was selling crack cocaine . . . nothing more, nothing less. I tried my best to forget about the magazine covers, the video shoots, and all the cash I had blown through. Now was a time for holding guns, learning how to turn cocaine into crack, and running the streets.

I was unique in this sense; a sort of prize-winning puppy for the older guys that I kept company with who were deep in the life. I was certain they were looking out for my best interests from the way they gave me pointers that could never be taught in school. I imagine now, that while I cursed until I was blue in the face, they must have gotten a few giggles. I had just left a singing group called The Perfect Gentlemen . . . how murderous could I have been? A true killer I wasn't, but any guy from that lifestyle will tell you that the fastest one to shoot his gun is a young kid with something to prove. I had become that kid.

I made my first ten thousand dollars in 1989 as a professional entertainer. I was rich by 1991. At fourteen years old I made sure I always had at least $500 in my pocket. If I wanted a new piece of jewelry or expensive leather jacket, I would just call home and ask my mother to send me the money. For years my lifestyle had been a whirlwind of airplane flights, tour buses, hotels, concert stages, and girls. Now I was nineteen years old, in a crack house, with a newborn son to feed and no life skills. To say I was traumatized is an understatement.

I didn't really know Fizz and Paul well, but I trusted them because Fizz's uncle, Big Ran, was our boss and Big Ran and Big Chuck, my OG, were tight. We all knew where we stood with one another. There would be no tough talk or bullying from any of us without repercussions from the top. It was 2:30 in the morning. As I sat on the cigarette-burned sofa, my eyes darted back and forth from the small, dusty television on the coffee table to the middle-aged Puerto Rican lookout in the kitchen smoking up his payment. I could tell that he was once a decent guy. He didn't look like he used drugs, he just seemed frail and untidy.

Although this was supposed to be a stealth operation, there was always something going on in that little two-bedroom apartment. Whether it was crack being cooked in the kitchen, bagged in the living room, or smoked in the bathroom, there was never any downtime.

Usually, while the other two played cards, I would ask the broken souls who stumbled in and out the apartment a million questions. I was curious as to how human beings who were once functioning mothers, fathers, daughters, and sons could become zombies. I wanted to know, "What happened? What triggered it? Who were you before this? Why . . . when . . . how?" The questions never stopped. I didn't know it then, but this was my natural disposition attempting to push itself to the surface. However, it would take me years of psychological pain and suffering before that burning desire to help others would manifest itself full circle. For now, my ego and false pride overpowered any instincts of civil thinking I may have had.

My Puerto Rican coworker and I had some decent conversations. I would usually let him do all the talking because I knew he wouldn't believe me if I told him about my past. He would sit on a milk crate, peeking out the side of the window, watching out for detectives who routinely drove by and slowed down when they reached our spot.

We were on the fourth floor of a brownstone, and they knew what we were doing. I guess they weren't yet prepared to come and get us and we weren't smart enough to get the hint. Whenever they turned the corner my Latino friend would signal us and we would turn off the television and lamp and sit quietly until they crept down the block. This went on all night.

I was fresh from the music business. I had been in it as a professional since I was thirteen years old. I was completely fascinated by all this decadence. I would pull up a crate next to my Latin buddy and start my interrogation. He had come to America to find good employment twenty years before. After struggling from menial job to menial job for ten years, he quit working altogether. He told me that he started selling drugs and spent most days in the house smoking marijuana until that wasn't enough.

Eventually, he started smoking crack and shooting heroin, until ultimately our paths crossed. Now he spent his days working for pennies as a temporary laborer and his nights working for crack as a lookout guy for punks like us. He had his raggedy girlfriend with him, and after she would take a hit he would grab the pipe, wrap his lips around it, inhale deep, and hold the smoke in his chest until he was overcome with a coughing fit. The smell made me nauseous. Over and over, they took turns until they were both on their hands and knees, combing the kitchen floor for any cocaine dust that they could stuff in that pipe and suck up.

I watched as Mona, the pregnant woman whose house we had turned into a crack den, begged Fizz for more "bumps." Her brain-damaged seven-year-old son sat on the bed staring into space while Mona argued about the crack-rent owed to her. Short, plump, with an aggressive swagger, she was no pushover.

Even though Paul and Fizz would complain about her constantly interfering, she would hang all night with us, running in and out the apartment with her drug-induced friends. Some nights she was all jokes and stories and some nights she was grouchy and cold as ice. We would each give her a few bumps for the night, and she would start off satisfied until her high began to dwindle.

After Mona came crashing down from her high, she would curse out Fizz, grab me by the arm and pull me in a backroom to ask for more drugs. I never argued with her, I just gave her what she wanted, and she knew I would. She was eight months pregnant, and I was shutting her up with crack-rocks.

I found out through one of my interrogation sessions that Mona was an ex-police officer who was caught shaking down drug dealers and keeping their product. After being fired, Mona eventually dove headfirst into the underworld and now she rented her apartment every night for free drugs.

From seven at night until seven in the morning the routine never changed. Me, Fizz, and Paul would take turns "serving fiends" every time that door buzzed. When I left in the morning, it was usually with a pocket full of crumpled money, about seven hundred dollars.

As I took it all in, I felt a sense of humiliation and accomplishment all at once. How did I go from performing on world tours and being a guest on the *Oprah Winfrey Show* to sitting in a filthy apartment interviewing addicts? How did I go from being on the cover of cereal boxes to this?

One crisp May morning, as I made my way up the narrow wooden staircase to the fourth floor of the brownstone to start my 7 a.m. shift, I noticed things seemed abnormally quiet. I would usually knock on the door and Fizz or Paul would open it with no problem. But this time when I knocked, a white lady with curly blonde hair answered. She was a police detective. She was dressed in jeans and a dark blue windbreaker. She had a black nine-millimeter holstered on her hip and a walkie-talkie in her hand, and I could see a few other detectives in the background bustling in and out of the bedrooms. The sound of police radios filled the air. Fortunately for me she thought I was a crackhead. She stood at the door, looked me up and down, and said firmly, "Don't come back here anymore, they closed shop!"

I was scared to death. My heart almost climbed out of my mouth it was beating so fast. She didn't even give me time to respond. She just shut the door in my face. Then I was running so fast I should have fallen headfirst down those four flights of stairs. When I made it outside, I began skipping like a child, not out of happiness but out of desperation to get as far away as possible without drawing attention to myself. This is when it all began to hit me.

I had no one to grab me by the collar and help me exploit my own talents. All the men up to that point in my life had been broken. Each had managed to cover me in some form of dysfunctional love, but nevertheless it was incomplete.

As a child, I loved to read those huge encyclopedia sets that every family used to have tucked away somewhere in their home. I would turn to any random page and just start reading. I learned about all kinds of plant life, animals, and historical people from those dusty old heavy books. I loved words. I loved to think. Ideally, for a boy, a father is the one who is supposed to recognize those signposts in his son and push him in the right direction. Mine had walked out on me long ago.

My mother divorced him to protect us children from his tyranny. A mean, cruel father is as good as not having one at all, or maybe worse. I don't regret him leaving, I regret him not trying to be a better man.

Back then my mom was a secretary for a company that managed public housing. She was, for me, the most kind, loving, and caring person I'd ever known up to that point in my life. Fair-skinned with long silky hair, I remember thinking she was the most beautiful woman in the world. She would treat me like I was a precious piece of uncut diamond. She raised us six children on $14,000 a year in the 1980s. She was able to manage that money down to the last dime because she grew up poor in the south end of Boston in the Cathedral Housing Projects. She knew all about the 'hood. But somehow, she managed to make us feel like we weren't in the center of madness in our little one-family house in Roxbury.

She was protective of me and my siblings and managed to teach us the value of having good character, being courageous under all circumstances, and respecting everyone, from the janitor to the doctor. I got a lot of attention and love because I was the youngest. And my mother taught me to dream the impossible from day one.

When I was about eight years old, I was obsessed with Daredevil, the superhero. I wanted to be him. One day I went around the house gathering a metal hook, some duct tape, and a few wooden sticks to make a makeshift Daredevil utility belt, complete with a long rope I tried to swing from. It didn't work.

I went into my mother's room and sat down on her bed, feeling discouraged because my taped hook wouldn't stay on my rope so I couldn't swing properly. I was sulking. I said, "Do you think I'll ever be able to really be a superhero?" Her answer influences my thinking to this day. She sighed, shrugged her shoulders, looked me in the eyes, and said, "You never know . . . if you work hard enough every day, someone might appear to you and say, 'Now is the time. I choose you to be the next superhero.'"

I was blown away! She finally confirmed what I believed all along. I had a chance! There *was* a mystery I could unlock if I worked hard enough! There *were* real superheroes! There *was* someone who chose others to become super! She gave me my hope back.

We weren't the type of siblings to fight one another. And that emboldened me. I never felt scared in my neighborhood because I knew if I was going down, there were five other people going with me. My oldest sister Wanda was twelve years my senior, and next came my brother Melvin, who was eight years older than me. After that there came Veronica, Ginene, and Tina. We were all very close.

Just before I entered middle school things started to change big-time for me. My mom got involved with a man we called Popps. He was a few years older than her; a strong, silent street-guy from Alabama.

He was a carpenter by all accounts, but in the 'hood he had a serious reputation for leading a group of crazy country hustlers who did whatever needed to be done to make a dollar. He was always very respectful to us. Our financial situation improved drastically when he entered our lives. He didn't move into our home or even sleep over. He just visited. And when he came, he made sure there was abundance, whether it was groceries, clothes, or money. We never went without after he entered our lives.

However, in retrospect he was a broken Godsend. I think my mother deserved more and so did we. Although Popps was good to us materially, my mother didn't have real companionship and we children didn't have guidance. I learned a lot of good values from him, but I also picked up negative traits from his absence. Adolescent Black boys inadvertently learn maladaptive behaviors from the Black men in their lives, even if the experience is positive.

To note, Tunis Campbell, one of the first Black men freed after the Civil War, became a representative for Freedmen, a term used for recently freed slaves. On his first trip to the US government–sponsored Freedmen's Bureau, he asked for three things so that Blacks could start their lives: yams, land to plant them on, and marriage licenses so that they could start real families. Mr. Campbell intuitively knew that if the newly freed Black community wanted to thrive, Black boys needed both a mother and a father living under one roof. But I imagine even back then it was too late.

Professor Libra R. Hilde writes in her book on Black fatherhood and slavery, "In terms of parenting however, it was harder to be an enslaved father and maintain sustained contact with one's children. Fathers were more likely than mothers to live at a distance or be permanently separated from children. Slave holders might congratulate themselves on keeping families intact and yet apply that practice only to mothers and their children."

Because of the transgenerational slave practice of fathers being deliberately prevented from participating in their families, this became normalized in Black households. Popps was a man of honor and yet, from his lack of emotional range and intimacy with my mother, I learned unhealthy principles like money can be a replacement for time, masculinity is defined by a lack of emotion, and paternal absence is nothing to frown on as long as bills are paid.

Popps never raised his voice. He never talked bad about anyone. He never talked down to us. But he was also an archetypal ghetto boyfriend: distant, living more than one life, and infrequently present. In terms of authentic, positive, Black male mentorship, my brother Mel and I were on our own, and thus entered the mentorship of music and all the wolves and foxes that come with it.

Mel was the first to become involved in music, in 1984. In 1986, every day after school I found my ten-year-old self in the basement with Mizzy, Mel, and a host of older thugs. None of them were under the age of eighteen. Don't ask me how or why they accepted a kid in their crew, but they did. I learned to be mature very fast. I was caught between pursuing my lofty intellectual pleasures and being seduced by the mundane street life that had hypnotized all those around me.

Mel and Mizzy would produce a new song, and we would all take a half hour or so to write our raps, and then we'd all pile in the tight little square room that we made soundproof by hanging quilted sheets on the walls. There'd be six or seven guys in the room surrounding one microphone, chanting a chorus. Then, one by one, each of us would step to the front of the microphone to deliver a verse. When it was my turn, my brother would pick me up while I said my rap because the microphone was too high for me to reach. We called ourselves the "Block Boys."

We had a host of hooligans who would come to the studio to drink and smoke while we recorded. There was T-Bone, who was my sister Wanda's boyfriend, and Fat Rat, the local drug dealer who always had a nice shiny, fast car, and a thick gold chain around his neck. T-Bone was a real street guy. He protected me and my siblings. When Mel got into problems with any other 'hood, T-Bone would go straight to the problem and do what needed to be done to solve it and keep Mel safe. When my mother was being harassed by some guys during her nightshift at work, T-Bone went there and straightened them out. He was also a broken Godsend to us.

We used to play a game in my neighborhood called "right-hand snatch." If anyone caught you holding something in your right hand—food, snacks, a drink et cetera—they could grab your wrist, yell "right-hand snatch," and it was instantly theirs. You had to fork it over without any protest. It was a fun, clever way for the hungry to eat.

When I was about seven years old, I used to beg all my siblings and their friends to let me play, and they would always tell me no. I would protest until they told me yes. Then I would get my food snatched and freak out.

One day, while I was throwing a tantrum, after my friend Dru had taken a honey bun from me, T-Bone came walking up the street. I was chasing Dru around cars, yelling and screaming at him to give me back my honey bun! T-Bone asked what was going on, and everyone told him, "Ty can't handle when he loses."

He caught me mid-stride, grabbed me by the arm and yanked me toward him. He wasn't angry but aggressive.

"Wait, Ty. You can't get mad cuz things didn't work out for you today. I thought you was tougher than that." I was huffin' and puffin' with my arms folded, on the verge of tears. "If you're tough, then you make a deal and stand strong even if you lose out. You ain't standin' strong right now. He got you today. Tomorrow, you get him. That's life. But what you're not gonna do, is act like a baby out here with me around."

My breathing calmed. It made sense. I begged to play, and I lost. That's what everyone had been saying to me, but somehow when it came from T-Bone, it sounded like real wisdom because, even at seven years old, I knew he lived his life on those principles.

T-Bone had that effect. He had a cache of integrity with us street urchins. Even though his integrity wasn't based on universal morals like getting an education, finding a good job, and living a clean life, nevertheless, his value system was virtuous to us: don't be a tattle tale, don't go back on your word, don't run even if you're afraid, and always be loyal to your friends and family. He lived it. And when you live it, it's easy to convince others of its value.

This was the environment I grew up in. We were products of a combination of the emergence of crack cocaine and the 1980s politics of Reaganomics, which cut social services to salvage government spending and even petitioned to have ketchup packets in inner-city schools classified as a vegetable.

These young thugs and gangsters were my role models. They loved on me. They encouraged me with huge high fives and pats on the head when I wrote a good rap. They protected me from danger and provided a level of brotherhood that Professor Jordan Peterson emphasized when he remarked, "Every man needs a gang."

In the mid-1980s, there was no emphasis on education in my neighborhood. There were no after-school tech programs for me to attend. There were no internships. There were only opportunities we created for ourselves, using the resources that were available to us. We were desperate kids trying to understand our world and make a way for ourselves in it.

Although my mother did absolutely everything she could for us children, any woman can only do so much to make a man. She tried hard to give me balance, but she was outnumbered and outgunned by the influences of pop culture even back then.

For many single Black mothers who fear losing their Black sons, there's a point where they transition from disciplinarian to distant admirer when their boys reach the early teen years. It's such a delicate dance to stay in their sons' lives to monitor them, but also not encroach in a way that would force these young men to push their mothers out completely. White school administrators and judicial system workers don't understand this dynamic and easily turn every negative situation involving a Black boy into a moral monologue about uncaring households. It's far more nuanced than that. My relationship with my mother was making this subtle change. Thus, she allowed me to make the decision to turn down a prestigious scholarship to Buckingham Brown and Nichols, a private school in a suburb of Boston, because I thought it would interfere with my rap rehearsal schedule.

When I consider the poverty and violence that surrounded me in my childhood, what stands out is the tragic component of vanity. Young Black boys in the 1980s and 1990s grew up in an age of consumption. We watched television shows like *Lifestyles of the Rich and Famous*, *Silver Spoons*, *Diff'rent Strokes*, all about wealth and indulgence, and then we came outside and lived a blighted existence.

The Black American experience of being poor but wanting to present a façade of wealth gave our narrative a molested and lethal volatility. We didn't have enough food and possessions to rise above the poverty line, yet we would never starve. And when you're young, with your stomach half full and being influenced by a dog-eat-dog society, you have just enough energy and time to kill one another and not enough hope and education to consider tomorrow.

In 1989 there wasn't much to the music scene anywhere in any ghetto, let alone in Boston. Maurice Starr was the music impresario who had originally created the R&B music group New Edition in 1980, but later lost them to MCA records over a money dispute. He had recently gathered five white kids from Dorchester, a low working-class neighborhood adjacent to Roxbury, and formed another New Edition-esque group.

These white kids would be in the grimiest parts of Dorchester and Roxbury singing and dancing for the rowdiest crowds. Back then they were known as Nynuk but the world came to know them as New Kids on the Block.

Maurice was a golden ticket to us Black kids in the 1980s. He was giving his annual "Hollywood Talent Night" show and it was the biggest thing in town. We told everyone in Roxbury that the Block Boys were performing in a talent show and that they should come and support us.

We came in with an entourage wearing leather coats, gold chains, and fashionable sunglasses—confidant and ready. The room filled up quickly and when the lights dimmed so the show could begin, the smell of marijuana filled the theater. There was a sea of hoodlums and their girlfriends—stepping over each other, slouching in the chairs, and listening to their own portable boom boxes.

When Mel and Mizzy J took the stage, I stood next to the curtain waiting for my cue, peeking out at the audience. It was full of Kangols, sheepskin coats, Gazelle glasses, cheering guys, and screaming girls. When the second song started, I burst out with my coolest strut, just as Mel had told me to do. "Yo, yo—hold up—what do you think you're doing? How are you gonna' do a show without me?" The crowd went berserk.

At barely a hundred pounds, I was so much smaller than the other guys and my voice sounded like a chipmunk. I felt empowered and cocky up there, looking out at all those people. I wasn't the least bit uncomfortable and, in fact, I took the lead, walking back and forth, commanding the crowd to wave their hands. When it was all said and done, we came in first place and I was hooked.

After our father left five years prior, we had no guidance. My brother Mel had demonstrated genuine leadership ability. He convinced street thugs to put down their guns and pick up microphones to support us in the 1980s. This was before mega fame and wealth was accessible to young Black people. My brother had cracked the code, and we were on our way to fulfilling our dreams, or so we thought.

How many big brothers in the 'hood have had to assume the role of father to their younger siblings while still trying to find their own identities? This is no easy task. Can you imagine the burden of being sixteen years old and trying to find a way forward for your family, when you don't know the first thing about employment and you have no employable skills yet? Mel was my father, my mentor, my role model, and everything I aspired to be, even while he struggled to find his place in the world. There was a period when he was hanging with T-Bone and it could've gone all bad, but even T-Bone saw Mel's potential and would discourage him from trouble. To that point, T-Bone was a blessing, albeit a broken one.

Nevertheless, the streets have their demands and if one doesn't want to be victimized, one must respond aggressively. I remember one day the local ice-cream truck came driving down our tiny street with that familiar whistle tune blowing out its speakers. It was a hot summer day, and all the goons were out. I was no more than nine years old, so Mel was only seventeen.

After he bought my ice cream, I went to sit on my front porch. I heard Mizzy shouting at the ice-cream truck drivers, who happened to be Latino. As I licked my ice cream cone, I saw one of the drivers hop out the back of the ice-cream truck with a huge butcher knife. Mel, who was on the porch with me, jumped over the banister and ran toward Mizzy and the ice-cream truck. Soon there were knives pulled and a lot of shouting. Murder was in the air. I was shocked and frozen with fright.

I found out later that the ice-cream truck drivers were using the truck as a front to go to different neighborhoods and sell drugs. Mizzy somehow got into a beef with them because of a deal gone bad. Ultimately the Latino guys, sensing that things were getting out of hand, retreated to their truck and sped off. I never had a taste for ice-cream trucks after that. One of the most pure and innocent parts of living in the ghetto is the ice-cream truck experience, and now I had knives, drugs, and violence associated with those trucks.

I thought they were going to return with more people and weapons. If I was outside playing kickball or tag with my friends, every time I heard the faint whistle of an ice-cream truck in the distance, I grew anxious. Even now, when I approach an ice-cream truck with my own children, in the recesses of my mind, I think of those drug dealers and their butcher knives hopping out the back of that rusty, old, colorful step van. And I think of Mel ready to risk it all for his friend.

Mel was always soft spoken and easy to get along with. He was tall, brown-skinned, slim, and a magnet for women. He wasn't a gangster; he was an artist to the core. But he was forced to be a protector to his four sisters and younger brother. The trauma of a young man being forced to face down knives and guns when he is not a natural brute can be life-shattering. I've seen Mel do all of that. He was a creative genius stuck in a barrel of crabs, with no ladder to climb out. As the late great Nipsey Hussle rapped,

> *Young black n---a trapped and he can't change it*
> *Know he a genius, he just can't claim it*
> *'Cause they left him no platforms to explain it*

Until today any creativity or productive idea I possess is just a branch from the tree he planted long ago.

That night, at Jamaica Plan High School, we became ghetto superstars. Maurice Starr was sitting in the balcony. He made his way down to see us. He pushed through the crowd of well-wishers, leaned in, and whispered, "I'm planning to put my son Maurice Jr. in a group, and I want to know if this little guy (me), would like to be in it. They're going to be huge! Bigger than New Edition! I'm going to make sure these guys take it all the way! You saw what I did with New Kids. I just got off the phone with New York. We're planning the biggest tour the world has ever seen! It's going to be sponsored by Coca Cola, and McDonalds!"

In 1989, under the guidance of a single mother desperate to save her sons from an early grave, an older brother who dreamt of getting us out of the hell hole of Roxbury, and a host of broken male identities cheering me on from the sidelines, I became a young Black entertainer, like dozens before me who had visions of overnight success. But I had no idea how long the night would be.

3

LOST BOYS

Black Dreams in a White Construct

IT WAS THE summer of 1990 and, as The Perfect Gentlemen, me, Corey Blakely, and Maurice Starr Jr. had already scored a pop hit with our teen ballad, "Ooh La La." The song peaked at number ten on the Billboard Hot 100 and number twelve on the R&B/hip-hop charts. Our debut album, *Rated PG*, on Columbia Records, was on its way to gold status, which means we had sold close to five hundred thousand copies. We were preparing to embark on the largest tour of the year, the New Kids on the Block Magic Summer Tour.

The New Kids had already gotten to the point where they were worthy of stadiums. We had spent the previous three months as the opening act for them on their Hangin' Tough tour, performing in venues of sixteen to twenty thousand people, but this was different. We'd be in front of fifty, sixty, seventy, and eighty thousand people every night. From June to September, we performed in one hundred cities. Four months of nonstop traveling.

I didn't even have a moment to think how all this happened so fast. Six months before, we had been performing in local talent shows with no more than two hundred people in attendance. Now we'd be earning ten thousand dollars a show. I was overwhelmed.

During our press tour, while conducting interviews for teen magazines, filming music videos, and doing a barrage of photoshoots, the group lived in New York on West 52nd Street in a penthouse owned by Maurice. I got so used to living a life of luxury that within months I unconsciously left my poor beginnings behind me. I began to think that, because I stayed in the best hotels, traveled in limousines, ate the best food, and wore tailor-made group uniforms, somehow these things were by my will and not God's. I thought that the trappings of success were mine to claim in perpetuity.

Back home, all my friends were feeling the heat of a violent 1990 summer, whereas I was rubbing elbows with powerful people and traveling the globe. I thought this would be my lifestyle forever. In fact, I didn't even think it, I knew it. I'm just special. I'm different; chosen even. A year prior I would've been stumbling drunk in my older sister Wanda's apartment with my friends at twelve years old. We'd drink Private Stock all night until the sun came up. Now, I left that toxic behavior behind and exchanged it for a toxic mentality instead. I grew an out-of-control ego and a sense of entitlement until I became rotten to the core. I thought I was self-sufficient.

To top it off, Maurice put together a band of young musicians to play in the back of us which consisted of the rest of his sons and his nephews: all from the 'hood like me. There were about eight of us. We were like the military schoolboys from *Lord of the Flies*, stranded on an island with no adults. Sure, there were adults available if we needed them, but they weren't disciplining us.

In retrospect, the adults were more lustful and careless than we were. These were men I looked up to who were supposedly righteous people, but they were as crooked as any crook. They were using drugs, stealing our merchandising items, sleeping with underaged girls, and abusing our tour budget. They would sneak us condoms every night. We were too young to have any kind of moral conscience, but the adults functioned as facilitators of iniquity.

Out of all the adults on tour with us, there were only two who seemed genuinely concerned about our behavior and our well-being: our Irish tutor, Pete McClain, and our Black American tour manager, Ibrahim Duarte. Pete grew up in Dorchester and was a middle school teacher. He was thirty-five and had a wife and two boys. All of us really liked him because he accepted us and treated us fairly.

Pete was the first white man I trusted. I just knew he was a good man. Whenever he saw me going off the deep end, he would pull me to the side and gently remind me how much my mother cared about me and wanted me to be responsible for myself. He called me to think on a higher level. I would have to say that, had it not been for Pete's gentle public love for me and the rest of the guys, I might have never allowed myself to trust any white man. Because up to that point, all of us Black boys were taught to stay as far away from white men as possible.

The concern he showed me carried me out of religious bigotry twenty years later. When I was in the prison working alongside several racist, Islamophobic white staff, my childhood relationship with Pete wouldn't allow me to blame an entire race of people, despite my inclination to do so. Our relationship enlightened me that no individual or even large group of haters represents an entire race. Pete gave me an advantage over many other young Black men in that way.

Ibrahim, our tour manager was an orthodox Muslim. He was a former horn player, who used to sing with a famous group from the 1970s called the Kay-Gees. He had seen the glitter turn to gutter. He knew there was no room for Black dreams inside the construct of whiteness. He was the only critical conscience on that tour.

Ibrahim would get us alone, smile, and say "All of this—the tour, the New Kids, the Perfect Gentlemen, the screaming little white girls, the illusion of wealth and status—is pure madness and none of it will last."

Of course, our response was always, "Well why are you out here with us? Go home then!"

Ibrahim was a nice guy. He kept his distance from the stench of the music business and tried to warn me often. He didn't use the language of the Academy or of Islam, but he certainly explained to me in depth about the construct of whiteness. He said, "Brother, this is all *haraam*." That was the Arabic/Islamic way of saying this lifestyle of fast girls and celebrity worship was prohibited according to his Islamic belief. "These little white girls live in a state of blindness brother." He was always very dramatic, as if he were giving a speech to just me. "They don't even see you. All they see is your shiny polka dot suits. They don't care nuthin' 'bout you and where you really come from."

It took me almost three decades to understand his sentiment. Ibrahim was trying to say that one component in the construct of whiteness is the inability to recognize the racial overtones of being Black in America and the incapacity to empathize with the Black struggle, but instead only see what we offer them for stimulation: cool dance moves, catchy songs, and creative ways to dress. He was emphasizing that, because of those shortcomings, I could never sustain an authentic life within this dizzying world of glitter and dazzle.

"What will you do in three years when you're seventeen years old, and all washed up from this music? You better have a plan." I didn't pay it any attention, in fact none of us did. How profound those words would become.

Allah had always been gently nudging me toward Islam. My mother was never a religious woman, but she taught me how to believe in God. She used to say, "Just because you get dressed up and go to church, doesn't mean you know God." I paid it no attention, but it was still a point of view and one that would grow on me.

I used to hang out in Ibrahim's room and watch him pray. He seemed to know God. He was so centered. Just watching him bow and prostrate in a quiet hotel room brought me such inner peace. He'd pull out this little colorful rug and spread it out on the hotel floor and go up and down, up and down, softly reciting the Qur'an, Islam's holy scripture, while standing, and bowing. It reminded me of my days with Ms. Bilal.

Ms. Bilal was my sixth-grade art teacher. She managed to center my heart on Islam through her weaving amazing religious tales into her everyday vernacular. She wasn't like the others. She wore bright clothes and colorful jewelry and headscarves. Her classroom always had realistic-looking skeleton displays, green plants, flowers, experiments, and other interesting things a step beyond just art, and a breath of fresh air in that stale, dusty old school. She would rarely teach anything. She would act more as a moderator for class discussions.

She was a tough woman. I knew she was not to be played with, but she never had to act any way but kind to us because we all respected her so much. She let us think. In fact, she taught us to question everything. Why do trees grow straight up and not sideways? Why is the sky blue and not red? We loved her.

Ms. Bilal would keep us after school, giving us these impromptu lessons about all different kinds of weird things. In addition to being an art teacher she was also a mortician, so she knew much about the dead. She would use the chalkboard to explain things like the process of embalming a dead body. She'd take us out on field trips to the Museum of Science and the Museum of Natural History.

Twice a year, Ms. Bilal would pack us into her car and drive us to the hospital where she would donate blood. She would come wobbling out of the hospital room with us four or five kids waiting to grab her and walk her to her car. Then she would take us for ice cream.

If a kid came to school smelly, she would bring him some new socks the next day. If she observed that a kid was always hungry, she'd bring him a lunch. But here's the thing—she kept a closet full of resources, but she gave nothing away to us for free.

She knew we all had candy money, so she would tell one of us, "Put a quarter in the jar and go in the closet and get you some socks brother." She was teaching us the value of a transactional relationship. Nothing is free in life, and she knew the sooner us Black children understood that the better off we would be.

She didn't give us a lot of theological terms. She loved us in real time and demonstrated true chivalry. We watched her back down hardcore gang members to protect her students. We would feel safe when she was around. She said to one well-known thug who came to the school with murder in his eyes for another student, "Now brother I don't know what this man has done to you, but I know you have a mother and I know she taught you that life is precious so go on back home." He saw that she was just as serious as he was and left. She used to say to us, "Don't come across my table," meaning, *don't die out in these streets where she would have to embalm one of us.*

She would weave stories of the prophets into our little minds as if they were rappers or superheroes. Ms. Bilal knew we didn't know the Qur'an so, after narrating one of her prophetic stories from the Qur'an, she would say "And it's in the Bible too!" to legitimize the Qur'an for us.

She once told the story of the prophet Solomon. And she blew my twelve-year-old mind and changed the way I viewed myself from that day forward. There were about a dozen of us students seated at a round table, with her in the center of all of us. Apparently, there was a great prophet-king named Solomon. In as dramatic fashion as a Black woman could, she described the prophet as "this fiiiine brother with long silk robes and the power to control the *jinn*." The *jinn* are spirit-like creatures that are created by Allah and exist on earth with humans. Some good and some bad in Islamic theology.

We were wide-eyed and silent the entire story. She continued. In describing the prophet Solomon's courting of the Queen of Sheba, Ms. Bilal told us that, in the Bible in the Song of Solomon 1:5–6, the prophet Solomon says to Sheba, "I'm Black, but I'm comely!" When she made that statement, my eyes watered up.

Imagine this type of mystical narrative being told to young Black children in 1987, when the world around us was burning in flames of crack and gun violence. It was so beautifully relayed. The picture in my mind of a Black prophet-king was so far removed from the current miserable existence we dealt with daily that it was almost too much for my little heart.

She was magical for us: a physical connection to another dimension. She inadvertently converted several of us to Islam over a span of ten years.

In retrospect, she was the only master teacher of Islam I've ever known. All the rest were overrated. She gave real *dawah* according to our social context, *dawah* being the equivalent Arabic word for Christian proselytizing. Those values she imparted to us stayed imprinted on my heart even while I ran wild on tour and later in the streets of Roxbury.

Out of all the kids on tour, I was the worst child of all. I took all the decrepit lessons I had learned in Roxbury and just packed them in my bags with me. Touring was a chance to let loose and act a fool. I was uncivilized in the truest sense of the word. A person is only civil when he can successfully combine his freedom and the choices he makes with moderation and balance. I had become a maniac. Left alone and given the tools to destroy itself, the soul will easily grow dark without the guidance of God.

Me and the rest of the *Lord of the Flies* crew were so far removed from the 'hood that we just assumed that nothing from that aggressive environment would or could ever touch us out here in what seemed to be a traveling Disneyland vacation.

Donnie Wahlberg was the main attraction in the New Kids on the Block. I looked up to him because he reminded me of the guys from my neighborhood. He was a very jovial, loving guy. He and I both loved Adidas sneakers and clothing. He said my brother Mel influenced his dress style back in the Nynuk days in Dorchester. He took me under his wing earlier on and would pick me up in his limo late at night and we'd cruise the city hanging out looking for something to get into. He was having a hard time adjusting to his newfound wealth and fame, like my adjustment but on a much higher level.

Believe it or not, he was one of the first people after Ms. Bilal and Ibrahim to introduce me to Islam. He had a beautiful gold ring that said *Allah* in Arabic. Allah simply means *God*. He showed me where to get one and I ordered it right away and kept it on my finger up to the day I converted to Islam many years later.

Back then, he was thinking about converting because hip-hop had exerted a heavy Islamic influence on our generation. We bonded beyond music. We used to talk about life, relationships, women, religion, and fame. He is a profound thinker.

Even today, I always encourage him to speak publicly about his very illuminated views on politics and society. But he's clear on what he wants his legacy to be, and what his mission is. And I respect his conviction. When my life came crashing down, Donnie's friendship was important to me.

My mother was busy struggling with her life back in Roxbury. I honestly forgot all about her. I didn't care either. I was a boy living a grown man's life. I had money, clothes, women, I was traveling . . . and no one in my family knew where I was or what I was doing.

Sure, my mom had an itinerary, but she would have to call around and find me if she wanted to speak with me. Mobile phones were a luxury few people had back then. And every time my mother did track me down, I was rude and aggravated. She was a reminder of who I had been just a few months back. She reminded me that I was just a child, not with her words but with her very presence. So, what does one do when a person's very existence makes one uncomfortable? Tune that person completely out of their life. And that's exactly what I did.

I barely spoke when she came around. I would grimace and give her blank stares when she had anything to say to me. I hated for her to come around. She seemed to just want to destroy my life. I liked the dream world I was in. And even though I did see her sporadically while on my travels, it must have been painful for her to watch her child being kidnapped by fame and superficiality.

One time we were all in Florida with our parents. I hadn't spent any time with my mom in months and, when I finally did, she was so excited to see me. I shrugged her off and did my best to avoid her the entire trip. She stayed for three whole days, and I didn't spend more than twenty minutes with her.

On the last day of the trip, she came to my hotel room to talk to me before she left. When I saw her, I sighed heavily. I was playing

Nintendo and didn't feel like being bothered. I had some friends in the room so she said, "Ty, can I speak to you in the bathroom?" I sucked my teeth out loud, dropped the game controller, and stormed to the bathroom where she was waiting. She immediately shut the door and started to cry. I was numb as the tears rolled down her cheeks, messing up her eyeliner.

The sight was absurd. My mother was all dressed up, here to visit me in Florida, crying in a hotel bathroom, with me—the son she had nurtured and protected his entire life—giving her a cold scowl. She grabbed my face, "Tyrone, what's wrong?"

She was convinced that there was some underlying issue that was bothering me. Was I being sexually abused? Did someone threaten me? Was I being treated unfairly? But it was none of those things. I was just a brat, spoiled and rotting every second.

"Nothing," I said. "Then why are you acting like this with me? I want to help you." She must have been feeling like this for a long time and now it was all coming to the surface. I just stared at her. She shed a few more tears and said a few more things, but I don't even remember what.

When she saw that I wasn't budging, she cleaned herself up and opened the door. I crept by her and sat back down to my game. She left even more upset than when she came.

The Perfect Gentlemen were on television every day: videos on BET, performances on *Arsenio Hall*, *Joan Rivers*, *Rick Dees*, *Soul Train*, *Dance Party USA*, and even a guest interview and performance on the *Oprah Winfrey Show*. Things were out of hand and all my dreams had come true, but our finances didn't seem to add up.

We got a contract to be on the box of Golden Grahams cereal. I was excited because our album had sold five hundred thousand copies, and we still hadn't even heard about getting a dime from that or from the gold status of our first single, and I thought there must be cash involved in this deal. Our only money came from constantly touring. We were worth something as a brand now.

So, on the day of the Golden Grahams photo shoot I asked Maurice, "We can't get any money from them using our faces all over the place?" I was never good at biting my tongue, so I told him clearly, "I just want to get some money for all this." I wasn't afraid to speak my mind, but I didn't understand the business enough to have a valid, informed point of view. I just wanted money. "The money is coming buddy. New Kids had to wait twice as long as you guys before they did anything like this. In fact, three, four times as long and now look at them. We have to do these things for free in order to get you guys' name out there, then we can ask for the big bucks. Besides that, I've been putting you guys in the best hotels, buying you wardrobes et cetera. I have to recoup that money first."

How do you argue with a person who is feeding you well? How do you ask for what you deserve when you're not sure what you deserve? How do you sift through a contract that is three hundred pages long and make sense of it all? How do you demand compensation for your work when you're riding in limousines everywhere, eating steak dinners, and staying in the Four Seasons wherever you go? Maurice was right.

Even though he spoiled us, in the recesses of my mind I felt that I would rather not be spoiled and would prefer to choose how, who, and what I owed, rather than owe without say so. I believe if there had been a responsible adult man in my life to make sense of the contracts, and keep me grounded, both Maurice and I would have behaved differently under those circumstances.

While I was a chaplain in prison, there was a young Muslim man (who has since been murdered) who asked if I had access to the prison mug-shot system so he could see his father's face. His dad was a notorious criminal who had been incarcerated for his son's entire life. He said, "I haven't seen him since I was a toddler." When I looked his father up on my prison computer, the young man's eyes lit up when he saw his face, "Yup! That's my dad!" He was happy. It was a very pathetic moment of clarity for me about the fragile state of Black sonhood.

I'm convinced that if even 70 percent of Black men were released from prison before their children were teenagers and placed back in the household with a restorative mindset, all the juvenile Black-on-Black violence across America would disappear. It's that simple. Black fathers save Black families.

The poor fans were no exception. The more they screamed for us while we were on stage, the more I felt like they were mindless zombies. They'd wait all day in the hotel lobby just to get a glimpse of us coming and going. There were some girls who convinced their moms to load up the family van and come on tour to every stop we made within seven hundred miles of their homes. They'd follow our tour buses, check into the same hotel as us, and stake out the lobby until someone from our entourage came down.

I began to feel like I was Michael Jackson. I'd see signs in the audience with my name written in glitter and it made me feel like a superstar. After several dozen times, it became no big deal that someone cared enough about who I was that they'd sit down and take the time to write my name to show me support.

If I had a bad morning, then everyone had to taste my displeasure all day. If I left the hotel in a foul mood, I'd just ignore any fan who said a word to me. They'd be running up to me, smiling and jumping up and down, "Tyrone can you please sign my shirt!" I'd just keep looking straight and act like I didn't see them.

Perfect Gentlemen was just a glitch. We weren't even super famous or well-accomplished. We were simply the dust from the New Kids on the Block sandstorm. But I was acting like I was the biggest star in the world.

On one occasion, I was being escorted out of my hotel by my bodyguard, when a young white girl around fifteen years old with her blue jeans rolled up, wearing penny loafer shoes and a Perfect Gentlemen t-shirt, ran up to us and begged me, "Tyrone please sign my paper!" I was having a bad day, so I said, "No!"

She just skipped alongside us and kept asking, "Please Tyrone! Please don't let me go home without your autograph! Come on, please?" I stopped abruptly, "You want my autograph?" I snatched her paper and pen from her hand and scribbled my name on it and then stabbed the pen through the paper and gave it back to her and kept walking.

She was shocked. She didn't know what to do. She just stood there with her mouth open, looking down at the paper and back at me, as I walked away scowling at her. My bodyguard scolded me, "Why would you do that? She is the reason you're out here! You can't treat the fans like that Tyrone, it's gonna backfire on you." I felt untouchable. "I don't care!" I responded.

As we grew in popularity, I grew in insolence, with the fans, the staff, my family, and even my group members. I began to get into fist fights with the members of my group if I didn't like the way they'd act in rehearsals. Imagine that! They weren't half as bad as I was but, since there was no one to check me, I became the sheriff, the lawyer, the judge, and jury.

By 1993, the New Kids were getting tired of dragging us around the globe. They were growing and going in a more mature direction, and we didn't help with our bubblegum songs and teeny-bopper image. Things began to get tight for us. We stopped getting paid for shows and our per diem was decreased from fifty dollars a day to twenty-five a day.

Our band of brothers had to leave the tour because of budget reasons. Bright new acts were opening up for New Kids, so our time got cut from an hour-long show at first, to forty-five minutes, then to half an hour, then to a pitiful fifteen minutes. I could feel things changing. There were no more friendly exchanges between the New Kids and us. It was all business.

We had watched these guys go from neighborhood talents to multi-millionaires with financial burdens, accountants, budgets, staff, et cetera. We were still just three kids under Maurice's wing. Even the New Kids staff stopped fraternizing with us.

It wasn't long before our record label, Columbia, also got fed up with us and dropped us from the label. We were on tour number three with the New Kids, and we were still wearing the same old suits, doing the same old routines, to the same old songs. It had been three years since we had a hit record.

When the tour ended, we were happy. It had been almost four straight years of constant traveling. By the end of the tour, even the screaming girls began to grow bored with our tired dance steps and lip-syncing. The deafening screams became half-hearted shouts until one day, as we were performing, I realized that the girls were sitting in their seats and talking to each other. . . . It was over.

Maurice packed us up and we moved to Florida for a spell, then to LA. I enjoyed my time in LA, but eventually I was dropped off back in Boston. I had spent most of my money and only had about twenty-five thousand dollars in the bank. By mid-1993, I was back in Roxbury like I never left. Except now I was just famous.

I had been a dreamer without a plan. Like many Black entertainers and musicians, from Frankie Lymon, the teen heartthrob who died in 1968 at the age of twenty-five of a drug overdose spawned by a broken heart after a fall from popularity, to any contemporary rap artist who's been senselessly gunned down because of a lack of living strategically, I didn't have a long-term plan.

A dream is what talented Black kids in the ghetto want to happen for them. It's helpful in the beginning, but it's not useful after you've arrived at the wildest dream you imagined. I had no thoughts about what happens after you've sat on Oprah's couch, after you've finally purchased all the diamond rings and gold chains you dreamt about, or after you've constantly performed in front of eighty thousand people every night for months on end. I had not been intentional about my goals as an entertainer. I was just happy to be on stage, getting paid to jump around and lip-sync to my songs every night. Now it was over.

I often juxtapose the dozens of one-hit-wonder rappers of today, who end up back in the streets or dead, with my own experience. Like me, most of them had no strategy. They just wanted money and fame. That's not enough. There must be a reason that comes after those things.

The only deceased rapper who seemed to have a real plan was Nipsey Hussle. He was buying real estate in his neighborhood, giving people jobs, creating tech programs for young people, and building a community-minded legacy. Everything Tupac spoke about, Nipsey accomplished. He was Tupac 2.0.

I had just started to get familiar with his music in 2018, but I really became a fan of his disposition and mentality more than his music. There was something extremely relatable about that young man. He had the signs of intelligence on his face. When I got the news that he'd been killed, I went in my room and cried. I still don't know why.

People think that his mistake was that, after all the fame and money, he was still touchable and that his accessibility was the cause of his death. In some respects, yes it was. But from a prophetic stand-point, particularly in Islam, leaders should be accessible even if it gets them killed, because being held accountable by your own constituency is mandatory.

The *sahaabah* or disciples of the Prophet Muhammad, including Umar, Uthman, and Ali, were all assassinated because of accessibility. I don't consider that a deficit, because some covenants mean more than life itself. Allah controls life and death and what is written will take place regardless of whether you have bodyguards or not.

Nipsey Hussle did, however, make a mistake that I believe we should all learn from. As wise as he was, as much leadership as he displayed, he continued to identify with a low-vibration lifestyle and affiliation. I respect the 1970s origin of gang culture: to protect the neighborhood from corrupt law enforcement and from marauders coming from other neighborhoods. But we all know now what that culture has devolved into: murder and treachery. Einstein said, "No problem can be solved from the same level of conscience that created it." A man can't solve a social problem using the same language and tools of destruction that created it in the first place.

I believe Nipsey had evolved from his original criminal mind-state to one of illumination. But he felt as though he had to keep his affiliation as a credential. However, those who evolve are held to a higher vibration and must disassociate themselves not necessarily from the people of their past, but from the negative choices those people make.

One who is given great gifts must answer the call of God with wholeheartedness and clearly delegated lines of right and wrong, with no moral gray area. Nipsey had subjected himself to mixed energies, thus becoming vulnerable to the darkest parts of those energies.

I mention this with the highest regard for him and his family. His legacy is intact, and I am in no way aiming to tarnish his body of work. That wouldn't even be possible. But we must learn from our martyrs and saints, in the roster of which he is now certainly included.

As tragic as every death is, some hold more weight with us because of the potential we see. Nipsey's murder was weighty for our culture because of who he might've become and what he might've accomplished. But Allah's wisdom is perfect. And it was that wisdom that took me off my high horse, with nowhere to go but down. Ibrahim, my tour manager, had warned me about dreaming Black while in a white matrix.

The construct of whiteness decides who deserves to be famous, who gets the contracts, and who is no longer a viable product. This construct defines acceptable norms, like when three little Black boys can get a record deal because of their wholesomeness, and when three older ones can get a record deal because of their violent language and volatile behavior.

There's a highly nuanced racial subtlety to entertainment. All I saw were screaming fans, but Ibrahim saw the dichotomy of Black fame in a finnicky white world. He saw where I was headed because he had been to the same sunken place as a member of the Kay-Gees twenty years prior. Black dreamers never survive in a white construct and that's why he insisted that I save a nest egg.

I didn't, though. And many Black entertainers before me didn't, and still don't. One time the original lead singer of the legendary Temptations, Eddie Kendricks, came to hang out with us backstage for a few shows. Mr. Kendricks had spent thirty-plus years as a superstar and yet he was backstage looking not just sick, but broken. He had suffered from drug abuse, alcoholism, and a myriad of other challenges he was never able to fully recover from. The typical plight of a Black dreamer. He held his dignity together, but I could tell there was nothing material left. The fame was gone, the money probably never was what it should have been, and his heart had come to terms with that.

Our handlers introduced us to him as he sat on the couch and smiled with that big, soft, friendly smile he was known for. We barely paid him any attention. I was familiar with him only because I was a fan of early Motown. As we kids danced around and wrestled one another in our dressing room, all Mr. Kendricks kept repeating was, "I remember those days."

It must've been bittersweet for him to see us. I remember hearing about his death only a few months later. Another Black dreamer in a white construct who died broke and with a broken heart. I have wondered to myself if Mr. Kendricks's statement of "remembering those days" was a warning for us or simply a moment of reminiscing for him. Did he understand where we were headed, but felt words of caution from him would have gone over our heads?

It wouldn't be the last time I'd witness a legend in winter. One of the Blue Notes from Harold Melvin & the Blue Notes, the famous seventies act who gave us timeless songs like "The Love I Lost," "If You Don't Know Me by Now," and "Wake Up Everybody," would hang around whenever we came to Philadelphia. He would make sure he tagged along for a meal and would ask for a plate to go. Then he would, without shame or fail, ask our tour manager or bodyguard to

"Hold a twenty." It was nauseating to see a pioneer in such desperate need for something as basic as food.

I could go on naming famous Black dreamers I've seen humiliate themselves at the tail end of their fame run. I would become one of them and would probably have been dead by now had Allah not guided me.

Another Black entertainer we spent some time with was Lionel Richie, the legendary singer and songwriter. He used to visit our hotel room to meet with Maurice during our extended stay in LA. He was always humble and kind. His energy was always generous. He was intentional about showering Maurice with genuine compliments and praise. His vibration was not adversarial, but always as if he were a novice watching a grand master. Maurice would play him one of our new songs and he'd say "Maurice how do you do it? You're a genius man. I just don't understand it."

Mr. Richie wasn't a dreamer. He was a proven strategist of the highest caliber. He started as a singer in a marginally successful group called the Commodores in the 1970s. But he somehow managed to break through the mediocrity and, if you were alive in the 1980s, then you know Lionel Richie's fame and regard was comparable to Drake's today. You couldn't turn on a television without seeing a commercial with him in it or watch an awards ceremony without him hosting. And you couldn't turn on a radio without hearing his voice. He wasn't the greatest singer, and he wasn't a sex symbol. He was talented, yes, but more than that he was a strategist. And almost fifty years later, he's still relevant.

Although today he is worth hundreds of millions of dollars, more importantly he raised a family and managed to carve out a value system for himself, even after some very public mistakes. The difference between him and Eddie Kendricks was stark.

If I had to mark a distinguishing factor between Black dreamers and Black strategists, I would say one cares about the moment and the other cares about himself.

Caring only about the clothes you're wearing for the day, the money in your pocket, and what woman you're going to lay with that night is the hallmark of the Black celebrity-dreamer. He cares only about the moment.

A dreamer doesn't want to feed his family more than he wants to rap or sing. If he has the choice to get a job or do a show for free, he'll do the show because the show has lights. He'll chase the stage until he is in his eighties. All he hears is the applause. He looks forward to the fleeting moment of dropping the top on his convertible and driving down the strip, even though the vehicle is rented and must be returned in the morning. He doesn't have the mind or moral conscience to care about the children he's left in every state or the credit bills piling up. He's looking for the next show so he can stand in the purple-and-blue spotlight. He has the same repeating dream at fifty years old that he had at fifteen.

Some would say, "Well that's his gift, leave him alone." Maybe it is a gift, but if a gift prevents you from living up to the role of father and husband then it's a curse. You can't keep dreaming while you're making children and placing the burden of bills and rent on your woman. That isn't a gift, that's selfishness.

However, people like Lionel Richie, Jay-Z, 50 Cent, and a minority of other Black entertainers care about themselves. They enjoy the accolades and the perks of wealth and fame, but they also know when to turn it off.

Years after The Perfect Gentlemen had fizzled out, in 1997 I briefly became a ghostwriter for hip-hop icon Dr. Dre, through my OG, Big Chuck. Chuck took me all around LA to parties and premieres. When we went to the movie premiere for *How to Be a Player*, Chuck introduced me to Jay-Z. Jay-Z was just starting to heat up. He and Chuck had some history together from the 1980s.

The profound part of our meeting was that Jay-Z's name had somehow gotten caught up in the Notorious B.I.G. and Tupac rap beef. Tupac had rapped some disparaging things about Jay in one of his last diss records. Jay-Z never responded formally. Instead, everywhere he went he cleverly began performing pieces of a freestyle where he dissed Tupac. The rumors about how good this freestyle was were beginning to spread. So naturally Chuck asked him to recite some lyrics for me from the Tupac diss, and he did.

However, Jay never recorded the track and released it. Here was an up-and-coming rapper who was only regionally appealing at that time, who had an opportunity to associate his name and talent with the two biggest names in the history of rap music, but he declined to seize that moment. Jay-Z cared about himself.

Even though Tupac was deceased by then, Jay had enough sense to know that transient association with these two icons could possibly lead to more foolish violence, which in turn could hold him back or, even worse, take his life. I knew even back then that he wasn't a dreamer like I was, but was instead a master strategist.

What did I learn from being a dreamer? I learned its opposite: how and why strategists come out on top. Although I'm addressing dreamers that I've witnessed in entertainment, these lessons can be applied to anyone, from any walk of life.

If their pasts don't reflect their current state of mind, then strategists distinguish themselves from their former dark personas with clear intentional words and actions. They're mindful about the places they go, and instead of a twenty-man entourage they keep their circle tight. They invest in their children. They don't often "hang" in night clubs or other public platforms. They know their paperwork. They don't just sing and dance, they also create products that have a life beyond their names. They save more than they spend and constantly reinvent their public personas. It's not that they could ever escape the white construct of entertainment, but they recognize it for what it is and learn to navigate it with mastery, so that it works for them and not against them.

That's what Ibrahim was trying to teach me: to care about myself more than the moment; to see the matrix for what it really was and then interact with it accordingly.

We love to make our Black bodies a brand, just like chattel slaves. We can't see beyond our own desperate vain desire for fame and a red car. Even if it costs us our own souls. We dream in months, rather than in decades like white people do. We dream in clouds of glitter, rather than black ink on white paper like white people do. And we dream for ourselves and not for our great grandchildren like white people do.

But for me, there was a way out. I just had to stumble to it.

4

FAKE THUG

The Idolatry of Guns, Drugs, and Money

WHEN YOU THINK of Black revolution, Boston is not the first city that comes to mind. But, in fact, it set the tone and shaped the hearts and minds of many pioneering Black leaders dating back 250 years.

A Black man named William Cooper Nell was the first legal beagle to squash school segregation in Boston. He used the Massachusetts judicial system against itself in 1855 and was able to start a national trend. This was fifty years before Plessy v. Ferguson. Nell studied law but was never admitted to the bar because he refused to swear allegiance to the United States Constitution citing it was a proslavery document.

The 54th, the second Black regiment in the United States, was also straight out of Boston. They saw action that killed almost half of their unit while defending Black freedom in the Civil War. It was the free Black residents of Massachusetts that recruited Black soldiers to fight for their own freedom and the freedom of all Blacks in every state. Frederick Douglass had two sons who were among the first to enlist.

Of course, Malcolm X lived in Roxbury, which is my neighborhood in Boston, during his early years. He later opened Nation of Islam Temple Number 7 in neighboring Dorchester.

Boston native and close companion to Malcolm, Hakim Jamal, founded the Black revolutionary group, "US," after Malcom's death, and was actively engaged in the national struggle for Black liberation until he was murdered in Boston by a rival Black nationalist group in 1973.

When King was assassinated in 1968, it was the Black residents of Roxbury that set fire to the city during James Brown's historic concert, where he petitioned Black residents to remain peaceful.

Black Boston has never been soft when it came to acting on Black freedom. But perhaps the most haunting for Black people, but least recalled, is the extrajudicial killing of Crispus Attucks.

Attucks was the first Black man to be killed by law enforcement while participating in civil disobedience when he was martyred in Boston after protesting the presence of British soldiers in 1770. By all accounts, he was the first Revolutionary War casualty. His murder and the subsequent acquittal of his murderers continues to stain the collective psychic well-being of all Black men in Boston, even while most of them would hardly make that spiritual connection.

Ironically, and not unlike the criminal justice system of today, the British soldiers who murdered Attucks were successfully defended by John Adams, who later went on to become the second president of the United States. Adams, also a Massachusetts native, accurately characterizes the racial tension between Blacks and whites that still exists between Boston's Black community and white political structures in Massachusetts.

In his final statement in the murder trial, Adams said,

> *now to have this reinforcement coming down under the commando of this stout molatto [Attucks] fellow, whose very looks was enough to terrify any person, what had not the soldiers then to fear? He had hardiness enough to fall upon them, and with one hand took hold of a bayonet, and with the other knocked the man down: this was the behavior of Attucks, to whose mad behavior, in all probability the dreadful carnage of that night is chiefly to be ascribed.*

The white claim of Black men's superhuman strength will continue to be conveniently utilized as a valid argument in court. They've emasculated themselves with this construct because, although it's not true, they're now forced to implement extreme violence on Black bodies because of feelings of inadequacy that they themselves are responsible for creating.

Eric Nelson, the attorney for Derrick Chauvin, the white officer who was convicted of murdering George Floyd, argued that George Floyd exhibited what Nelson called "excited delirium," saying, "Mr. Floyd was able to overcome the efforts of three police officers while handcuffed, with his legs and his body strength."

The language in both trials is the same. Adams uses the term "mad behavior," Nelson, "excited delirium." These are phrases spoken 250 years apart, yet they echo the same sentiment of inherent fear and racial disdain for Black men.

By 1990, Blacks and whites in Boston were still reeling from the violence that resulted from the court-ordered desegregation of Boston public school busing that lasted from 1974 to 1988. During that time, there were compulsory busing policies implemented between white and Black areas of the city. Many Black students were beaten by mobs of white adults, dragged off buses and regularly assaulted. The tumultuous period changed public school demographics and catapulted white people into the suburbs, leaving Blacks full of resentment, and weary of local government.

When I returned to Boston in 1993, no one cared about revolution, only survival. Roxbury was on fire with gangs, drugs, and a murder rate that hasn't been as high since. There was a constant stream of traffic jams from the perpetual construction, half-finished buildings, and a bastion of whiteness in state and local government that had no concern for Black lives except to hold them accountable for being the super-predators that Hillary Clinton had labeled them as.

Things had changed. People weren't wearing flashy Adidas sweat suits that fit perfectly like Run DMC. Now everyone had on black oversized Champion hoodies and dark Karl Kani jeans. There seemed to be a dark cloud emerging over every neighborhood. Hip-hop was no more. Gangsta rap had taken over.

When I left Roxbury in 1989, the ghetto was listening to Queen Latifah, De La Soul, Public Enemy, EPMD, and LL Cool J. However, by 1994, every public housing window and fast car blasted Cypress Hill, Onyx, Wu Tang Clan, Scarface, Ice Cube, Notorious B.I.G., Nas, and Snoop Dogg. The culture had shifted from Black empowerment to Black angst. In retrospect, I understand why.

The human will is fragile. It meets at the intersection of race, class, religion, culture, and hope. If any of those constructs becomes damaged, the entire soul is damaged. I was back in the 'hood and had lost hope myself. I was a teenager grappling with my own identity, while witnessing the racial bureaucracy of the Rodney King verdict and O. J. Simpson trial in a universal sense, and experiencing the particularities of daily Black-on-Black violence and police harassment. I didn't want to be in a pop singing group. I wanted to be with my people, in the trenches of the vile and dark marginalized space we'd been cast into. Gangsta rap allowed me a gateway into that space.

In Roxbury, where I went to school at Boston High, I had to readjust to life in the ghetto as if I never left, only now everyone knew me because of my fame. I had settled into carrying a gun at my waist every day. I accepted that I could be shot down or that I might have to shoot someone to protect myself. I was a target because everyone thought I was loaded with money. I wasn't. Nevertheless, more than one rumor said that some of the more dangerous guys at my school wanted to "jack me" for my BMW. I had to stay ready.

One day a white middle-aged English teacher, Mr. Johnson, seeing me grim-faced, dressed in all black, walking with my pregnant sixteen-year-old girlfriend down the dusty hallway, pushed me in a corner, got close to my face, and told me, verbatim, "You'll never be s--t. You're gonna ruin that beautiful girl's life because you're depressed. You wear black every day. You walk around grimacing with your pants hanging off your butt. I wish you would just leave her alone."

I *was* depressed, and, in his hatred for the young Black male, instead of asking how he could help me, he had betrayed his duty as an educator. The collective Black experience had taken a toll on me and all my friends. The Violent Crime Control and Law Enforcement Act (1994) that President Clinton had issued that year had dampened our spirits because it emboldened law enforcement to pull us over and drag us out our cars, off the sidewalk, and sometimes out of our clothes without accountability.

The new crime bill was the reason I watched my childhood friends Jermaine, Fat Steve, and others get mandatory life sentences with no eligibility for parole. Not one of them was older than twenty-five at the time. It was the reason my friends were being arrested at sixteen and being charged as adults.

So yes, we wore black, talked tough, and fed into what sociologist Robert K. Merton called, "self-fulfilling prophecy." We were being criminalized by the entire nation, so we drank forty-ounce beers every day after school, we got high, and we looked for trouble because we had no fathers, no mentors, and no positive examples of brothers making it out successfully.

I needed Mr. Johnson's public love. I was seventeen and carrying around the pain of being abandoned by my father while in the midst of an acute identity crisis and I didn't even know it. Mr. Johnson was supposed to be in the business of saving lives, but instead he implicitly taunted me to take my own. I was shocked and numb. I had forgotten about the blatant racism I experienced from white police officers before I went on tour. It didn't take long to remember.

One night, as I left my girlfriend's house, there was a Massachusetts state trooper waiting for me on the bottom steps with his car blocking mine. I had just been gifted a new truck by Big Chuck. He had gotten it tricked out to resemble a Mercedes-Benz. It looked like the Batmobile, painted all black, with twenty-inch gold rims and remote-control doors that popped open. By then Big Chuck was the closest thing I had to a father figure. He looked out for a small group of us and showed me how to survive in the street, but he was also a victim of circumstance. We were doing our best with the tools we were given. His demonstration of love for me was in the only form he knew at that time: giving me weapons, jewelry, and cars. Some might criticize him, but I needed that kind of love in that moment.

There are thousands of Big Chucks all over the country, taking care of young men and teaching them to survive a brutal system set up by those who would call them manipulators and predators. On the contrary, these men are stuck in the same system as their younger counterparts. They're trying to figure out how to be resilient after a life of victimization by policies that leave them with no choice but to choose the streets. We were all we had and the truck he gifted me must've upset this state trooper.

When I made my way down the steps the officer asked me, "Is this your vehicle?" I nodded and said, "What's the problem?" He was a young white officer, probably in his mid-twenties. He said, "Your tires are a little wide and it's illegal to drive because of the regulations of car tires protruding from the car, and your tint is too dark. Can I see your license and registration?" When I popped the door open with the remote, he smirked. As I reached into the glove compartment to grab my registration, he looked in the back seat. He saw a plastic baggie with some white residue in it. When I handed him my registration, he told me to step away from the vehicle and take a seat on the sidewalk. By now, my girlfriend's mother was leaning out the window screaming at him, "He didn't do anything! You're just harassing him because he has a nice car!" The entire neighborhood was outside watching.

The officer used his flashlight and began to pick up all the little crumbs on the floor and examine them. The plastic baggie with residue in it was left-over cookie crumbs from my toddler son. He didn't care and kept searching. When I realized he was going to push the issue until he had probable cause to arrest me, I said, "So what exactly are you looking for?" He turned to me and grabbed my arm, "Alright, put your hands behind your back, you're under arrest!" As he threw me against his vehicle I asked him, "For what?" I felt the cold steel cuffs tighten around my wrist as he shouted, "For resisting arrest!" Huh? I hadn't even done anything suspicious, I'd just asked that one question. I cooperated the entire time.

All the neighbors started shouting to the officer and laughing at him, "Ah man you're just racist!" "You're jealous cuz he has a better car than you!" "Go solve a murder, why are you bothering him?"

In the back of the police car, on the way to the station, the trooper tried to make small talk with me. "Bro, where did you get a car like that?" I said nothing. "How could you afford that? I'm not trying to bust your balls, but you shouldn't have given me a hard time." The white man's curiosity for Black strength and intelligence knows no bounds. He had the upper hand, I was charged with a crime and under his arrest, yet he was curious about how I survived in the jungle of Roxbury. He couldn't help himself, he had to ask.

At the station, I was booked and left with a white female officer. It was late at night in Cambridge, a predominantly white city just outside of Roxbury. When the female officer knew we were alone, she looked both ways and told me to pull my jean shorts down because she had to search me to make sure I didn't have any contraband. I refused at first. "What? I never heard of that! They just searched me and took my shoelaces, my belt, and all that! Why would you have to look up my backside?" I was nervous, but upset. She was nervous too, but I sensed she was desperate to either humiliate me or fulfill a perverted fantasy. "Look, I can have you sitting in a cell for days if you refuse. Then we'll come in with a team and strip you anyway." I unbuttoned my shorts and shoved them to my ankles. I was looking at her eye to eye. Her eyes glazed over and reminded me of a hungry fox as she looked me up and down. "Turn around," she mumbled. "Now bend over." I did. She said, "A little more." When I did, she didn't touch me, but instead just told me, "Okay all set, get your things and go wait in the bullpen." I was only a year or two from being considered a star and now I was a common criminal. That's what happens to a Black dreamer in a white construct.

Another time, I was accused of stealing from a neighborhood bodega by a clerk because I walked in the store with my portable car stereo in a plastic bag. He assumed I was filling the bag up with food. As I walked out, he started shouting at me, "Hey get back in here!" The store was next door to the police station in Egleston Square and, as I got in my car and took off, two detectives gave chase. I sped up and tried to outrun them, but it was no use. After just a few minutes, there were several police cars surrounding me.

The two plain-clothes detectives—one white and one Black—approached my car with their guns drawn: "Put your f-----g hands on the steering wheel!" the Black one shouted, as he approached the driver's side. When I didn't comply, he put his black nine-millimeter gun an inch from my nose. "Put your f-----g hands on the steering wheel or you'll be eatin' my nine (millimeter)!" I slowly put my hands on the wheel and kept looking straight ahead. I was enraged.

They made me sit on the sidewalk while they destroyed the inside of my car looking for whatever they thought I stole. I heard them laughing when they found promotional rap photos of me in my trunk. After a half hour or so, they told me I could leave. As I got back into my car, the Black officer said, "Do me a favor, make sure you *do* steal something next time, so I can blow your head off."

Those moments happened to someone in my circle almost daily. How could we feel good about the police? When we listened to music, we heard the same stories from Ice Cube and Tupac. It made me believe my destiny was to become a rapper. How I would go from Perfect Gentlemen to believable gangsta rapper didn't occur to me.

All I wanted to do was rap. Rappers were physical manifestations of the way I felt. Not the rap I grew up on, but the gangsta rap that fed my angst during that time. I wanted to show Mr. Johnson that I could be better than him. That I could achieve. And when Notorious B.I.G. said, at the beginning of his song, "Juicy," "This album is dedicated to all the teachers that told me I'd never amount to nothin'," I felt his vindication. I wanted my own vindication, and because music was all I knew, it was the only thing I believed in.

For me, gangsta rap felt more religious than religion. There was something deeply spiritual about the lyrics and the content. It wasn't just about aggression. Here were young Black people articulating stories and narratives that sounded like elegies to Nat Turner and rebuttals to those who would have their lives snuffed out. It was truly poverty's poetry: a type of gospel music for the condemned. And they delivered it with prophetic tenacity.

I didn't have these revolutionary thoughts back then. All I knew was gangsta rap gave me an identity and a disposition of resilience that responded to the times of the 1990s. When Tupac rapped:

> *Who you callin' rapist? Ain't that a bitch*
> *You devils, are so two faced*
> *Wanna see me locked in chains, dropped in shame*
> *And gettin' stalked by these crooked cops again*
> *F-----n' with the young black male, tryin' to stack mail*
> *And um, stay away from the packed jails*
> *I told the judge I'm in danger*
> *And that's why I had that fo'-five with one in the chamber*
> *F--k the world*

I felt he was anointed.

By the time Tupac wore it, the crucifix had lost its religious significance and took on a new meaning for Black values in the twentieth century: wealth, power, violence, and voice.

I was only on tour for four years, but I was raised around thugs my entire life. Those lyrics felt right for me and the condition I found myself in. However, in my teenaged ignorance, I had mistaken my love for writing and my thirst for self-expression as a passion for rapping.

So, when Big Chuck called me from California with the legendary producer Dr. Dre on the phone, I was ready to do whatever it took to stand next to him.

Big Chuck had moved out to the West Coast just after famous rappers Tupac Shakur and Notorious B.I.G. were murdered. Dr. Dre had just left Death Row Records and he hadn't quite developed his new label. Big Chuck was helping him put things together.

Shortly before he was killed, Tupac accused Dr. Dre of being a closeted homosexual. At that time in rap that was one of the worst things you could be accused of. Big Chuck wanted both of us to benefit from his new home in LA. He called me one night and said, "Listen, I want you to write a serious record for Dre." I interrupted excitedly and said, "Going against Tupac?" Chuck said, "Write whatever you want and I'm gonna call you in two days so have it ready!" I hung up the phone and got started. I wrote a five-minute tirade of words exposing what I thought was every weakness or flaw in Tupac. I was ready.

Sure enough, a few days later Big Chuck called me from Las Vegas with Dr. Dre on the phone. He said, "Hold on, I have someone that wants to talk to you." Suddenly I heard that familiar baritone voice, "Yo, who dis?" It was Dr. Dre. My dreams had come true!

"Whas up Dre, this is Ty Ty from Boston. I wanna spit something for you." I was full of nervous excitement, but I played it cool.

"Aight, go ahead," Dre said. I tore into a five-minute scathing verse dissing Tupac, hoping Dre would buy into the ignorance I was trying to sell him.

When I finished rapping he asked me one question, "When can you come to LA?" I was getting picked up from LAX three days later.

Los Angeles has two sides. One is the bleached hair, plastic surgery, tanned skin side, and the other side is the khaki pants, colored bandana, Converse sneaker side. I would experience both on this trip.

I had been to LA countless times before, but this time felt different. It felt like I had never been to LA in my life. The night sky seemed more sinister. The lights from the city gave off an intense aggression.

The music coming from the cars seemed louder. The name of Dr. Dre's new record label was Aftermath.

This period for Dre was before the famous rapper Eminem had even been discovered and Aftermath was just a small hopeful label. As I drove in the back of Dre's white Mercedes coupé, we talked about some of the projects he wanted me to work on. I would first ghostwrite some songs for the Hughes Brothers documentary *American Pimp*. Ghostwriting entailed me writing all the lyrics to a song and allowing Dre to use them. It was a behind-the-scenes writing job.

Dre mentioned to me on that drive that he didn't want to pursue me writing a song for him against Tupac because, as he put it, "Too many people love him." I agreed. I loved him also, but I was desperate to get in the business and I would've risked my life for it. Why not? I was already risking my life back in Roxbury for much less.

It's easy for older, more stable Black Americans to criticize young rappers killing one another and bragging about it in rap songs. Those young men have nothing to lose. If the record labels will pay them millions to put on a show of violence, then they'll put on the same show they've been putting on in their neighborhood for free. It's an easy business decision.

I had already considered the possibility of violence as a valid business decision. I was and still am a huge fan of Tupac. He was the greatest rapper that ever lived, in my opinion. He combined righteous anger, masculinity, courage, and revolutionary thinking to make the perfect machismo cocktail for my generation.

When he spoke to a huge crowd of his generation at the 1993 Black Expo, he screamed and scolded his own community. "Little Latasha got a bullet in her back and ain't none of y'all do a mother ------- thing!"

Tupac was looking for like-minded and like-hearted revolutionaries and bounced around from state to state embracing first Black Panther ideology and Islam-centric views, then Crip gang culture, then New York hustler swagger, to finally settle with the MOB Piru. He wasn't spineless, he was just young and confused, searching for the right team to accomplish his lofty community-centered goals. But his twenty-three-year-young self didn't see the pitfalls and distractions of searching for such a team in the rap music industry where the lure of a flashy lifestyle could easily divert the most disciplined of revolutionaries let alone a poor Black kid.

When Minister Malcolm X lost the support of the Nation of Islam, it was a physical, financial, social, political and emotional loss. Even though his tenacity and bravery compelled him to continue pushing, his last days were ostracized. He had no money, no security, and no fraternity in a worldly sense. As a result, one who might be uneducated in the spiritual disciplines would conclude that he died unprotected.

We learn from the lives of our forefathers whether subconscious or not.

When Tupac got shot and robbed in New York, that moment for him was akin to Minister Malcolm receiving numerous death threats in the weeks leading to his assassination. Rather than be a sitting duck, Tupac sought what Malcolm had the spiritual insight to intentionally *not* seek; a group of virile men who were just as recklessly courageous, rich, and dedicated to violence as his enemies were. At the point of his shooting in New York, the revolution that Tupac often spoke of would have to wait until the smoke cleared.

The tragedy of Tupac was not that he died from gang violence but that there were no responsible, community-minded Black men courageous enough to come to his rescue like the MOB Piru and Death Row Records were. He went where he was embraced, and it ultimately cost him his life. His blood is on the hands of all the so-called Black elders and leaders of the 1990s who failed to protect and guide the young Black voice of an entire generation. I view them as negligent cowards.

Record corporations are funding urban terrorism, why would they help someone like Tupac find direction? Being a dead rapper is an entire standalone industry separate from music now. The merchandise of deceased rappers like Tupac, Pop Smoke, XXXTentacion, King Von,

Young Dolph, and Nipsey Hussle generates tens of millions of dollars for the owners of these rappers' images. Many of their families still live in abject poverty while these corporate bloodsuckers live off their dead sons' likenesses. These corporations make use of them dead, as they did when they were alive. And in many respects a deceased rapper is more profitable in the ground than on stage.

But in 1997 I was ready for fame, fortune, and war if need be. If Tupac's friends wanted problems because Dr. Dre wanted me to diss him, then I was ready for violence, because my only other choice was to go back to raggedy Boston. I would have rather shot it out in the street than end up a cashier at a fast-food restaurant.

Whenever a person chooses violence, it's not only a moral failure, but it's a bad business decision. If you're killed or sent to prison, which is always the outcome of violence, then your family loses a breadwinner. Your children lose mentorship and protection. Your mother loses an asset, and you lose tens of thousands of dollars in annual income because you're in the grave or sitting in a prison cell. Violence is always a horrible business decision but sometimes, for Black men stuck in inconceivable circumstances of poverty, it's the only decision to choose.

My time with Dre continued. He'd pick me up and take me shopping or to a nice restaurant and we would talk about the music business. Sometimes he would drop me off at the studio and I'd record demos for a few hours and then someone would take me back to the hotel, where I'd roam around Universal Studios alone. It was around this time that I became aware of a subtle change inside of me.

Things became clearer for me one day when Dre picked up me and Big Chuck and took us out on the town. We stopped at a restaurant to eat lunch. At the table was me, Chuck, Dre, and his friend. While ordering our meals, Dre ordered a Long Island Iced Tea, which was an alcoholic mixture of hard liquor and cold tea. Chuck ordered the same and so did Dre's friend.

Although Big Chuck and I had drank together countless times back in Boston, when it was my time to order I said, "I don't drink." I don't know why I said it, or where it came from, it just came out. This made everyone at the table uncomfortable. That was the first sign of trouble. Dre asked me, "Oh you don't drink?" He wasn't trying to be a bully, he just seemed curious. I said, "No." Reflecting on that one moment, I would have to say that is when my outlook and attitude started to make a major shift toward some semblance of a moral compass.

Big Chuck had an emergency and left town for a few weeks. Dre became my full-time host. He took me to a few nightclubs that were full of celebrities and rich gangbangers. We partied hard, but I grew more uncomfortable by the day. I became increasingly apprehensive under every circumstance. There wasn't any physical fear, instead, it was my conscience. It was eating at me.

Dre took me to his home. I met his wife and children, and it appeared that things were looking up for me, and yet I didn't feel good. I felt like somewhere in those smoke-filled parties with the lights dimmed and the half-naked women, there was someone watching who really knew me: knew my inner thoughts and fears, knew the humiliation, and the struggle I was going through back home. With my baseball hat tipped to the side, my Timberland boots unlaced, my gold chain swinging on my neck . . . it wasn't real for me. Every picture I posed for I stuck my middle finger up and gave my meanest face. It was all too much work for me. I was uneasy and it began to show.

I spent years honing my rap skills. I must've memorized ten thousand lines of poetry, but now I had severe writer's block. I was supposed to deliver a song called "King Midas" for Dre the next day. I stayed up all night writing, scratching out and rewriting; probably the worse raps I ever put to paper. Maybe it was the shock of meeting my rap idol and getting to know him in such an unexpected and short period of time. Or maybe my true nature was attempting to push itself back to the surface. What that nature was, I didn't quite understand.

The next morning the driver came and picked me up, brought me to an empty studio and put on the music for "King Midas." I crashed. Not only did I lay down the most inferior lines ever, but I also managed to deliver them in the most insecure, monotone, bland style. I didn't intentionally do it. I just choked.

I imagine Dre winced upon hearing my song because eventually I was abandoned in that hotel room. No one called, no one came to pick me up, and I just sat. A few days passed until one night a girl from Dre's office called. "Hi, Dre is not going to be using your services right now, so you're booked on a flight to Boston in the morning. Please be ready to leave at six a.m. in the lobby." I was hurt, shocked, and relieved all at once.

I wasn't ready to leave California behind, but I was ready to go home. Sometimes the one thing you crave from a distance can be so ugly and distorted up close that you lose interest. The fragrance of the gangsta rap world smelled sweet from afar, but when I was near, its stench was too much for me to bear.

I wanted the clothes, women, cars, jewelry, and money because gangsta rap taught me that those things were expressions of power in a world controlled and dominated by the white cisgender male. However, I've come to learn that it's those very things that are in fact expressions of powerlessness and that the only real power in the world comes in two forms: organized money and organized people. Laws and policies aren't passed with guns, but with lobbying and votes. However, I would later find out I was primarily interested in a third kind of power: faith.

I returned home and everyone congratulated me as if I had already made it. Little did I know that my journey of "making it" would take on a prophetic meaning.

Gangsta rap was not lost on Allah. Poetry was a major cultural attraction for ancient Arabs, whose language is rich with nuance and layered meanings. Before Muhammad was commissioned with prophethood and cleansed the Kaabah in Mecca, which serves as the first house of worship built by Abraham and his son Ismael, all the greatest poems of the day would hang from its walls. Not unlike the poetry of our times, ancient Arab poetry addressed social ills, political disputes, and boasted tribal superiority, thus Allah saw fit to highlight the importance of poetry in the Qur'an.

There's a chapter in the Qur'an called "The Poets." In one verse of note, Allah says, "As for the poets—the deviant people follow them. Do you not see how they ramble in every style? And how they say things they never do?"

Allah doesn't condemn the poets entirely. However, he takes issue with the way they manipulate the masses to follow them into an abyss of nothingness. The Qur'an condemns the hypocrisy of poetry's purveyors, who encourage violence and use violent imagery, which in turn evokes young impressionable minds to believe that imagery to be a fact of life and an inevitable outcome to their blighted existence, which in turn causes them to make short-term decisions involving violence, which often leads to immorality or death.

Allah continues in the same chapter, giving context to the poets: "Except for those who truly believe and do righteous deeds and remember God often and defend themselves after they are wronged."

Hanif, a young Muslim man I mentored in prison while he was serving a ten-year sentence for murder, is now home and on his way to becoming a well-known and respected rapper. He has all the qualities that make someone great; skill, charisma, good looks, and street credibility, but he insists on rapping about a lifestyle of drug-selling and crime. I love his music and lyrics when they hit high points, and although we've had discussions about his strategy to deliver a cloaked positive message, it's hard for me to get past the glorification of vice in his lyrics. He reminds me of my former self in that he has yet to tap into his purely intellectual side.

In the year 2001, after I had been Muslim for only a year, me and about eight brothers from the mosque took a weekend road trip to an Islamic conference in Philadelphia. Accompanying us was an older Black psychologist named Dr. Brown. He was a new Muslim convert also. Dr. Brown was a small man with wild gray hair and very eccentric ways. He wore suspenders and a bow tie everyday and often spoke in parables.

We returned from our trip Sunday night and unloaded the van. When everyone went inside the mosque to pray Dr. Brown grabbed my arm and didn't allow me to walk inside the mosque with everyone else. Instead, he aggressively pushed my chest up against the brick building until my back was flush. I was taken aback. Dr. Brown got up in my face almost violently and pointed his tiny finger right at my nose and said, "Stop being afraid to be an intellectual!" My eyes widened. I didn't understand. He continued, "I see you." I was quiet. "You're still trying to be Joe Blow but God wants you to grab hold of your mind and use it young brother! Read *Moby-Dick!*" He turned his body to walk away with his eyes still focused on mine and rushed into the building just like that. I was so confused.

I followed him into the building to pray, albeit slowly. I didn't know what he saw in me then until I met Hanif. Today, as I encourage Hanif to change his lyrics and rap about something substantive, I find myself not wanting to be like the so-called responsible Black clergy and community men who abandoned Tupac for his lack of moral integrity. There's a space between gangsta rap and responsibility that Black men must find if we want to bridge the gap between a generation of self-righteous men of religion and the young wild-eyed poets who control the narrative.

Even Allah is not as stiff as that old generation who claims rap music is devil music and that all rappers are useless. Rather, knowing the importance that human civilization places on poetry and its value in a society, he puts clear conditions on its use. His contingencies are based on a universal code of conduct and on justice, and not on contractual obligations.

That said, I believe gangsta rap and the backward culture that derives from it are the primary causes for the moral decline of Black people in the twenty-first century. If one were to judge gangsta rap from a purely monetary perspective, then of course an argument can be made that rap music has empowered Blacks, given them access to wealth and leverage, and provided financial security for hundreds of families. All of that is true, but at what cost?

Allah says, "And do not trade Allah's covenant for a small price. What Allah has for you is far better if you only knew."

My experience with music, and gangsta rap in particular, has left a sour taste in my mouth. I admire some of the rappers today, but I admire them for overcoming the poverty and despondence they faced, and not for what they rap about.

The respect that Allah has for humankind is remarkable. In the hierarchy of creation, the human being is the deputy of God. He was created to have free thought and action. We don't see anything in the physical world that has the freedom that the human being has. Therefore, what we choose for ourselves must be superbly appropriate because we're representing God on earth.

Across all our collective sorrows and troubles through the centuries, one consistent theme in the ethos of Black liberation has been *moral faith*, not monetary compensation. However today, for Black culture, everything boils down to the proverbial *Bag*. It has us killing for it, stripping for it, dancing for it, and betraying one another for it. The Bag is the twenty-first century's Golden Calf.

There is an idiom of *fiqh*, or Islamic jurisprudence, that reads, "Matters are to be determined by their objectives." This means anything that leads to transgression is mandatory to abandon, even if that thing is benign in and of itself. For example, music with vulgar lyrics is prohibited in Islamic law not simply because of the words but because of what it leads to.

The Prophet Muhammad said, "Toward the end of time music, alcohol and fornication will become normalized." This is because each one leads to the other. We can't have a good time without music. Music isn't as sweet without alcohol and the night isn't complete if I don't leave with someone to sleep with.

My life was miserable for a period of almost seven years, from 1993 to December of 1999. This was partly due to the social conditions of the 1990s, but I must hold myself and my culture accountable by confessing that my hope for a better life had become intertwined with a molested version of the hip-hop culture I had come to know and love and, in turn, it darkened my spirit. I became possessed by darkness. I was not possessed in the way we see in horror movies, but instead in a truer sense by satanic forces taking hold of my mind and heart until my body had no choice but to obey. But it wouldn't be long before there was a literal purging of demons from my chest, and Allah gave me my life back. The time had come.

5

SUBMISSION

Embracing Islam

I STARTED MY twenty-fourth birthday by driving to the barbershop in the early afternoon. That's when I spotted Deuce. He was a guy I attended high school with, but we never saw eye to eye. I heard from a few people that he was telling everyone he robbed me one day when I was in his neighborhood to visit a girl. Deuce was not a threat, and I knew I'd get a chance to see him, and then he'd have to tell me to my face that he took something from me. After a few months of rumors, there he was standing on the corner with a girl, waiting at the bus stop.

I drove by him, made a U-turn, and parked my car. I got out and walked toward where he stood with the girl. When he saw me, he tensed up and got ready to argue but when I got close enough, I smacked him as hard as I could muster. The girl started to scream. Deuce was shocked. He expected me, the pop singer to say, "What's this about you telling people you robbed me?" But I had graduated from conversation years ago and learned to act first. He stumbled back and got into a fighting stance. By then I had taken his spirit, and we both knew it, but he had to save face. We threw a few punches and, within seconds, the ladies working in the hair salon came out and told us they'd called the police. I walked back to my car while still facing Deuce. I was feeling satisfied. I yelled to him, "Now, go tell everyone you got smacked, punk!"

I drove back to my mom's house and there was a police car in front of the house. It was a family friend, Al. He had recently become a police officer. I knew he was there for me, but how did he find out so fast? It had been about ten minutes since the incident. I was more worried about him telling my mother what happened.

I gathered my things out the car and made my way to them with a half-smile on my face. My mother had her hands folded and looked very worried for me. I know she was so disappointed that her little lawyer-turned-entertainer was becoming this dark, hopeless person. Al pulled me to the side. "Ty, what are you doing man? I just got a call that you beat some guy and girl up on Tremont St." Deuce had told on me. Al said that the police were looking for me, so I thanked him and left. I had to get my haircut because I was headed to the Essex Club that night.

Deuce was the archetype tough guy. If he had a gun on him, he would've shot me, I'm sure of it. Lucky for me, he didn't have a gun, so he did the next best thing and told on me. He was the only one present that knew my full name.

In my years as a prison chaplain, I've met dozens of Deuces: murderers who are really just confused kids full of anger from lack of having a father. A lot of them snitched on their codefendants. I wish youth in the 'hood could see them after the shooting, arrest, and conviction; when they're living in what is essentially a bathroom for the rest of their lives, humiliated for being labeled a snitch.

The streets are a myth. I mean that the idea of living the life of an outlaw without boundaries is a false construct. The "streets" are an amalgam of violent, selfish, hypocritical actions, hyphenated by indiscriminate fratricide, compounded by a cowardly fear of police and vacillating moral code.

The invisible rules of the streets are fluid according to who they apply to. For instance, the "no snitch" rule applies to everyone unless you're really a tough guy who can fight or are willing to stab or even kill in prison. Then you can walk around the prison camp with autonomy. No one cares enough to risk being beat up by a snitch who can fight or, even worse, lose their life at the hands of one. But if you're weak and you snitched, then you'll be singled out, isolated, and targeted. Other prisoners will run in your cell and take your property, blackmail you for money, and assault you.

Street life is a very strange type of hypocrisy with its own warped logic. Even the many hip-hop activists who march for new laws to be passed and speak on their social media platforms against police brutality still find themselves condemning snitches and promoting the "free such-and-such person" slogan. But why should any criminal be free?

I understand that people despise snitches because they have no personal value system and no honor when they commit a crime and then weasel out of the repercussions by snitching on other people. However, the people they're informing on are murderers, drug dealers, and community pariahs who make neighborhoods unsafe for women, the elderly, and children. Why should they be freed? What is the benefit?

And if you were to argue that the "system" is corrupt, so therefore no Black or Brown person deserves to be imprisoned, then I would rebut that and say that systemic corruption doesn't give us license to molest our own people and communities.

Where is the spirit of the Black Panther Party, who attacked the drug dealers and punished the pimps? Today we have a bunch of T-shirt slogans and rap songs about justice, but no reality, because the streets are confused and hypocritical. They'll be no real peace or progress in the Black and Brown community until we hold the streets accountable for their hypocrisy.

But leading up to my twenty-fourth year on earth, I wanted in.

Me and my buddy Dru got to the Essex Club at about 11 p.m. We bought drinks and pushed our way through the crowd to make our way to the other end of the room, only to push our way back through again. This is all any guy does at a night club: either pushing through the crowd or leaning against a wall. But this time, when I made my way to the other side there was a guy waiting for me. He was staring dead at me. "What's up," he said. I was too drunk to know if he was someone that I previously had a problem with, so I responded in kind,

"What's up." We both stared at each other. He said it again, "What's up?" This time I put my drink down on a nearby table and responded more firmly, "What's up!" Just then, his friend interrupted our stare down, "What's up, Tyrone!" Now I was really confused.

Dru had just made his way through the crowd and, when he saw those two guys, he cracked a huge smile. They shook hands and hugged him. Apparently, they were guys from our high school, but I didn't recognize them. I was still upset. "Why the hell y'all playing games, coming at me like that?" I yelled over the loud music. "Yo Dru, get your man before someone gets hurt up in here." They didn't take kindly to my harshness. Dru apologized and grabbed me by the arm and took me to the other side of the club, where I spent the rest of my birthday mean-mugging anyone who made eye contact with me.

My life was on its way to becoming a cautionary tale. I had become a composite character of all the street thugs I had known. I wanted to make a name for myself by any means necessary, and at that point death or prison would've suited me fine. I was spiraling out of control, and it was only a matter of time before I met someone willing to call my bluff.

The night that changed my life happened a few days after my birthday. Dru and I had been smoking marijuana in his grandmother's parking lot while sitting in my car. We hadn't been there ten minutes when the street was filled with police lights. The two patrol cars pulled into the lot and shined their lights on us. They weren't surprised to see two fools sitting in a car trying to hide the fact that they were high on drugs. When Dru told them he lived across the street, they just told us to go indoors.

Instead of listening to their advice, we drove down the block to my house and parked in my parking lot. We were laughing hysterically because a huge raccoon had appeared out of nowhere and he was standing on two feet, digging in someone's garbage barrel, and opening empty boxes with his hands like a human. We got a kick out of that. We couldn't stop laughing. Suddenly, out of nowhere, a tremendous sadness swept over me. I immediately stopped laughing. This was my life. I was nothing. I was wasting my life away. I had never become so sad so suddenly. It was as if my entire twenty-four years flashed in front of me. All the good that had been bestowed on me, all the ease and comfort, and all the luxurious times flashed through my mind in one instant. When Dru saw my change, he said his goodbyes and got out the car and walked home.

I sat there for ten minutes, reviewing my life in my mind. I had been given so much in such a short time and yet I had nothing to show, not even gratitude in my heart. Then I started to remember all the terrible little things I'd done: the way I treated people who cared about me, selling drugs, behaving violently. I burst into tears. I didn't deserve to be happy. I was a rotten person.

I opened the door of my car and ran to my house. When my mother opened the door I fell into her arms, "Oh God, Ma I'm so sorry!" I was sobbing uncontrollably. My mother held me tightly and although she didn't know the specifics of what made me come to her, she knew what this was about in general. I had been negligent, hateful, and irresponsible and now it was time to repent. I cried like I never cried before or since.

I begged her to forgive me. She held my head and said, "I forgive you baby." Her words ran through my soul, and I could feel a burden in the depths of my spirit lifted off me. "I want God to forgive me Ma!" I cried harder. "He forgives you Tyrone."

She comforted me. Each phrase of hers cut like a knife into something buried in my chest. With each affirmation she made I could literally feel things leaving my body. Something profoundly evil was being removed from my soul that night and I felt it in my chest. Physically, I felt a light breeze that released me with every word of remorse I uttered. That night in my mother's arms, I was set free by Allah.

The next morning, I woke up feeling like a new person. My heart was as light as a feather. I was restored. I had been redeemed in one night. I can't completely articulate what happened to me that night, but I know it was the workings of Allah's grace.

Over the next few days, I separated myself from everyone and stayed isolated in my room. I knew I needed to be connected to God, so I started by calling an old high school friend of mine name Gary Bugg. Gary had been saved as a Protestant Christian when we were still in high school. I had known him since the first grade and, boy, did he change. He went from this quiet, mean, tough kid to a bright, energetic friendly person. He attributed his change to the blood of Christ. I wanted that change for myself.

Gary picked me up one night and took me to his church for service. When I entered the building, I noticed it was very large, neat, and didn't contain any statues or religious iconography. There were a few musical instruments set on a small stage: drums, a piano, a guitar, and other instruments. Gary introduced me to the twenty or so people in attendance and I took a seat.

There was a mixture of mostly white people, with a few Blacks including myself. When the service started, Gary took to the stage and grabbed a set of tambourines. The pastor spoke about Jesus redeeming our spirits for only ten minutes before he sat at the drums and the other men grabbed their instruments on the stage and began to play.

Gary was in complete ecstasy. "Jesus loves me . . . Jesus loves me!" He and the other members of the church were singing their hearts out. The pastor's words were substantial enough, but my heart wasn't affected, nor did the environment provide me with a feeling of reverence. The uncoordinated four-piece band stumbled through the song while everyone sang. I was in the front row, pleasantly smiling as I watched them perform.

I sat there feeling empty and sad. This wasn't the place for me. *I wanted it to be.* I began to think that maybe religion wasn't for me. I respected Gary's transformation and those people in attendance were very sincere. I was polite and attentive the entire service, but I wanted to go home.

I tried not to be discouraged and I thought maybe I needed to attend a more ethnic service. The following Sunday, the first Sunday of December, I woke up early, put on my best suit, went to the local Baptist church, and sat in the back pew alone. The preacher spoke well. I listened closely, trying to hear those words that would transform my heart. *Nothing.*

At the end of the service, the preacher requested those who wished to be saved to come forward. Several people got out of their seats and bashfully made their way to the front, while the people in the pews praised God and some clapped. I almost got up. I thought to myself, *This is your chance, Tyrone. Don't be disheartened because you don't feel some wonderful spiritual trance. This may be it. Get up!* I couldn't bring myself to lift from the bench. It didn't feel right for me. I stayed seated until the service was concluded, filed out, and went home.

The next day, as I sat in my room and thought about what I would do next, I got a collect call from my friend Apple in prison. Apple and I had been running partners for a few years before he got a thirteen-year prison sentence for home invasion. He was already just about halfway through his sentence by now. We had become good confidants. I told him that I was ready to change my life and that I had been to several churches, but I didn't feel the spirit to submit.

Since being in prison, Apple had rediscovered his birth religion. He was born Muslim, and his true name was Abdul-Alim, which means "Servant of the All-Knowing," the *All-Knowing* being one of Allah's ninety-nine Attributes. Apple now insisted that people call him Abdul-Alim. He had been trying to convince me to accept Islam since he'd been in prison, but I would tell him, "Wait until you come home, we're going straight to the strip club!" But now here I was explaining to him that I was ready to find peace in worshipping God. But I didn't know which religion was true.

I told him I wanted to go to a mosque to check out Islam. I had been intrigued by it since my middle school days with Ms. Bilal, and later the time I spent with Ibrahim on tour. I thought I knew enough about Islam and that I didn't want to be a Muslim because it seemed too strict and had a tinge of hypocrisy when it came to the treatment of women. However, I wanted to give every faith an equal chance to possibly touch something in my heart that had been untapped. Abdul-Alim gave me the address of the mosque in Roxbury. I hung up from him, got my coat, and drove down there.

At first, I couldn't find the mosque, because I was looking for some grand building. After all I was in the 'hood, this was an area I knew well. I had driven around the block a few times when I saw a man on the sidewalk with a kufi, which is the small religious cap Muslim men wear on their heads. He was standing outside of a brownstone. I knew that was it.

The mosque was founded by a group of Black American men in the 1970s. They were fresh from the Black Power movement. They were ex-criminals and drug-users who were looking for a new way of life to exist off the grid, even while they were still very much physically in the ghetto. They didn't have much formal, scholarly information about Islam back then, only references to a vague form of Sufism, which is a sect in Islam that is more concerned with intention and the internal meaning of physical things, rather than pure Islamic law.

Following this iteration made these pioneering Muslims morally ambiguous and generally antiestablishment. They could rob a bank to finance buying a building and justify it as ". . . taking back what America stole from our ancestors." In the seventies, they had a Black Panther/revolutionary attitude about Islam and how it related to an American construct.

They weren't the best at following the letter of Islamic law, but they had courage. Many had migrated from the strange heterodoxy of the Nation of Islam and, because of that, still harnessed a fiery attitude about being aloof from American capitalism. They used that self-determination to pool their resources and purchase several buildings to open masjids. *Masjid* is the Arabic word for mosque. As one old Black American pioneer in his eighties told me, "Back then, we had courage without knowledge, today you young Muslims have knowledge without courage."

He was referring to the general nonchalant attitude we contemporary Muslims have about applying Islamic values and principles to our public lives. In the 1970s, they were shaping what it meant to be an urban Muslim: one not influenced by the blasphemous theology of the Nation of Islam, yet not fully emerged and accepted by a growing Muslim immigrant narrative.

The building was very weathered and there was a tiny restaurant attached to the corner of it. I first went inside the restaurant. Inside it was vacant and unkempt. There was a dark African man behind the counter cleaning dishes. When he saw me, he smiled and welcomed me in. I didn't know what to say until he beat me to the punch, "As-Salaamu alaikum!" I knew enough to respond, "Wa alaikum as-Salaam." This is the traditional greeting in Arabic meaning "Peace be upon you," and its return, "And upon you be peace."

I was nervous and felt out of place. He asked me my name. "Tyrone," I said. He was used to guys like me coming in. I told him I was interested in learning more about Islam. He smiled a big smile and said, "I thought so."

His name was Samba. When he told me his name, I immediately thought of the *Lion King* movie, and I was not interested in being in an eccentric African cult. I was very shallow-thinking and without any sophistication in my conclusions. Surprisingly, Samba's personality disarmed all those thoughts. He was charming in a mundane way. He was a tall, thin man who had been in America for several years and had ended up being the assistant to the masjid imam. The imam is the religious leader who holds the same position as a priest in Christianity. I didn't ask him many questions because he was listening to a lecture on an audio CD.

He gave me some date fruits to eat, and I sat and listened with him, intrigued by the entire environment. This masjid was clearly lower- to working-class, and I felt at home.

I learned later that almost every masjid in the world ascribes to a very distinct *manhaj*, which is the Arabic term for "prescriptive ideology."

There is the Salafi *manhaj*, with its focus on imitating the early generations of Muslims; the Tablighi *manhaj*, which is characterized by groups of Muslim men peacefully visiting other Muslims at their places of business or in their homes to remind them about living a prophetic lifestyle of worship, service, and humility; the Sufi *manhaj*, which advocates for spiritual ecstasy and unconventional worship practices outside of orthodoxy; the Ikhwani *manhaj*, which is more focused on Muslim civic engagement and secular education to establish Islamic norms and customs in a non-Muslim society; or the Warith Deen *manhaj*, which emphasizes a benign Black American, scientifically driven milieu of Islam.

However, there are always a few masjids that don't ascribe to one understanding of Islam. They may allow several different versions of Islamic practice in their masjid. One day they may emphasize politics, another day it's spirituality, and yet another day secular progress is underlined. In theory, this sounds enticing and liberating, but I've found this type of approach to be problematic because it becomes difficult to achieve true religious knowledge and gain mastery in learning a particular set of Islamic values when there's no central theme and distinct canon of previously researched Islamic data to drawn on.

This masjid was of the latter ilk. There was no central theme of religiosity, but more of a hodge-podge of urban culture, anger politics, and random Islamic ideas. Nonetheless, the masjid still served a noble purpose in that it was clear that this was the place that all the lower-class, urban Muslims came to find peace, inclusion, faith, and reassurance about their identities.

The imam, or Muslim leader of the masjid, was a tall handsome man in his early fifties named Imam Abdullah. He was a former street guy who had accepted Islam in the 1980s and turned his life around. He was a true leader; courageous, generous, and innovative. I was immediately drawn to his identity but eventually discovered over time that I needed to stop searching for a father figure in transient Black men and ground myself in values and principles I found to be true based on my own personal growth experience. I had stopped idolizing the likes of Big Chuck, Fat Rat, and T-Bone. I wasn't going to fall prey to anyone else, even an imam. I was going to blaze my own trail this time.

The following day I went down to the masjid again and sat with Samba. This time he had another gentleman with him who was clearly a Muslim. He had a full beard, and he was wearing traditional Islamic clothing, including a thobe and a kufi. He was Black American, and his name was Shareef. He shook my hand and looked me up and down. I had on a black leather coat, a gold chain, a gaudy diamond and gold ring, and two diamond stud earrings in both my ears. Gold is forbidden for men in Islam because it is considered effeminate and signals unwarranted attachment to the transitory things of this world. He didn't say anything to me about the way I was dressed, but he knew I wasn't Muslim. "My name's Shareef, brother." I told him my name and we smiled genuinely at one another.

Samba told Shareef I was interested in Islam, and he wasted no time. "Well, are you ready to take your *Shahaada*?" I knew what that term meant because of Ms. Bilal. It is the formal words of testimony from a person that takes him from being a non-Muslim to being a Muslim.

To be the Muslim who administers another person's *Shahaada* into Islam is one of the greatest honors in Islam. Unlike Judaism, and closer to Protestantism in this case, Islam advocates conversion. Muslims love to be the first to offer someone to become Muslim because they genuinely believe that salvation lies with Islam and Islam only.

This type of attitude can present as arrogant and self-righteous if one isn't careful. I would later become just that kind of Muslim. But today I was on the other end of the spectrum, looking for salvation, searching for inner peace and a safe identity I could adhere to that gave me liberation from who I had become.

I still wasn't quite sure I was ready to dive in. Shareef said, "Follow me." He took me next door and into the masjid prayer area. I followed him up two flights of stairs and when we reached the top, he told me to remove my boots. I removed them and stepped into a simple, spacious room with wall-to-wall green carpet. It was very quiet and reverent. I saw a few men making *salaat*, which is the formal Arabic term for Islamic prayer. They prayed in the same way I had witnessed Ms. Bilal and Ibrahim pray.

There were two things that struck a chord with me. The first was that there were only five or so people in the room, and all of them were of different races, all praying quietly in separate parts of the room. When I saw those different men sharing the experience of prayer, I knew I was on the right track.

The second thing that amazed me was that two of the men had holes in their socks. It may sound strange, but when I entered the room, I honed right in on their socks and noticed that they had a few holes in them. When I had attended church a week earlier, I felt the same social pressure of being "in style." It's difficult to focus on God when you're in an environment that emphasizes style and you keep showing up poor, with the same dusty shoes and raggedy suit. But in the masjid, I saw jeans, hospital scrubs, and T-shirts. There were cab drivers, laborers, and doctors all lined up in the same prayer. Now I was convinced that this path was the way that led straight to God: men of different races and places gathered for mutual worship, not concerned about the superficiality of looks.

My entire life I had been burdened with image. How I looked, how I walked, talked, acted. It had driven me almost insane. Seeing those "holy" socks was a strange confirmation that this was what I'd been searching for.

Shareef took my hand and guided me to a corner, and we sat down on the rug facing each other. He said, "Do you believe in Allah?" I said, "Yes I do." He then told me the basic beliefs of a Muslim, which seemed like it took forever but was probably only about ten minutes.

Shareef had given me an earful of information that I didn't even really understand. But I did believe that there was only one God and that I needed Him now more than ever. The other things I'd learn later. Shareef explained the six articles of faith in Islam.

The first was that Allah was the God of all the prophets including Adam, Noah, Abraham, Moses, Jesus, and Muhammad, and that he was alone in his Lordship. He said, "A lot of people think Allah is a moon god or a strange god. They think we worship a different god other than the Lord. But Allah says, 'Do not prostrate to the sun or the moon, but prostrate to Allah who created them both, I you truly worship Him alone.'"

Shareef explained that the name *Allah* was merely the Arabic equivalent to saying *The God*. He said that Arab Christians also called God *Allah*, and it is written in the Arabic Bible as such. He was trying to ground me in the idea that this shouldn't feel strange because Allah is timeless and he has been the same from the beginning, only we've changed his names according to our languages. He said, "Do you believe that?" I said "Yes." He said, "Good."

He then explained that the second article is to believe in the angels created by Allah. They are created from pure light and have no free will to disobey Him like we humans do. He said the angels guard human beings by protecting us from harm and evil. He said they do not enter a room in which there are images of animate beings or one in which there is a dog, not because dogs are evil but because they are unclean.

I had often wondered why Muslims didn't like dogs. He explained it wasn't that they don't like dogs, but that the saliva from a dog is *najas* or filthy, and that if it rubs its nose or tongue on a Muslim's clothes, he or she must wash those infected places before he or she can make *salaat*, the formal prayer, and because of that Muslims generally like to avoid getting close to dogs.

Continuing with the same point, Shareef told me that Satan is called Shaytan in Islam, and he was not a fallen angel but instead part of a third creation after humans and angels, called *jinn*. *Jinn* were created from the fire of a smokeless flame and had free will as humans do. He said *jinn* dwell on earth with humans, some Muslim, some Christian, and some other than that, as Allah mentions in the Qur'an, saying, "And jinn we created before from smokeless fire."

Shareef explained that the third article of faith was to believe in the holy scriptures sent down by Allah from the beginning of time. He said that the Torah and the Gospel were both sent by Allah but had since been corrupted by the dark intentions of men. As a result, Allah sent down the Qur'an in an Arabic tongue as an affirmation and completion of the previous scriptures.

Shareef emphasized that while we do not follow the former books, we must respect them as having been revealed by Allah. He said the reason Muslims constantly recite their prayers in Arabic is so that the original language of revelation remains alive and uncorrupted. He was proud to tell me that there is a chain of men whose recitation of the Arabic Qur'an can be traced back from teacher to teacher until it reaches the Prophet Muhammad himself. "This," he said, "ensures that the Qur'an will never be corrupted as the previous scriptures were."

He then explained the fourth article, which was to believe in the prophets sent by Allah. He said that all the prophets were divinely inspired but they did not have a divine presence. Shareef stopped and looked me in my eyes and asked me, "What do you think about Jesus?" I didn't know what to say, so I said the first thing that came to my mind, "He was a great man." Shareef smiled and continued, "Yes, he was, but he was not the son of God. He was not one of three but rather he was a prophet and messenger of Allah who was given divine miracles."

Shareef explained that Allah had no need for a son and that, the same way he created Adam from dirt, without a mother or a father, and later Eve from Adam—which would be from a male without a female—he created Jesus from Mary, essentially creating from a female, without a male. He said Allah can do anything because he then took a male and a female and created all of us in perpetuity. It made sense to me.

He said, "The fifth thing we believe is in the Day of Resurrection. That is the final day when every human being will be resurrected and made to stand before Allah: barefoot, naked, and uncircumcised. They will answer for all the actions and beliefs they held in this world." I couldn't imagine being naked in front of all of mankind, and Shareef sensed my doubt. "Everyone will be too afraid about where they're headed to be concerned about nakedness, brother." He gave a rebuttal to my thoughts.

And finally, Shareef said the sixth belief was belief in Divine Decree: that whatever was meant to reach me from Allah, no one could ever prevent it, and likewise whatever was destined to miss me, no one could ever make it touch me good or bad. He said everything that happens on earth was written fifty thousand years before anything was ever created. Shareef said it was all written down in a Divine Book called *Al-Low Mah-footh*, the Preserved Tablet.

Shareef said Divine Decree was very complicated, because even though our human actions are already written and Allah knows what we will do, at the same time he has given us limited free will to choose our own paths. He stressed for me to submit to this concept without giving it too much thought because it can be discouraging to the human mind.

After giving me a brief overview of Islamic theology, Shareef told me I have five duties as a Muslim. These are called the five pillars.

The first is to testify with my tongue and believe in my heart that nothing deserves worship except Allah. This was the *Shahaada*, which I would be soon taking. The second is to pray five times a day perfectly, and at fixed times of the day according to the movement of the sun. This is *salaat* or formal Islamic prayer.

The first prayer is called *fajr* and it was at dawn, the second is called *thuhr*, at noon, the third is called *asr*, in the afternoon, the fourth is called *maghrib*, at sunset and the fifth is called *ishaa*, at nightfall.

The third pillar is to fast the month of Ramadan, refraining from eating any kind of food or drink and engaging in sexual intercourse from dawn until the setting of the sun for thirty days. He made it clear that, after each daily sunset, it was permissible to eat whatever I wanted if it was *halal*. *Halal* means *permissible*. In Islam things like alcohol and pork can never be made *halal*.

He said the word Ramadan was derived from the Arabic word *Ramada*, which means *scorching heat*. The purpose of this month was to purify the Muslim from a year of transgression and mistakes so that, the same way heat purifies animal skin, the heart of a Muslim is purified from the year's bad deeds. He said fasting would create discipline in me. And the same way heat shapes metal, the heat from hunger would shape my character into a more refined version of itself. He said we also fast so that we know what it feels like to be in perpetual deprivation, like 90 percent of the world's population who can't just randomly order a cheeseburger in the way we can. He said fasting grows a person's empathy.

The fourth pillar is my duty to pay *zakat*, an annual charity donation of 2.5 percent of my yearly savings to the poor and needy. He said the Arabic word *zakat* means to purify, and *zakat* is how we purify our wealth.

Last, he said the final duty of a Muslim is to make Hajj, the holy pilgrimage to Mecca to visit the Kaabah, the first house of worship built by Abraham and his son Ismael. He said I would only be obligated to travel there if all my bills were taken care of and that, if I never saved enough money to go, then the obligation was lifted from me.

He said, "A lot of people think Muslims worship the Kaabah because we circumambulate around it during Hajj. Nothing could be further from the truth. The Kaabah serves as a symbol of unity for Muslims who must all turn in its direction during our five daily prayers." He said that, at any given time during the day, there are Muslims from all over the world facing in the same direction of the first house of worship created to glorify God.

Years later I would explain this same framework to dozens of aspiring Muslims before administering their *Shahaada*. Today intermittent fasting has become a fashionable way of improving health, but Islam prescribed and institutionalized it almost two thousand years ago.

Shareef did a wonderful job of setting the expectations very clearly for me. He didn't sugarcoat things. I was worried that I wouldn't be able to fulfill all these demands after having spent most of my life undisciplined and unbothered by any sort of moral compass. He reassured me that it would all come naturally in time if I was truly sincere.

After giving me those details, Shareef then said, "Repeat after me." I listened and repeated the words, first in Arabic, "Ash-hadu an laa ilaaha ill-Allah, wa ash-hadu anna Muhammad rasuluLah—I bear witness that nothing deserves worship except Allah. And I bear witness that Muhammad is his messenger."

With those words, on December 8, 1999, my sins were forgiven, my life was changed, and a profound journey began for me.

Shareef hugged me tightly and then pulled back and looked me in the eyes and smiled with deep sincerity. I was happy. Although I was a little nervous that I wouldn't remember all the details, I was sure I wanted to try. Before we got up Shareef got serious and said to me, "Brother this means that from this day forth you acknowledge that Allah sees you, and everything you do. You can't smoke anymore, drink alcohol anymore, or date women until you're married."

That last statement was more shocking than all the other things he said to me. I was okay with no drinking or smoking, but I wasn't sure I could be without a woman, and I wasn't even sure that I wanted to get married. Despite my thoughts, I nodded to confirm that I understood. Regardless, I was Muslim, and it felt good.

Shareef told me, "Every time you do a good deed you get *barakah*. Every time you pray you get *barakah*. Every time you fast you get *barakah*. Every time you give charity you get *barakah*." I thought to myself that maybe *barakah* was some kind of special gift that other Muslims present to you.

I asked him, "What's *barakah*, and where do they keep it because there must be a lot of it?" Shareef smiled.

"No brother, *barakah* means *blessings from Allah*. Every time you do a righteous deed, there is a hidden reward that drops down from heaven from Allah. But you can only cash in all your *barakah* when you pass on to the *akhirah,* the hereafter."

I was shocked. Speechless. I felt the same chills I felt when Ms. Bilal explained the story of the prophet Solomon to me. For the first time in my adult life, I felt the presence of heaven and an afterlife. My imagination took me to an amazingly miraculous place in my heart.

I would later learn that Islam gives the most detailed and definitive description of Paradise from the three Abrahamic faiths. There are rivers of milk and honey, roads paved with gold, palaces and mansions made of glass, anything the heart desires beyond our imaginations. There are details of the conversations that will take place and even how pleasures will be fulfilled.

Allah says: "And no soul knows what joy for them has been kept hidden."

The emphasis on seventy-two virgins for every Muslim man in Paradise has no authentic basis in Islamic theology. Unfortunately, after 9/11, the concept of Muslim men who die as martyrs receiving seventy-two virgins has become the dominating narrative in Islam, but it is not mentioned in the Qur'an or in any authentic Islamic narrations.

There is a chauvinistic thread that has become interwoven in the public face of Islam that says women should walk three feet behind their men, women must wash their husbands' feet when they enter the home, men can beat women, and Paradise emphasizes rewards for men only. All false. Islam encourages complementarianism: the idea that men and women complement one another by having different strengths, but at no time is a man irrationally favored by Allah.

The Qur'an does address men directly, but for many topics including worship rites, inheritance, their duties, etc., and not simply the rewards of Paradise. However, the controversy surrounds several verses where Paradise is mentioned, and the operative phrase is "purified spouses," or *azwaaj mutahara* in Arabic. The word *azwaaj* means "spouses." The word *mutahara* means "clean and pure," and while it is in the feminine grammar form, there is no reference to virgins. For instance, when a Muslim performs ablutions for prayer, he or she is in a state of *tahaara*: meaning purity (from the same trilateral root of *mutahara*). This reward of having purified spouses in Paradise means spouses that are purified from all the earthly hygienic requirements and ungodly perversions, which will be true for both Muslim men and women.

This is why Shareef emphasized the Qur'an being preserved in Arabic, because when it is translated into different languages, translators take liberty to change many word meanings, one being "purified spouses" to "virgin wives"—a huge stretch and misappropriation of Divine Scripture.

Shareef patted my back and laughed, "But remember, *barakah* doesn't come down, unless good deeds go up first. Nothing leaves heaven until something leaves earth." I was awestruck. At that moment, Islam moved from the social/political themes in the hip-hop of my childhood to something deeply spiritual and intimate. *There's another side!* I thought. *And I've been only chasing this side of life. I better get to work . . .*

Shareef escorted me back downstairs, where the restaurant had suddenly filled up. I asked him what the special occasion and he told me, "It's the first day of Ramadan, the month of fasting. You became Muslim on a blessed day. It's time for us to break our fast because the sun has set."

I was sure that my life was about to change, and I was sure that these men were convinced that this way of life was true.

While I was eating at the table, a Palestinian man was facing me. He was eating too. He could tell I was a new Muslim by the way I behaved nervously, and from my clothing and jewelry. As he ate his food, he smiled gently at me, and remarked, "You know gold is *haraam* for men?" I didn't know. I shook my head. He said, "If I were you, I would take that jewelry off." I immediately complied on the spot, removing my earrings from my ears, my chain from my neck, my gold and diamond ring from my finger, and my gold watch from my wrist.

I stuffed it all in my pocket quickly as if everyone in the restaurant had not seen me walk in wearing it several minutes prior. I leaned into him and asked what I should do with it. He said, "Sell it and give the money to charity."

The next day I drove downtown, sold all my jewelry, and gave the money to myself. I hadn't changed all that much yet. I rationalized that I needed charity more than anyone I knew. Regardless of my thinking, I was set free. Liberated. I had submitted and it felt amazing.

By 2001, I was married, building my family, and taking odd jobs to make ends meet.

Walgreens pharmacy and convenient store needed someone to work security in the evenings and I had no choice but to take it. I was working as a demolition laborer during the day, cleaning basements full of dead rats and birds, but I needed more money because my second child was on the way.

I was a little hesitant, but I knew that this was a test from Allah. Would I submit to His Will and do what I had to do to feed my wife and family, or would I adopt the haughtiness of Shaytan and refuse an opportunity to earn good money?

When I arrived for my first day on the job, the store manager told me to just go stand by the door and make sure no one ran out of the store with anything. I felt like I was on the battlefield. I was going to slay my ego. It was refreshing for me. The two Islamic books I had been reading at the time both stressed humility and intention. Was I sincerely striving to please Allah or was I still a self-serving egomaniac only willing to practice Islam and be responsible when it was convenient? I was ready to prove I loved Allah, and stepping on my ego that night was part of that process.

The Walgreens that I was assigned to was in Mattapan, a working-class ghetto of Boston not far from Roxbury. As I stood by the door, I started to see too many familiar faces. They'd walk in and notice me in the corner. "Hey Ty, what's up?" I'd play it cool and answer, "Nothing at all. I'm just trying to survive." Most didn't realize that I was working; they'd do their shopping and wave to me on their way out. One girl that I had known well greeted me and then continued her shopping, and on her way out she stopped to chat with me some more. As we spoke, I probably looked a little nervous because she asked me, "Are you waiting for someone? Why are you just standing here?" I figured there was no sense in lying, "I'm working," I said.

Her neck snapped back, and her eyebrows went up, but she didn't want to make me feel too bad. "Okay then, I'm gonna let you get back to work," she said as she smiled and left the store. It was a great night, and I left my eight-hour shift exhilarated.

I did any job I could find. I delivered newspapers before the sun rose, I swept floors, and I helped people move into their apartments. All in the name of progress. I eventually settled into a warehouse job. It changed my life completely. I was working, coming home, reading, and taking care of babies.

Although I was always a present father, even for my firstborn son, Tyrone Jr., who had been born years before I accepted Islam, I still had never seen a Black man be a full-time live-in father and husband. Enter brother Ismail.

Ismail was a short, fair-skinned Black man just five years older than me. He had a long black beard that looked like a piece of silk that hung from his chin. He resembled a Native American, talked with a preacher's presence, and had a giant personality. He had left gang life to become a Muslim but was still very much rough around the edges. He wore the traditional Islamic thobe and kufi wherever he went, it didn't matter. Highly intelligent, and quick-witted, he was a force in any room he entered.

A week after I accepted Islam, Ismail happened to give me a friendly ride home one day after prayers on a Friday evening. The next morning, he was knocking at my door. When I cracked it open, I was surprised and a little freaked out. "Hey, let's hang out!" he said in his laid-back manner.

Ismail became my first teacher in Islamic masculinity. He would pick me up in a small car full of his young children, mostly girls. I'd tag along with him to the grocery store, the laundromat, and on other family-oriented errands. I watched him shop for his family and it was the first time I saw a Black man do that. It hadn't dawned on me that never in my twenty-four years of life had I seen a Black father in a grocery store with his young daughters, pushing a grocery cart and holding a shopping list. He became an instant paradigm of chivalry for me. He loved being a man and he loved helping other younger Muslims like me become men.

Not only did I pray my five daily prayers, but I found myself waking up at night to pray what is called *tahajjud* or night vigil. These are night prayers performed as an extra special time to reflect on life and make a deeper connection with Allah. I experimented with the "fast of Dawood." Dawood was the Arabic name for the prophet David. In Islam he is renowned for having fasted every other day, which is considered the most pious form of fasting but also the most difficult. I wanted to try every aspect of this new way of life. The fast of Dawood was in fact very difficult, but it did compel me to reflect on the creature comforts I so readily took advantage of. I didn't engage with the fast of Dawood for very long, though. I was far too spiritually weak, and still am.

I wanted to cleanse myself. I stopped listening to music to such an extent that if I was in the car listening to talk radio and a commercial with a jingle came on, I would turn it down until it was over. I had gotten rid of my television and only listened to the Qur'an and read books.

After a year of living a spartan kind of life, it became very difficult for me. I found the purely physical work to be redundant and the lack of innovation and intellectual rigor to be heavy on my spirit. I wanted to use my mind in a productive way. I wanted to be creative. I wanted to contribute to Islam. Instead, I was a picker of books and a packer of boxes.

I struggled with my feelings of frustration because I knew it was noble work and I didn't want to be ungrateful to my Lord. I was running myself ragged. I would leave the family station-wagon with my wife and take the train to work. On my way home I would see something that reminded me of the past worldly success I enjoyed. I didn't miss being in the spotlight, I missed doing something I really delighted in. I decided, I loved Islam now, and I enjoyed being Muslim . . . I wanted to do that.

But I felt as though my time had passed, and I would work at Harvard Business School Publishing warehouse now for the rest of my life. How could I argue with my Lord, who had been so generous to me and given me a good wife, a safe home, healthy children, and an honorable place to work?

However, it was an internal challenge to come to terms with my new mundane life as being a permanent condition. After all I had been through, was this it? Would I be picking books and racing back and forth trying to beat the clock for the rest of my life? I was feeling selfish and ungrateful and because of that I would feel as though my heart hadn't improved at all.

I would ride the train with my feet literally swollen and aching from walking for seven hours on a hard concrete floor. I began to have major back spasms from lifting all the heavy loads and I would wake up some mornings paralyzed by pain for hours. In addition, I began to have stabbing migraine headaches.

The walk from the train station to our modest apartment was all of fifteen minutes. I would get off the train and cry all the way to my front door. Those tears had no sound. They would just slowly trickle down my face. It was a release of all my frustrations and a shower for my inside. When I reached the doorstep I would wipe my tears away, take a deep breath, and put my key in the door so that I could enter my home without burdening my wife with my personal sorrows.

An American Muslim usually converts to Islam for of one of two reasons: they've grown to hate themselves, or they're attracted to the political undertones that have been highlighted through the life of Malcolm X.

However, I was still struggling to understand exactly why I should be Muslim: Was it for brotherhood? Was it because of the disciplined lifestyle and clean living? Was it because of its political and social implications? I was receiving mixed messages from every Muslim I met.

In my thirst for reading, I decided I'd gather any title that would help me be more "spiritual" or politically aware. I read Mahtma Ghandi's *My Experiments with the Truth*, Frances Fox Piven and Richard Cloward's *Poor People's Movements*, George Jackson's *Soledad Brother*, Neale Donald Walsch's *Conversations with God*, and so many more books with conflicting philosophies that I became more confused than before. When other urban Muslims would see me with these titles, most would praise me and tell me to keep "seeking knowledge." But little did I know the content I was reading contained no guidance for a Muslim.

A proverbial window opened when I began to listen to a series of tapes by a Black American Muslim scholar named Abu Usamah at-Thahabi. He was ten years my senior and from the 'hood in New Jersey. After graduating from a Saudi Arabian Islamic university, he returned to the states to teach Islam to urban Muslims. His delivery, down-to-earth disposition, and practical approach to learning changed my life. He exemplified what it looked like to keep your Black identity yet honor classic Islamic values. I would spend the next twenty years using his early example as a guidepost for my Islamic leadership style.

In one of the Islamic books of *fiqh*, I read that Muslim men should grow their beards, so I immediately began growing my facial hair. The wisdom behind the ruling is that every male species is decorated with a natural adornment: for male lions it is their mane, for male peacocks it is their bright feathers, and for male humans it is their beards. In addition, all men of faith had beards in the past. I even noticed in Christian images that Jesus wore a beard, and his mother covered her hair like a Muslim woman. It was all fascinating to me.

I had been participating in correspondence courses with the Salafi brothers through Albaseerah International Institute by way of telelink, which was an early version of Zoom, where multiple people could be on one telephone line and a scholar from Saudi Arabia would teach an entire course on Islam over the phone, while another person translated his words from Arabic into English.

I traveled to Mecca in 2006 to receive certification in Islamic studies. The trip changed the trajectory of my life. On August 17 I arrived in Medinah! I was asleep on the tour bus when a fellow student shook me awake, "Brother, look!" There was the prophet's masjid . . . Masjid Nabawi!

It was the most amazing sight I had seen in my entire life. I saw a towering brown mortar structure surrounded by bustling traffic and busy storefronts. It looked like a huge palace. Amazing!

We dropped our bags in the hotel and headed to the local shops to buy some thobes, which were Islamic dress. The first time I heard the *athaan*, which is the formal call to prayer that blasted from loudspeakers over the entire city, my eyes bubbled over with moistness. This wasn't a dream. The beautiful voice of the caller echoed with the sweet melody of "Haya alasalaah, Haya alaal falaah," which meant "Come to prayer, come to success."

The people flocked in their thousands, all the men in white and all the women in black. It was *maghrib*, the sunset prayer, and the lights of the masjid, which I had seen so many times on postcards and in photos, began to come to life in front of my eyes.

Then, to the shock of all the American students, we were given an exclusive tour of Masjid Nabawi, the Prophet Muhammad's original masjid, where he lived, and where he was buried. We were taken through the masjid control center and security center, and given an oral history of the original construction work complete with museum-style displays.

As if that wasn't enough, we were then escorted into a plush private theater inside the masjid where we were treated to a screening of a documentary film of the history and legacy of Masjid Nabawi. We sat in these huge leather chairs and waiters brought us tiny cups of Arabian coffee and tea. As I sipped my tea, I thanked Allah for favoring me out of billions of souls and inviting me to His House.

Every night we were there was spent in prayer in the masjid for as long as our eyes could stay open. I prayed as much as I could, and I tried to remember every person I loved, liked, had known well, or had spoken to briefly, and asked Allah to forgive them.

At some point I visited the Prophet Muhammad's resting place. Considering that his house was attached to the original masjid when it was still very small, he was buried in it. Now after over one thousand years, the masjid had expanded and his burial place was not in the masjid at all, but instead it was sectioned off and surrounded by several walls facing away from the *qiblah*, just in case anyone might get the idea that Muslims pray to Muhammad.

"As-Salaamu Alaikum, Messenger of Allah," I whispered to him as all Muslims are instructed to do upon visiting his grave. My heart was smiling, and I had become overwhelmed with a calm joy. I touched the gate to the Prophet Muhammad's grave and bent down and stuck my face into one of the large openings and looked inside. I was in the presence of a great man. Inside was a small narrow hallway with a gray cement floor and what looked like a rectangular outline. Perhaps it was signaling the exact spot he was buried. I wasn't sure.

I couldn't believe that, as ignorant as I had been and as backward-thinking, selfish, and violent as I had once lived, I was now standing as a Muslim in the presence of my Prophet Muhammad. Praise Allah!

It was there, in the Holy Land of Medinah, that I finlly could be myself for the first time since I was a child. There was no false façade of bravado that I needed to project to ward off would-be schemers, and no worry about being accosted by the police. I felt like an eight-year-old boy again; innocent, even.

The following day our tour included an exclusive trip to "The King Fahd Complex for the Printing of the Noble Qur'an." We toured the huge factory and saw Qur'ans in every language being printed.

The next day we traveled to Mecca where I made Umrah. As a pilgrim I could only wear one thin white towel draped over my shoulders and one thin towel wrapped around my waist, with nothing underneath, like I had just gotten out of the shower. It is called *ihram.*

This dress is part of the religious rites of Islam when visiting the Kaabah, which is the first house of worship built by the prophet Abraham and his son Ismael. One of the goals of Umrah and Hajj is to come before Allah with nothing, whether you're a king or a poor man. So, the donning of simple white clothes symbolizes the poverty of mankind before Allah who is Rich and Free of need.

When we arrived in Mecca it was midnight, but none of us were tired. The masjid had several levels that wrapped around the Kaabah and we were on the ground floor. The closer we came to the center, the more I saw. Then finally . . . the black square appeared in my view, right in the middle of the masjid! Tall and majestic, the Kaabah is magnetic in its attraction. It pulls you to it. It is one of the symbols of Allah and of course we don't worship it or pray to it, but it holds a special place in the hearts of Muslims.

As I got closer, I realized that there were thousands of people forming one large moving circle as they made their way around it, praying to Allah. We put our *ihram* under our armpits, which is part of the rites of worship, and we joined in the circuit! I made my seven rounds around and each time I passed the Black Stone, which is encased inside a corner of the Kaabah, I waved to it. I couldn't believe I was praying at the Kaabah! I was here!

Before that journey, I had assumed that I would continue working in a warehouse picking, packing, and shipping books for Harvard Business School Publishing. But now I felt a higher calling. Little did

I know that ten years later, I would return to Harvard as the first paid imam and lecturer at Harvard Divinity School.

We began our wrap-up lessons before the major tests. The lessons I learned from the great scholars of Islam or *ulema*, were profound. I learned *Kitab Tawheed* (The Book of Monotheism), an integral book in the Islamic creed from Sheikh Fahad Al-Fuhayd. The noble elder and scholar Abdullah Ghudyaan taught us lessons from *Arba'een An-Nawawi* (Forty Hadith of Imam Nawawi), which were the essential forty narrations of the Prophet Muhammad on faith and actions. We delved into *Mustalah hadeeth* (hadith terminology) with Sheikh Abdullah Musallam. We were taught some of the intricacies of *fiqh* by Sheikh Wasiullah Abbass, and the sciences of the Qur'an by Sheikh Saalih As-Sadlaan.

We were visited by the Grand Mufti of Saudi Arabia, Sheikh Abdul-Aziz As-Sheikh, a direct descendant of the polarizing Muslim cleric, Muhammad ibn Abdul-Wahhab, about whom much has been written and spoken.

In addition, a member of the *Kabaair 'ulema* or Council of Senior Scholars, Sheikh Al-Luhaydaan, spoke to us about our role and responsibility in the West. He stressed that as students of knowledge, we must have patience and beautified character, with no trace of harshness or enmity toward the non-Muslim.

Some of those great men have since passed away and I ask Allah to forgive them and reward them with good for taking the time to teach and encourage the likes of myself.

⚜ 6 ⚜

AMERICAN MUSLIMS

Intrareligious Tension

OBVIOUSLY THE FIRST Muslims in America were Africans imported through the Atlantic slave trade, who were literate in Arabic and practiced in secret. However, historian Kambiz GhaneaBassiri writes in *A History of Islam in America* that, by the end of the nineteenth century, American-born children of slaves did not identify as Muslim. Islam had faded from their lives as they were compelled in many instances to accept Christianity.

But there was an influx of immigrants from Muslim-majority countries, who voluntarily migrated to America in the early twentieth century partly due to the industrial revolution and the need for railroad workers and other laborers. In fact, the first mosque in America was built in Chicago in 1893 as a temporary display during a state fair on a fictional "Cairo Street," meant to depict a neighborhood in Egypt. The second, more official, mosque in America was built in 1921 by immigrant Muslims in Highland Park, Michigan. Regarding the intentions of those early Muslim immigrants, historian Sally Howell writes:

> *Built by Muslim migrants for use as a place of worship, this mosque, like the one on "Cairo Street," was intended to represent Islam to American observers, but the Muslims of Highland Park hoped to create a very different impression of their faith. The Islam to be practiced in the Moslem Mosque of Highland Park would not be exotic, foreign, or a thing of*

*spectacle. It would be an American faith tradition not unlike
those found in nearby churches and synagogues. It would
attract worshipers who were American citizens.*

Islam didn't suddenly appear in America just before the tragic
9/11 terror attacks on the World Trade Center as a strange, foreign religion bent on destroying the West. It's clear that the ideal to assimilate
has always been at the forefront of immigrant Muslims.

However American Muslims are not a monolith. Based on my
more than twenty years immersed in a very diverse Islamic mosaic, I
would assess that there are essentially two distinct categories of Muslims living in America today, and each has subcategories.

Immigrant Muslims

Subcategory 1—Immigrants from lighter-skinned countries: These
are Muslims who migrated to America from Egypt, Morocco, Turkey,
Pakistan, India, and other places in the 1960s, 1970s, and 1980s. They
typically came to America for a better quality of life, including educational opportunities and wider career choices. These immigrants
went to college and became doctors, engineers, and dentists. Likewise,
their children, who were born in America, have also become educated,
working professionals.

These immigrants are the builders and funders of most of the
contemporary American mosques. They celebrate their success by
founding Islamic grade-schools and cater their programming to "young
professionals," which has become a euphemism for Arab-only events,
including matchmaking events, family outings, and other social occasions. These communities—Arab, Turkish, Pakistani, et cetera—are
very insular.

I've heard from enough of them myself: "Why can't Black
Americans just work hard like we did?" They don't understand the
dichotomy of American racism and American accommodation. One

suppresses Blacks through racial bureaucracy and the other encourages immigrant achievement through student loan programs, grants, and filling nationality quotas in universities.

Frankly speaking, these immigrant Muslims owe their success to Black people who spearheaded minority rights during the civil rights movement.

The Immigration Act of 1924 favored European immigrants. Muslim-majority countries were not even a factor to consider for immigration until Dr. King and the civil rights movement compelled the United States to pass the Immigration and Nationality Act of 1965. This act banned national quotas and shifted to an immigration system based on family unity and skilled laborers, thus allowing an influx of Muslim migrants to come to America and aspire to a white construct.

In a 2017 Pew survey of American Muslims, 40 percent of respondents are categorized as white, although half of those in this group are of Middle Eastern or North African descent. This is because the census currently codes these people as racially "white," even though no scientist or anthropologist would deny these people are of African ancestry.

Because of their "white status" they carry the assumption of white privilege, and it affects how they view Black people in America. This construct of whiteness in an Islamic context has less to do with color, and more to do with a fluid ideal that allows those who hold dominant power to set the religious norms, to decide who fits in and who doesn't, and to shape a narrative with huge intrareligious deficits and cultural blind spots.

Once, after I'd appeared as a guest speaker at a local mosque, the immigrant imam invited me to have dinner with his congregation in the mosque basement. During our open conversation, he proceeded to tell me the harrowing story of his first time traveling to America. Apparently as he entered the airplane and checked his ticket, he saw a beautiful white woman with blonde hair and blue eyes in a seat nearby.

He said, "I prayed to Allah that he did not test me by making me sit next to this beautiful woman for the entire flight. And as I prayed, I checked my ticket and stopped at my seat, and Allah answered my prayers! He sat me next to a Black woman!"

I didn't say anything, and nor did the many African Muslims present. I thought to myself, *Does this man not realize that my mother is a Black woman? My wife? My daughter?* How supremely tone-deaf he was.

For this subcategory of immigrant Muslims, the sophisticated nuances of racism are lost. They believe if they don't use the N-word, then they couldn't possibly be racist. They define inclusivity as counting the number of Black Muslims in the room, and if the total amount falls shorter than what was hoped for, then they invite more. However, being invited doesn't mean that these Black voices will be heard, or their opinions considered. It's a numbers game for them.

Subcategory 2—Immigrants from darker-skinned countries: These are primarily darker-skinned immigrants from the African continent, including Sierra Leone, Senegal, Sudan, Somalia, and other places. These Muslim immigrants are given refugee status in America due to famine and civil war in their countries. They're also given access to federal and state assistance programs like monthly food vouchers and public housing. They usually become cab drivers, laborers, or small business owners.

Keeping in mind that Senator Durbin stated that President Trump referred to Haiti and African countries as "shithole" countries during a White House meeting with twenty-three members of Congress, a Pew Research study showed that Somalis had the highest immigrant arrest rate under the Trump Administration. This is not a coincidence. Research shows that darker-skinned immigrants are targeted and given less access than those from lighter-skinned countries like Egypt.

According to a study at the University of California, US immigration authorities locked detainees from African and Caribbean countries in solitary confinement cells six times as often as the population at large. Detainees from these predominantly Black countries made up just 4 percent of detainees in US "Immigration and Customs Enforcement" custody from 2012 to 2017—but 24 percent of all solitary confinement stays.

American-born Muslims

Subcategory 1—White Muslims: Whiteness in America is fluid. During Jim Crow, the "One Drop Rule" stated that if you had even one drop of Black blood, you were considered Black. Professor James Horton states, "Virginia law defined a Black person as a person with one sixteenth African ancestry. Now Florida defined a Black person as a person with one eighth African ancestry. And Alabama said, 'You are Black if you got any Black ancestry, or any African ancestry at all.' But you know what this means? You can walk across a state line and literally, legally, change race."

To qualify this subcategory, by white Muslims I mean converts born in America who have European ancestry, not Moroccans designated as white by the US census.

According to a 2017 Pew research study, 62 percent of white Muslim converts are men. According to an American Muslim poll in 2020, white Muslims are more likely to support former President Donald Trump (in terms of presidential job approval and favoring him as a candidate in the 2020 election) and they favor building political coalitions with conservative groups.

Experiencing these conservative leanings has been at the crux of my relationships with white middle-class Muslim converts. They are, for the most part, oblivious to the plight of Black American Muslims as it relates to intrareligious racism and social marginalization in general. While some are devout, many of the ones I've encountered move with religious impunity, not wearing *hijab* or even offering formal prayers. The immigrant Muslims designated as white considerate it a great honor to have white people incline toward Islam, even at the expense of implementing the fundamentals of faith. Many of these white converts behave outside of the Islamic norm. It seems they convert to Islam for the culture and exoticism without having any real theological attachment to the faith.

Many lighter-skinned immigrant Muslims and white converts hold a hidden contempt for Black Muslims.

Subcategory 2—System-affected Muslims or SAM: I am a system-affected Muslim; however, system-affected Muslims are not just Black people. A system-affected Muslim or SAM, can be any race, including white. They are characterized by an entirely unique historical and/or social circumstance consisting of any of the following:

- poverty
- violence
- broken homes
- mental/physical abuse
- drug addiction
- social deprivation
- discrimination

All the above are the results of institutional racism, transgenerational trauma due to the legacy of chattel slavery, and social marginalization that results from poverty. And because the legacy self (the part of our subconscious minds that possesses the knowledge of an ancestral connection to a larger narrative of achievement, cultural identity and tradition passed down from generation to generation) has been decimated, SAMs are without a collective cultural identity of any significance.

The Black SAM was created after the post–civil-war reconstruction effort was sabotaged by the emergence of the KKK. There were no opportunities for Black people. Many of them returned to work for their former masters as sharecroppers. As a result, Black families left the south in droves, discouraged and searching for hope in the north.

The US government began to build public housing projects in the 1870s because of this displaced population of freedmen. They needed a place to store all these newly freed Blacks, whose chance at interracial democracy had been cut short by waves of terrorism in the form of vigilante violence. These buildings took their architectural structure from the classic chicken coop. For the first time, people would be living stacked on top of other people. Many moved into these public housing units, called "Projects," and thus were perpetually isolated from the breadbasket of goods and services that America offered the rest of her citizens.

Those who don't think objectively like to undermine the post-slavery trauma that still affects Black Americans and the Black SAM in particular. They think electing a Black president or having Black billionaires in America somehow replenishes centuries of disenfranchisement. That is hardly the case.

Black Americans at the turn of the nineteenth century were in a constant struggle to build and maintain enough mental fortitude and momentum for survival. For those who arose every morning in a country that hated them, where the laws were designed to sabotage their progress, and where their children could be killed by any number of environmental hazards, the appeal of worshipping a Jesus who looked like their oppressors waned rapidly.

These adverse social conditions created an urban environment ripe for *therapeutic theology*, that is, a religious creed that suited the social/emotional needs of a disregarded group, answered their mysteries, quelled their fears, and affirmed their identities and struggles. Enter Noble Drew Ali and the Moorish Science Temple of America.

Born Timothy Drew in 1886, Drew was said to be the orphaned son of two former slaves from North Carolina. He eventually left home and joined a traveling circus that made its way to Egypt, where he was exposed to Islam. Upon his return, he claimed to have been taught by an Egyptian high priest and given magic powers.

In 1913, he started the Canaanite Temple in New Jersey. His doctrine stated that Black people were all Moors, descended from an ancient tribe in Africa. He encouraged Blacks to use mind power for personal transformation and to reject being called Black or colored. He later settled in Chicago and founded the Moorish Science Temple of America in 1925.

At the time of his death in 1929, one of his original followers, Wallace Fard Muhammad claimed to be a prophet reincarnated and became the teacher of Elijah Poole, who later changed his name to Elijah Muhammad and founded the Nation of Islam in 1934.

The Nation of Islam, using a combination of reverse racism, the Bible, and the Qur'an, and a pointed dress code far from the gypsy-inspired attire of the Moorish Science Temple, attempted to reframe the stereotype of the dimwitted Black person with notions of Black supremacy. At that time, their religious movement was only sixty years removed from the Reconstruction era. The wounds of being denigrated and tortured were still fresh in their minds, in the same way as the wounds of the civil rights movement (which we're only sixty years removed from) are fresh in ours.

Their parents were victims of the Reconstruction sabotage and would tell them stories of being tortured and harassed, just like our parents were victims of the civil rights movement and they too tell us stories of being discriminated against. It is understandable that 1930s Blacks, staring at an unfulfilled destiny and a scathing stereotype, would want to gather around a religious narrative that empowered them.

However, after the death of Malcom X in 1965, and then the death of the Nation of Islam's founder, Elijah Muhammad, ten years later, the trust from the Black community that once was a hallmark for the Nation had begun to dissipate. Elijah's Muhammad's son, Warith Deen Muhammad, emerged in 1975. Imam Warith Deen had apparently spent some amount of time overseas studying orthodox Islam, and it's said that his father had planned for him to reestablish the Nation of Islam upon orthodoxy after his death.

Imam Warith Deen single-handedly dismantled the Nation of Islam upon the death of his father and declared himself and his followers to be Sunni, mainstream, orthodox American Muslims. However, it was this fracture in the Nation of Islam that catapulted Minister Louis Farrakhan into the spotlight after he resisted Imam Warith Deen's orthodox assertions and rekindled the Nation of Islam that exists today.

Imam Warith Deen, while certainly a hero to many urban Muslims for converting an entire community of tens of thousands of families to orthodox Islam in the 1970s, fell short of appreciating the *sunnah* in its entirety. The *sunnah* is loosely defined as "the lifestyle and example of the Arabian prophet Muhammad of 1,400 years ago." The *sunnah* is his implementation of Islamic ritualsin daily life that have come to be the crux of Muslim ritual and law. Orthodox Muslims derive the name "Sunni Muslim" from this concept.

To reconcile the exaggerated Black supremacy mythology of the Nation of Islam, Imam Warith Deen adopted a scientific approach to Islam and subsequently rejected any hadith or qur'anic verses that spoke of divine miracles. In his version of Islam, Moses didn't really split the Red Sea, it was metaphoric. He feared his congregation would be susceptible to falling back into Nation of Islam folklore if they accepted any religious ideas that defied science and logic.

Over the following two decades, this misstep ultimately led his congregation to misinterpret qur'anic meanings and undervalue the significance of the prophetic lifestyle found in hadith.

Resenting the incomplete Islamic application that the Warith Deen community offered SAMs in the 1970s and 1980s, the Salafis then appeared in the early 1990s to try to establish a true understanding of orthodoxy through an exaggerated appreciation for the hadith.

Salafis are categorized as "Muslims who adhere to the belief and practice of the *Salaf,* or first three generations of Muslims, from the advent of prophet Muhammad's first generation in 610 Common Era to the third generation in approximately 800 Common Era."

The first three generations of Islam are categorized by a pure monotheistic creed, unadulterated by cultural beliefs and foreign worship practices. Salafis today lean heavily on hadith narrations to shape their entire belief and daily lives in accordance with the life of the earliest generations of Muslims.

As a former Salafi myself, I find many of their qualities appealing, such as their love of learning and their meticulous attention to detail when it comes to worship. During my years as a Salafi, I met some intelligent and sincere Salafi brothers from whom I benefited tremendously.

However, some attributes of the Salafi methodology are problematic for me today, such as remaining aloof from politics, placing too much emphasis on hadith literature, dogmatizing faith, and condemning any other iteration of Islam.

Paradoxically, when overseas Islamic educational institutions began accepting American students in the 1980s and early 1990s, many young SAMs began traveling to study Islam.

The results were disastrous, in my humble opinion. Many of the young men who were chosen to study traditional Islam with a Wahaabi/Salafi lens had tumultuous childhoods. They were former gang members, or naïve sycophants who hadn't addressed their own emotional/intellectual deficits. When they returned to the United States and went back to the ghettos, during their lessons and sermons they took the words of the Middle Eastern scholars, twisted them into half-truths, and used them to verbally abuse all Muslims who didn't adhere to their understanding of Islam.

They used rude terms to refer to their non-Muslim family members, labeling them "stinking, filthy disbelievers," and even to other Muslims, calling some "dogs of the hellfire."

As SAMs, people who have been deeply damaged both psychologically and spiritually by the constructs of other races, why would we believe that we could adopt a dogmatic Islamic framework and successfully transpose it onto our battered lives and be successful? Even the immigrant Muslims from the subcategories I mentioned adjust their Islam to fit a Western narrative.

I have seen what a caustic iteration of dogmatic Islam can do to SAMs. If we follow a rote Islamic framework, we'll only be safe within the walls of the masjid, but when we leave we will be at risk of all the dangers and vices of our neighborhoods: drugs, alcohol, promiscuity, delinquency, false ego, violence, and vile habits.

SAMs must climb out of colonialism, self-deception, and racial exploitation while simultaneously worshipping God, and worshipping God cannot come at the exclusion of those factors.

SAMs need to be submerged in a faith that is friendly to all people, because SAMs are conditioned to welcome confrontation, so compassion should be emphasized as a religious principle. They need a faith that keeps their struggles at the forefront, because the SAM is always balancing a tightrope of family problems, financial struggle, and personal challenges with little-to-no social tools to address them.

The Moorish Science Temple, the Nation of Islam, the Warith Deen community, and American Salafis have all tried to address these problems. Where we had no traces of legacy, we created them. Where we saw no divine protection, we generated folklore. And where we felt no community, we built it, one city block at a time. The SAM is born out of this tenacious and troubled narrative.

W. E. B. Du Bois writes,

After the Egyptian and the Indian, the Greek and Roman, the Teuton and Mongolian, the Negro is a sort of seventh son, born with a veil, and gifted with second-sight in this American world,—a world which yields him no true self-consciousness, but only lets him see himself through the

*revelation of the other world. It is a peculiar sensation, this
double-consciousness, this sense of always looking at one's self
through the eyes of others, of measuring one's soul by the tape
of a world that looks on in amused contempt and pity. One
ever feels his two-ness,—an American, a Negro; two souls,
two thoughts, two unreconciled strivings; two warring ideals
in one dark body, whose dogged strength alone keeps it from
being torn asunder.*

Du Bois suggests that Black people see themselves in two ways
simultaneously: through their own sense of self, which is more fluid
and not as clearly defined, and through the reflection of a white construct, which views them with amused contempt and pity. I would
argue that the SAM, surrounded by a prevailing immigrant narrative,
suffers the same psychological turmoil.

Until now, there has never been a balanced, nurturing, and
knowledgeable approach to orthodox Islam from an urban perspective because the urban personality has never had an affirming, positive
self-image. Many of us are quick to abandon our identities in favor of
thobes (the traditional, long dress-like garment of Arabs), sandals, and
turbans, assuming these things establish and reinforce a strong Islamic
presence.

While those items are useful in their proper context (namely on
special occasions or while living in Muslim lands) they do not serve the
purpose of edifying the mind and soul of the SAM and may only serve
as a kind of costume that we hide behind.

Arab Muslim scholars have long debated the equity of Africans
and Black people in general. To give context to Islam's view of slavery,
I want to mention the ninth-century hadith scholar, al-Bukhari (who
was Persian). This scholar took sixteen years to compile his hadith
collection. He implemented a highly scientific method of tracing the
names and identities of narrators, leading directly back to the words of
the Prophet Muhammad.

Bukhari compiled two books about slavery in his ninety-eight-book hadith collection; they were numbered as books forty-nine and fifty. The names he chose for these books are an indication of the Islamic position on slavery. They were called *Kitab al-'Itq* (The Book of Emancipation) and *Kitab al-Muktaba* (The Book on Contracts of Emancipation).

Bukhari was a jurist as well as a collector of hadith, and clearly his position was that slavery is to be viewed within the context of *freeing people*. Unfortunately, the traditional Arab view of the African can be found in *Lane's Arabic–English Lexicon*, an Arab-language reference book. In it, the term, *As-Sudan*, is defined as the following:

Negroes—that particular race who are the most stinking of mankind in the armpits and sweat; those who are eunuchs.

Ibn Qutayba wrote that Wahb Ibn Munabbih, a famous eighth-century scholar and convert to Islam, believed that Ham ibn Nuh (Ham the son of the prophet Noah) was a beautiful white man, but Allah changed his color due to Noah's curse. (This occurred in Genesis 9, when Ham allegedly saw Noah drunk and naked, so Noah cursed him and his descendants to be Black and rejected. This story does not exist in Qur'an or in Islam at all, yet many Arabs have adopted this construct in justifying the inferiority of Blacks as being "Allah's Will.")

In fact, James Sweet, a professor of comparative slavery at University of Wisconsin, concedes that it was from the Arab lands and from Iberia that these racial attitudes traveled to America when the Portuguese explained the Hamitic Curse to the Americans in the fifteenth century, just before the mass slave trade.

Ninth-century Persian historian, al-Tabari, in his *Tarikh al-Tabari* (History of Tabari) described Noah's son Sham's descendants as "Arabs, Persians, Byzantines and all who are good." He said the less civilized people were from Ham (Copts, Sudanese, Berbers), that is, the Black people.

Ibn Khaldun, another Islamic historian from the past, considered Blacks as dumb animals in his *Muqaddamah*. And there are many more scholars who believed Blacks were inferior.

As Muslims, we accept any rational ruling of purely legal content from any Muslim scholar of the *sunnah* regardless of race or background. However, when their personal opinions are passed off as sacred knowledge, we should do our own thinking based on our context.

This is because those great scholars were human beings, after all. They were influenced by the social norms of their time, which may have included constructs that weren't yet defined as nationalism and racism but were obviously prevalent. They were not immune to assuming (incorrectly) that their cultural norm was the norm of Islam.

Allah says:

> *O mankind, indeed, We have created you from male and female and made you nations and tribes that you may know one another. Indeed, the most noble of you in the sight of Allah is the most righteous of you. Indeed, Allah is Knowing and Acquainted.*

Arabs are a proud people with wonderful qualities of chivalry, loyalty, and hospitality. Today, I have many Arab Muslim friends who are paradigms of good character and come from wholesome families. However, as a collective people, they must look internally at their denial of the racism, chauvinism, toxic pride, love of wealth and power, and political ineptitude that has plagued them before, during, and after the advent of Islam.

Keeping Du Bois' definition of "A Double Consciousness" in mind, when an urban individual, possessing all this tragic history and internal trauma, discovers Islam with its lofty principles, he becomes enthralled by the dignity it instills within him. He then mistakenly conflates Islamic character with Arab or South Asian culture and deems it necessary to adopt their cultural norms to "legitimize" his Islam. Thus, he competes with his own self.

Not only does this have negative social ramifications, but we see Islamic theology shapeshifting according to the racial trauma of the American Black Muslim over the span of a century.

The damage done to the SAM is unquantifiable. He is confused in both who he should be as a Muslim (Black nationalist, Arab-like, or hip-hop), and what that representation should look like.

The ramifications of the much touted but false Hamitic curse have lingered in the modern immigrant masjids in America. We have witnessed the dismissal of our Black voices, opinions, and identities in immigrant Muslim gatherings. We have been disrespected and our children treated differently in Muslim shared spaces. We have been manipulated to be the "public face of mosque diversity" only when it benefits the immigrant narrative. We have been left out of meaningful decisions that affect the entire community. And the SAM pioneers of modern American orthodox Islam have been summarily left out of the historical paradigm of appreciation and honor after many of them sacrificed their very lives to establish Islam in America in the 1960s and 1970s.

❦ 7 ❧

GUILTY VICTIMS

Humanizing the Men inside Concord Prison

"MARTIN LUTHER KING Jr. can go to hell!" I screamed. I was giving a sermon to an audience of about forty men. They were killers, thieves, and drug dealers. Every day we gathered from 9 a.m. until 12 p.m., and then again from 1:30 p.m. until 3:30 p.m., in our small sacred space inside the belly of Concord prison. The year was 2006. We had a very nice worship area, provided by the state of Massachusetts. The walls were made of red brick, and we decorated them with beautiful Islamic quotes. On one end of the room was a huge wooden bookshelf built by Muslim inmates, where we kept a library of many different Islamic texts. You could find Qur'ans in Arabic, French, Spanish, and English, as well as books on Islamic law, finance, and family life. On the other end of the room was a long brown industrial coat-rack, flooded by cheaply made denim jackets stenciled with the letters DOC (short for Department of Correction) in huge white letters on the back.

All the inmates sat on the fluffy green rug, with their state-issued socks on display, in rows of Black and Brown faces, sprinkled with a few white ones. Some were grizzled by years of rough living, some young and fresh off the street. All were shocked by my words. Today I was teaching them how important Islamic theology was by emphasizing that even a man like Dr. King, who did so much good and sacrificed his life for it, was essentially useless because he was not Muslim. You would think convicted felons had no conscience, but most of them shifted their bodies uncomfortably. I wasn't done. "And the pope is gay! He slept his way to the top!" As I spoke, some of the younger men giggled, unsure how to take my words. Others grimaced openly. I didn't care. This was the truth as I saw it.

My Islamic education hadn't directly taught me those awful ideas, but I had been influenced by a sentiment of disdain for all things not Islamic.

As the men sat uncomfortably through my closing remarks, the officer on duty in the chapel opened the door to our prayer space and told us, as he routinely did, that we had five minutes until movement. The prisoners would have to head back to their cells for the day. As I concluded my lesson and stepped outside of the Muslim prayer space and into the chapel's main hall, where you could find dozens of Protestant and Catholic inmates bustling in and out of their own sacred spaces, as well as the rabbi sitting in a private office with a few inmates, one of the older African American Muslim inmates tapped me on the shoulder and asked to speak with me in the corner.

His name was Abdul Malik, but everyone called him Lucky. He was a hustler from the 1980s and 1990s who had been doing hard time off and on for decades. About my height at six feet tall, Lucky weighed about 210 pounds and was solid for a man in his mid-forties. He walked with a limp from being shot in the knee decades before. His skin was the color of mahogany and his face bore the traces of several scars, long since healed but still noticeable. Lucky wore the same white T-shirt and green state-issued prison pants as the rest of the inmates, but his were always immaculately clean and pressed. He had been Muslim since the early 1990s, about ten years before me. He wasn't a scholar, but he certainly was no dummy. He was well respected in the prison system.

When Lucky got me in a corner of the chapel, he looked me dead in my eyes and asked, "Martin Luther King can go to hell? Is that what they taught you overseas?" He was trying to be respectful, but his eyes couldn't hide his frustration. Before I could say a word, he continued, "Brother listen, you wouldn't be able to work in here if it wasn't for Dr. King. None of our people wouldn't even have rights if it wasn't for him. You can't be sayin' things like that to those brothers. Understand something . . . you are a light in this dark place. When you come in here you represent hope to us. We take your word as sacred. Anything you say we gonna hold on to. Why are you being so disrespectful? You don't have to disrespect the pope to make your point. We get it. If I can give you some advice; don't bring any negative language in here. Those guys are sitting here doing years in the dozens because of that kind of energy, brother. We all expect more from you."

It was like someone stuck a flashlight in my head. Why was I being so harsh? The scholars never mentioned a word about the pope or Dr. King. Where was all this negative energy coming from? Why did I feel the need to disparage other faiths and historical personalities to prove my religion's superiority? I didn't have the answer then, but in that moment with Lucky in the corner of Concord prison, I quickly became a student again. I shook my head slowly, "You're right. I apologize. Thank you, brother. I'll try to do better." And I did. But not all at once. There were layers to my ignorance, and it would take years of trying to find self-awareness to understand the dynamic that had just taken place.

When Lucky enlightened me that day about referring to Dr. Martin Luther King and the pope using derogatory language, I started to think about why so many convert Muslims in the West, especially those of African American descent like myself, were weaponizing Islam, not through violence but through subversive interpretations. I had to look at who I was before I accepted Islam.

Those thoughts took me back nine years prior to my conversation with Lucky. It was 1997 and I was twenty-two years old. I was in California with Dr. Dre, willing to risk it all to be accepted. But for some reason I flubbed and was sent home a month later. I know now that it was because, deep in my subconscious, I doubted the authenticity of my "gangsta rap" persona. Now I was being reminded that I wasn't a gangsta Muslim either. I didn't need to bring that low vibration into Concord prison.

Before Islam, I thrived on trying to be an ignorant street thug and I was never good at it. I would have too many second thoughts and instant regrets after I did something irresponsible. My heart was warm, not cold. I was a secret nerd, an intellectual in denial, posturing as if I was part of a hard knock life. I wasn't.

Since I was a child, I had been fascinated by T-Bone's violence, Fat Rat's money, and later Big Chuck's reputation. I wanted to be like those guys. I managed to appropriate many redeemable qualities from some of them. To survive in a setting as intense as urban life you have to be hyper-masculine in one way or another or run the risk of being a perpetual victim. And to that effect, T-Bone and Big Chuck taught me the meaning of loyalty, self-respect, bravery, and brotherhood in my late teens.

Men like them were prepared to do whatever they had to do at the drop of a hat. Big Chuck was very civilized and principled. Some of us young guys would party all night and crash on his couch, and in the morning he would get angry if he found out that one of us had urinated while standing in the shower because, as he put it, "People walk barefoot in there!" I'd watch him clean and clip his fingernails religiously. And if we went to a restaurant, he would ask for a glass of steaming hot water, then take his silverware and sit it in the glass to sanitize it.

Big Chuck gave me some insight into why street life is so seductive when, one night, Bunny, another good guy caught up in bad things, got into a fight at the Harbor Club while Big Chuck and I were there. Chuck knew the other guys and tried to make peace, but they insisted on wanting to fight Bunny. A few of us watched as Chuck and one of the guys from the other side shouted into each other's ears over the loud music. Chuck was trying for peace, but the guy wasn't having it. Bunny was raging in the background, ready to go. After a few minutes of failed negotiation, Chuck got fed up and told them, "Okay then, let's go outside."

Before we made it to the door, Chuck sent me with the keys to his car ahead of everyone else. I squeezed through the crowd and out into the night air. I made a dash to the trunk and grabbed a giant .9 mm from under some sheets. I stuffed it in my waist and ran back to the crowd. Chuck met me halfway and grabbed the gun from me, stuffed it in his waist and told me to pull the car up. He grabbed the guys who wanted to fight Bunny and he told them, "Listen, if there's a problem, let's deal with it now. If there's not, then don't let me hear that you tried to get him later." When they saw how committed he was to Bunny's safety, they agreed to make peace.

When he got in the car, I asked him why he said what he said. It was the intellectual side of me, always wanting to know one's intention and ethos. He responded, "How can I sleep if my friend feels like his life is in danger? If they want a problem, then all our lives should be in danger right here and now." I understood clearly.

When the world has turned its back on you, and you feel as though you're almost completely useless to the narrative of life, and someone shows up and stands next to you and says, "I'm with you until the end," you feel lifted up and seen. Those praiseworthy qualities of love and loyalty make gang life appealing for young men. How else can you express unconditional love to another man except through mutual bloodshed and protection? Love has never been so literal in any sphere as it is on the battlefield. Soldiers of any land can tell you that. It's the only way men can ever prove they love other men. So, we bond around the necessary evil of violence.

I learned later that there were other ways to express love but, for that time and place, we were who we were. In this manner I picked up small nuances from all the street guys I had been around.

But along with those positive aspects of these guys, I also carried the negative parts of their identities: arrogance, sarcasm, and a flagrant disregard for the feelings of others. Thus, these traits crept into my spiritual life and were cloaked in religion.

Religious men would do well to look at who they were before they were faithful. I've seen too many former drug users and sellers become Muslim and carry that negative energy into their religious life until it manifests itself in the form of arrogance and bigotry. Victims create victims. As for me, I had simply exchanged street slang for qur'anic rhetoric, *but the mentality was the same.* Instead of f--k Tupac, it was f--k Dr. Martin Luther King and the pope.

In Concord I was the wrong kind of Salafi—harsh, short-sighted, and essentially ignorant of the goals of Islam, which are self-purification, justice, and service—and instead focused on rote ritual and the emphasizing of dogma. But these men in Concord, some convicted of the worst crimes imaginable, were very sophisticated, despite my own intellectual shortcomings.

There was Taha, a Portuguese Muslim who had converted ten years prior but lost his way due to substance abuse. He was an excellent memorizer and could comprehend high-level theological concepts with ease. When he first came to Concord, he was thirty-four years old, short and stout, with a long beard that covered his chest. He had previously served a significant amount of time in prison and dreaded coming back. When he came into my office for the first time, he introduced himself with a stern face and, as soon as I shut the door, he burst into tears, expressing his regret in leaving his mom and sister to fend for themselves. His drug use stemmed from anxiety attacks that he couldn't manage. His anxiety stemmed from watching his stepfather physically abuse his mom as a child. He insisted he was no longer a criminal and that it was his attempt to control his anxiety that caused him to abuse narcotics, which in turn would lead him to commit petty crime to buy more drugs.

There was Taha's mentee, Abdul-Haqq, a twenty-two-year-old mixed-race kid who converted to Islam on his own at fifteen years old but, because of a broken household and chaotic childhood, found himself in prison for violence. Tall and lanky, he looked a bit awkward, was naturally goofy, and found it easy to get along with just about anyone. But he was triggered whenever he felt people were trying to take advantage of him because of his appearance. His feelings of insecurity would cause him to overreact with violence.

But perhaps the most prolific man I met in prison was Shakir Abdullah, a six-foot-tall, broad-chested, chocolate-skinned man with a salt-and-pepper beard. Shakir was originally from somewhere down south and maintained a southern drawl and easygoing disposition. What made him unique was his powerful but subtle presence. He never shouted, argued, or even debated with anyone. He is the only inmate I have ever seen command respect from both other inmates and correctional officers without a reputation for violence or the threat of it.

Shakir was falsely accused of murdering a man twenty years prior. He had a second-degree life sentence, which meant he could see the parole board and possibly be released after serving twenty-five years. Shakir had successfully commissioned the Innocence Project to take his case and was awaiting either exoneration or a successful parole hearing.

In addition to the classes I taught, I also held one-on-one counseling sessions. I spent hours comforting men who were sexually abused, abandoned by their mothers, disowned by their fathers, or forced into the most humiliating circumstances as children.

In one of my sessions, Abu Karim confided in me for the first time that he and his younger sister used to be made to sit in the kitchen while their mother performed sexual acts for the Johns who would randomly stop by every morning. He said, "She must have told each one to bring a box of cereal for us, because every man that came in the house came with cereal. We'd be so hungry, that we'd sit down and eat while we listened to our mother have sex in the next room. I hated the fact that the only way I could eat was through these men. I hated every one of 'em and began to hate myself because I couldn't help my mother, even though I was only ten years old at the time."

Hatim told me that his mother was strung out on drugs and was very neglectful. He said that when he was about nine years old and his brother was seven, they would be left alone in the house for days on end. "We had nothing to eat. Sometimes the neighbor would drop off some sandwiches. I used to be so afraid when nighttime came because the trees would make scary shadows on the walls through the window, and my brother was even more afraid than me, so I had to pretend to be brave so that I didn't make him more scared. We'd both fall asleep balled up in each other's arms."

Hatim said that, when the Department of Social Services would visit his house, he would protect his mother by lying to them so that she wouldn't be sent to prison or them taken out of the house. He said she didn't even ask him to lie, he just instinctively felt the need to protect her because, as he put it, "I knew she was being dragged around in the street by the men she dealt with, but she was still my mother."

I had a great childhood full of family, love, and hugs from my mother. Sure, my father was absent and there was occasional violence in the neighborhood, but I had no stories of sexual abuse, or being victimized as a child, tossed around the foster-care system. It wasn't until I entered prison chaplaincy that I realized this, however. Growing up in the 'hood, doesn't mean you're from the street. There's a huge difference. I was from the 'hood, not from the street.

I began to feel that Allah had exposed me to just enough of the street life so I could relate to these men, but not enough to break me completely. I was meant to be there, in Concord as a faith leader, to comfort them. I just didn't know what to give them beyond stale theological explanations and sterile jurisprudence.

I found myself weighed down by their problems. I would take them home with me. They would sometimes keep me awake at night. I would think, *How can I help Hatim understand that prayer is the key to solving his problems? What book can I give Abu Karim? What can I read that will inspire me to give Abdul-Haqq the right words?*

During my years in Concord, I met many brilliant, incarcerated persons who could've been doctors if not for their childhoods of horror. Their inquiries and questions about Islam and the secondary issues of theology and jurisprudence pushed me to research beyond my wildest endeavor.

Allah blessed me with a solitary several hours of intense self-study every day for almost seven years. During that time Allah increased my comprehension significantly. Outside of the prison I was able to study classical Arabic, as well as the fundamentals of Islamic law, with several Muslim scholars and institutions. During that process I received more classical licensure in Islamic theology and language. These lessons put me in an entirely new frame of mind and gave me more competency, but I still couldn't get over the fact that almost all the Muslim men who were released from prison during my tenure relapsed and/or recidivated. What was I doing wrong?

I would later recognize that I was a thirty-one-year-old idealogue. When I came to Concord, I had this idea that I would be "defender of the faith." I was young and inexperienced. I was still in the process of learning what it was to be a man. I was a new husband and father to a growing family. In a matter of a few years, I went from being a selfish, angry young man with an identity crisis, to attempting to be head of a Muslim household, and now an imam to broken men. I didn't even know how to grocery shop or clean the bathroom properly.

I was obsessed with the sciences of *aqeedah*, *hadith*, and *fiqh*. *Aqeedah* is the Arabic word that describes the entire ecosystem of Islamic creed, including the theological concept of *tawheed*. *Tawheed* of course, is the Islamic creed of God's singularity, which could get very complicated and scientific. *Hadith* are the narrations of the Prophet Muhammad. *Fiqh* is essentially the application of Islamic law, that is, how to make ablution, pray, the rules of fasting, et cetera, according to the Qur'an and hadith.

I read books about those topics, listened to lectures about them, preached about them, and taught lessons about them. Some books I even memorized in Arabic, verbatim from cover to cover. In my Concord days, I considered having the correct *aqeedah* as the nexus of Islam and of salvation, and I still do, but I understand it differently now.

I thought if a former drug user could learn *aqeedah* and *fiqh*, then his desire to use drugs would dissipate. I thought that if a gang member learned these sciences, then his life would be transformed immediately, and he'd leave drug dealing and violence behind. How naïve I was.

Take brother Demani, a studious Muslim who had a well-developed understanding of Islam. He had been in prison for the past seven years and was finally on his way out the door. Tall, dark, and handsome, Demani was always in the front row of any class I gave. He asked great questions, didn't use foul language, and gave great answers to other inmates when I wasn't present.

Demani presented himself as a leader. He was a former drug dealer who had gotten caught with a lot of drugs, but seemed to be completely reformed. Demani was even more obsessed with *aqeedah* and *fiqh* than I was. He was a stickler for following the letter of Islamic law. He would grow angry if a Muslim inmate shaved his beard, feeling as if they had betrayed Islam. He wouldn't speak to any Muslim who gambled or kept company with non-Muslim friends in prison. He was very judgmental.

Demani almost came to blows with another brother when the brother said he wasn't prepared to admit that his mother, a non-Muslim, was going to hell.

Now back then, I was strict, but I would never try and force a man to verbally condemn his mother to hell. It's just not my place to do that. But Demani was relentless. "Akh your mother was probably a nice lady, but the fact remains, she was a *kaafir*." Things got intense, and people were shoved and pushed because Demani insisted that the man's mother, as well as his own, were going to spend an eternity in hell because of their disbelief in Islam.

This was Demani's commitment to his version of Islam. He was a staunch Muslim with a very biting interpretation of how Islam should be practiced. However, it hadn't been two months after his release that he was caught in a whore house, smoking crack, surrounded by prostitutes. When he came back to Concord, you would think he would have been humbled, but instead, he returned to being a stalwart advocate of *aqeedah* and *fiqh* with a blatant disregard for his own shortcomings.

There was also Abdul Bari, another resolute proponent of pure *aqeedah*. He would berate anyone who had a different opinion than his and try to publicly humiliate them with his knowledge. However, one day, while we were talking about traveling to Mecca for the holy pilgrimage if he was ever released from prison, he remarked, "I don't know what I'm gonna do. I don't fly, man. That's a fourteen-hour flight. Too high in the sky for too long." I said, "But it's worth it, brother." He replied, "I don't trust no pilot enough for that!" It's almost as if for a moment he had forgotten his entire belief system and the way he intimidated everyone around him daily, using it as a battering ram.

An integral principle in *aqeedah* is reliance on Allah or *tawakkul*. If one becomes afraid, rendered powerless, marginalized, or falsely accused, *tawheed* teaches us to trust in Allah's perfect plan. Where was Abdul Bari's *tawakkul* in Allah?

Allah even says, "Whoever puts their trust in Allah, then Allah will be sufficient for him."

Thousands of people fly every day. Didn't Abdul Bari know that? It's technically safer than driving. It is Allah who carries those planes and flying them is just a skill he gifted to mankind. Even if the airplane were to come crashing down in a fiery flame, wouldn't he be given the reward of Paradise due to his intention of traveling to Islam's holiest land, Mecca? I began to suspect that although *aqeedah* was important, we had all gravely misunderstood it.

While I met some of the most brilliant and insightful men I had known in my life, they were also very broken. Prison is a giant middle school for boys in dangerous bodies. Some men, like Shakir, were highly evolved, but many were not. And now they had something as sophisticated as religion in the palm of their hands, and instead of using it to till land and plant seeds, they were wielding it like a wrecking ball.

They had spent a lifetime committing crimes—hurting people, taking their possessions, and poisoning their communities—but as soon as they accepted Islam, they were prepared to condemn their mothers, their aunties, and grandmothers to hell.

Sure, some of their mothers were negligent, but there were also a hundred stories of mothers who were resilient and patient. A lot of prisoners were raised by their grandmothers or aunts; Christian women who were prayerful and hard-working, not to mention still sending these men money in prison. I spoke to many of these old aunts and grandmothers. They were now taking care of their sons' children!

Most of the men came to prison with some semblance of faith because these women had taught them about an all-powerful God when they were children. That faith doesn't go away. It may not grow but it doesn't disappear, and I believe it was the seeds of faith that their mothers and grandmothers planted that allowed them to later submit to Allah. But let Demani and Abdul Bari tell it, and they were going to burn in hell. Or maybe it wasn't them telling it, maybe I was the problem because that's what I had been implicitly teaching.

I never doubted my belief system, but I did begin to question how I was applying it. I started to interrogate the narrative of "ritualistic Islam," even while I continued to teach it daily. I wasn't confident enough to declare that we were all wrong, but I knew that, somehow, everything was not in its proper place and that I needed to sort some of my own principles out.

I had the realization that many of the inmates who claimed to have changed because of Islam hadn't in fact changed at all, but only increased their verbal IQ.

This remains a general problem in Islam all over the world. If you are good with terminology and definitions, then you can fool anyone into believing you're deeply rooted in theology and morally committed to Islamic values inside and out: especially if you're articulate.

After all, *fiqh* is merely a science of verbs and adverbs—*wash thoroughly, bend deeply, stand tall. Aqeedah* is simply Arabic nouns—*tawheed, shirk, tawakkul.* If you could memorize and define fifty Arabic terms, you were considered well-endowed with Islamic knowledge in prison, even though your flesh hadn't been tempted, and your heart not yet fortified due to being incarcerated and not being susceptible to the desires, temptations, and fears of a real-world situation.

The *'ulema*, or Muslim scholars, say that if you take even the smallest finger, it is always bigger than the knowledge of all the people: meaning that every reality that Allah created (even the pinky finger) is always greater than human knowledge of it. And the Qur'an is not created as a book, rather Muslims believe that it is an Attribute of Allah, emanating from his speech. Therefore, how could such a lofty revelation, originated from a divine source, be relegated to verbs and nouns?

The men inside Concord prison had learned some religious rules, but many lacked spiritual guidance. I was at least partially responsible for that. Islam is nuanced, and I was teaching something I didn't fully understand.

I later came to understand that if *aqeedah* is an ecosystem, then an ecosystem is a biological community of interacting organisms and their physical environment. Context is everything. No definite conclusions can be reached from books authored by men. And while the Qur'an and the Bible are not written by men but revealed by God, they still need context because, without it, we get al-Qaeda, and the KKK.

Incarcerated people live in a six- by eight-foot cell, where they cook, eat, sleep, and relieve themselves for years on end, only exposed to other incarcerated people. You can't possibly claim to know true religious creed if you've been living in a bathroom for ten years and only reading books. You can say you've submitted to a creed, but not that you've fully understood it.

Allah says: "The Bedouins say, 'We have come to believe.' Tell them Muhammad, 'You have not come to believe; instead, you should say, "We have submitted" because belief has not yet entered your hearts.'"

Islam is a religion of praxis. Islam doesn't advocate monasticism. Muslims believe in interacting with the world as a means of spiritual struggle and purification of the heart. Otherwise, how does one prove fidelity to God when there's no temptation, only quiet meditation and contemplativeness?

That's when I started to pay heed to what Shakir, the prolific southern inmate had been trying to tell me. Shakir would patiently sit through my dry lessons on Islamic science, then he would later visit me in my office and read a verse from Qur'an in English. There was one verse that stood out.

There is nothing for man except what he strives for.

Shakir read the verse to me, and then pointed me to the footnotes about that verse. I remember what we read together, with Shakir's finger tracing every word as he read aloud:

> *Each individual is a product of his or her childhood.*
> *Each enters Islam with their own psychological and*
> *emotional trauma stemming from the circumstances of*
> *their youth, growth, and development. Thus Allah may*
> *have different expectations for each individual based on*
> *what they are capable of achieving.*

Shakir was signaling to me that Allah considers the emotional/psycho condition of each person and that we too must interrogate our own stories before we dive headfirst into theology and jurisprudence and then hastily become judge and jury over others. We had to do our own work first.

The gadfly in me began to stir. My restlessness was further exacerbated when I met Deacon Bruce Nickerson.

Bruce Nickerson was an Episcopal deacon who would volunteer in Concord for Alcoholics Anonymous every week. He was a short white man in his seventies who had seen a lot. He'd been a raging alcoholic who almost lost his entire family. He managed to get his faith back on track and earned a PhD. We immediately hit it off. He was blue collar, simple smart. He didn't try to put on an air of superiority or present himself as clergy. Even in his clergy collar, he told silly jokes that could be off-putting to some, but I found them to be amusing enough. He'd facilitate a circle of a dozen Catholic and Christian men who were recovering addicts. He'd tell his own story about how he was such an alcoholic; he would sneak and drink the wine reserved for Sunday mass.

Deacon Bruce and I began taking our lunch together. The first time we ate together I invited him in the prison masjid. I told him to take his shoes off and come sit with me. He was hesitant. He didn't know, as he put it, "if an infidel could enter a Muslim prayer space." We laughed, but he was serious, and I understood why.

There is so much propaganda in the world about Islam and Muslims. No one can separate fact from fiction. I told him that the Prophet Muhammad himself had invited two Christian delegations from Thaqeef and Najran, towns in Arabia, to enter his masjid. Some say he even allowed them to pray in it. People are under the impression that Muslims despise Jews and Christians but, frankly speaking, nothing could be further from the truth.

When the Prophet Muhammad first received the revelation of Qur'an, it was from the angel Gabriel. When he ran to tell his wife of the miraculous meeting, she encouraged him to visit her old cousin, Waraqah bin Nawfal. He was a wise man, who believed in the Messiah Jesus and wrote the Bible in Hebrew. He stood out as one of the only few Arabs who did not worship idols at the time. When Muhammad narrated the encounter he had with the angel Gabriel, Waraqah bin Nawfal replied, "This is the same angel to visit Moses. I wish I would be alive when your people drive you out of the land so I could support you."

Later, when the Prophet Muhammad's people, the pagan Arab tribes, rejected him and his small group of followers, Muhammad sent his followers to Ethiopia, a Christian land, and told them, "Go to Abyssinia, there is a righteous Christian king who will give you refuge." They were protected by this king, who eventually converted to Islam himself.

So, the first group who protected Muhammad and his followers were Black Christians. How could he hate them then and how could we hate them now, when Christian-majority lands are essentially still giving Muslims from war-torn countries refuge?

Likewise, when a Jewish man's funeral procession passed by the Prophet Muhammad and his disciples, he stood out of respect. His disciples reminded him that the deceased was a Jew. He replied, "Was he not a human being?"

The Qur'an is not antagonistic toward Jews and Christians. The verses of war in the Qur'an were against the pagan Arabs from Muhammad's own tribes. Those are the people who were fighting him at the time because they refused to accept monotheistic belief.

There are two main themes in the Qur'an about Jews and Christians:

1. There are some very pious men from among them.

    Allah says: "They are not all the same. Among the people of the Book is a community standing in obedience, reciting the verses of Allah during the night and prostrating in prayer. They believe in Allah and the Last Day, and they enjoin what is right and forbid what is wrong and hasten to do good deeds. Those are among the righteous. Whatever good deeds they do will never be denied, for Allah knows well the righteous."

    And Allah also says: "Among the people of Moses is a community which guides by truth and by it establishes justice."

2. The Jews and Christians should be invited to civil discourse about God.

    Allah says: "Say to the People of the Torah and Gospel, 'We must come to a common term. Let us worship no one except God, nor consider anything equal to Him, nor regard any of us as our Lord besides God.' However, if they turn away from (the Truth), tell them, 'Bear witness that we have submitted ourselves to the will of God.'"

One of the most criticized verses in the Qur'an is used to accuse Muslims of having license to kill Jews and Christians:

Fight in the way of Allah against those who fight against you but do not transgress, for Allah does not love transgressors. Kill them whenever you confront them and drive them out from where they drove you out.

This verse is specifically about the pagan Arabs who were fighting Muslims at the time. It is not a blanket command to fight and kill Jews and Christians, because Allah later says:

Allah does not forbid that you be kind and just to those who do not fight you because of religion and do not expel you from your homes—Verily, Allah loves those who act justly. Allah only forbids you from those who fight you because of religion and expel you from your homes and aid in your expulsion— He forbids that you make allies of them. Whoever makes allies of them, then it is those who are the wrongdoers.

The criticism leveled against Jews and Christians in the Qur'an is the same criticism that appears in the Bible. It is for sinfulness and transgression.

The Bible says:

All Israel has transgressed thy law and turned aside, refusing to obey thy voice. And the curse and oath which are written in the law of Moses the servant of God have been poured out upon us, because we have sinned against him.

The Bible says:

Jerusalem, Jerusalem, you who kill the prophets and stone those sent to you, how often I have longed to gather your children together, as a hen gathers her chicks under her wings, and you were not willing.

The Qur'an says:

They [The followers of Moses] were stricken with disgrace and misery, and they invited the displeasure of Allah for rejecting Allah's signs and unjustly killing the prophets. This is a fair recompense for their disobedience and violations.

There is no inherent hatred against Jews and Christians in the Qur'an or in Islam.

When the Prophet Muhammad was expelled from Mecca, and was declared the leader of Medina, he wrote a *sahifa* or Constitution. It is a long document. In it he mentions the Jewish tribes who lived alongside Muslims in Medina:

The Jews who join us as clients will receive aid and favor; they will not be wronged, nor will their enemies be aided against them. . . . The Jews of Banū 'Awf are a community alongside the Believers; the Jews have their religion and the Muslims have theirs. This applies to their clients and themselves. But whoever does wrong or commits treachery brings evil only on himself and his household. . . . The Jews have their expenditure, and the Muslims theirs. The parties to this treaty will aid each other against whosoever is at war with the people of this document. Between them is good-will and sincerity. And righteousness is easier than sin. A man will not act unjustly toward his client, and anyone wronged will be helped.

The Prophet Muhammad ensured that Jews could continue to practice their religion and even earn the support and protection of Muslims if an invader transgressed against them. He was a man committed to interreligious fellowship.

So, following that example, Deacon Bruce was a man of faith. Why *wouldn't* I allow him to come break bread with me in the masjid, when the correctional officers regularly came to search the masjid with dogs?

During our frequent lunches, we discussed history of religions, the current state of interreligious dialogue, and the failure of both Christians and Muslims to live out the precepts of their faith with sincerity. Allah says about Christians:

> *You will certainly find that the closest in friendship with the believers are those who say, "We are Christians." That is because among them there are priests and monks, and because they are not arrogant.*

Upon meeting Deacon Bruce I finally understood this verse.

As our friendship grew, I would meet him in Cambridge, a small city outside of Boston. He would allow me to accompany him on his walks through the train stations and bus stops where he would pay a weekly visit to the addicts and homeless to offer a Good Word and affirmation that they still mattered as human beings. The unhoused, with their layers of clothes and tons of shopping bags, would love to see him coming, "Hey Deacon Bruce!" They would shout. He would stay and chat with each one, making jokes, telling them to hang in there, and giving them hope.

He was the first religious person, after Ms. Bilal, that I had seen put their faith into action. I learned a lot about what religious work looks like, boots-on-the-ground accompanying Deacon Bruce. He didn't do a whole lotta preaching. He was plain. He used to say to me, "If this work kills ya, then what better way to die?"

In 2010, Terry Jones, a Christian pastor in Florida was planning to burn Qur'ans as a protest against Islam. This incensed Deacon Bruce. He said, "We gotta do something to counter that. Why don't you come and speak every Sunday at my church, during Lent?"

I raised my eyebrows, and said "Huh?" I didn't understand. "Well, let's educate people about what Islam really is. Let's tell them the truth," Deacon Bruce said. I was flabbergasted. Me speak to Christians in a church about Islam? About "truth"?

I was totally caught off guard. Up to that point I was very cautious around people from other faiths. They were mostly white, and I figured hostile toward Islam considering that 9/11 wasn't that far off. Sometimes, I would come to work in Concord and there would be a sign hanging on the wall that read, "Don't eat at such and such restaurant, they are Arabs who support the terrorists." Apparently if a correction officer was ordering a sandwich and had a brief exchange about 9/11 wherein the Arab clerks tried to engage in dialogue, which I'm sure wasn't in "support" of terrorism, but probably not articulate, the correction officers would grow hostile and assume they were defending Osama bin Laden. I saw those signs more than once, so I was always on guard.

Now I was having cognitive dissonance. How could I, a Muslim, be allowed to give *dawah* to Christians in a church? Nevertheless, I was invited to St Elizabeth's Episcopal Church during the Lent of 2010. I lectured for three Sundays in row to a crowd of working-class white folks who were eager to listen and ask questions.

In my first lecture, I explained who the Prophet Muhammad was. I was a little nervous, because I had never stood in front of a crowd of white people without breaking into a dance routine; now here I was delivering a sermon on a church lectern with a crucifix in the background.

I wanted to humanize Muhammad. I explained that he was born in the 570 CE, in the city of Mecca in the Arabian Peninsula. He was a descendant of the prophet Abraham through his son Ishmael, thus making him a distant cousin of Jesus. His struggle began even before he was born, with the death of his father while on a journey as a merchant. So, he was born into the world without a father, and lost his mother seven years later.

I went on to discuss the similarities in our faiths. I explained that Muslims perform ablution before prayer and remove their shoes and prostate like all the great prophets before them.

I referenced biblical verses to accentuate my points:

He placed the basin between the Tent of Meeting and the altar and put water in it for washing; and from it Moses, Aaron, and his sons washed their hands and feet. They washed whenever they entered the Tent of Meeting or approached the altar, just as the LORD had commanded Moses. . . .

The Qur'an matches that almost exactly:

O you who have believed, when you rise to perform prayer, wash your faces and your forearms to the elbows and wipe over your heads and wash your feet to the ankles.

I highlighted that in 1 Kings 18:42, as much as Christians want to claim Elijah was not doing anything similar to Muslims, instead he was praying to the "real" God, when he "Cast his face between his knees and his forehead touched the ground." This is the prayer that Muslims still perform today.

The lecture series humbled me and opened a window of opportunity that I hadn't considered before. I could maintain my identity and belief and build authentic rapport with those outside of my worldview. I was changed forever.

At the end of the series at St. Elizabeth's, I was presented with an award of interreligious fellowship by their openly homosexual priest, Father Joe. It was my first time encountering this kind of construct:

a gay priest who told me he was gay and celibate, who allowed me to preach Islam in his church. I had to rethink my position on what it meant to be tolerant in the face of living in a truly pluralistic land.

Some Muslims may read this and feel disgusted but, for me, ideology must meet real-world context before anyone can make proper judgment. That's not to say we should all compromise our theology to get along, because neither did Father Joe nor Deacon Bruce request anything other than to learn from me. Rather what I mean is that religious people should get out of their silos if they live in the West, not to water down their faith, but to understand how it functions in the world.

After that experience, Deacon Bruce would always tell me, "Taymullah, you have to continue your education. There's more work that you must do but you would be better prepared if you had more credentials." I didn't really see the benefit of education. To me, if I wasn't going to become a doctor, then why bother.

But one day one of my students in Concord, Abdullah, a twenty-two-year-old African American man was wrapping up a five-year sentence that he started when he was seventeen years old. He had been learning under me for a year. He was one of my best and brightest.

As Abdullah prepared to return into the world as a renewed citizen, who had not only paid his debt to society but had grown by leaps and bounds both spiritually and ethically, all the men lined up to bid him farewell. Those with life sentences looked forward to releasing young Black men back into the world primed for success. They lived vicariously through them. Abdullah shook hands, hugged some, and received small tokens of respect and affection from others. He took it all in.

The last day we were together, he shook my hand with a firm enthusiastic grip, smiled with his big white teeth and chocolate face and told me, "I'm gonna make you proud! Watch!"

It hadn't been six months, and Abdullah was back in prison. I noticed him in line for Islamic services in the prison chapel, in his green state-issued uniform, looking worn down and beat up by the world. I was immediately angry. I waved him into my office and when he shuffled in, head bowed, I shut the door behind him. Abdullah fell into my arms and burst into tears. "It was so hard out there! I had no one!" I didn't expect this reaction from him, and I wasn't prepared with any words of wisdom, so I let him cry.

After several minutes of me holding his crumpled body in my arms, he slowly took a seat and cleaned himself up. He told me that he had tried to find work for six months to no avail. He said he ran out of savings and couldn't even ride the bus. He wound up homeless, sleeping under the expressway overpass. When he grew desperate, he decided prison was the only safe and secure place for him to get food, clothing, and shelter, so he went to the suburbs, stole a car, and drove around breaking traffic rules until he was pulled over and arrested. He was relieved to have a place to sleep and something consistent to eat, even if he had given his entire future up.

That moment was the first time the thought of leaving prison ministry entered my heart. My original idea that real salvation was in teaching theological principles formed seven hundred years ago was fading further and further into the background.

Shakir's words about taking our social/emotional condition into consideration began to ring in my heart. I began to feel as though perhaps the real work was in diversion from crime, and not in salvation.

I started to recall all the times SAMs were released from prison and the largest mosque in Boston would call me because the men needed financial assistance. On numerous occasions I found myself at the ATM withdrawing money from my personal account to help these men. The mosque, with its wealthy endowment, would have nothing to do with them. It was clear that the socioeconomic challenges of the Black Muslim were being ignored, overlooked, or swept aside in favor of the dominant immigrant Islamic narrative which said, "if you're not a young professional or university student, then we have no interest in lifting you up."

I was part of that problem. I had been teaching the men how to follow rote ritual in worship and theology, while neglecting the fact that they were in prison as result of a myriad of social failures, including systemic racism and lack of access to the American breadbasket of goods and services.

I realized that Black and Brown men, in general, lack the proximate structural assistance necessary to overcome criminal history checks for employment, substance abuse, and poverty. They could worship perfectly after literally spending years in prison reviewing the details of Islamic ritual ablution and worship, but when they got up from the prayer mat, they still faced the perpetual social challenges of a Black man living in America.

In a 2017 poll, 33 percent of Black Muslims stated they had experienced discrimination from members of their own faith community. For many Black Muslims in America, the mosque has become obsolete because for decades it has failed to address the social needs of Black people. Instead, it has devolved into toxic trustee boards who hold on to imaginary power and perpetuate gender and racial hierarchy.

One year after Abdullah came into my office, I left Concord prison to start my own youth intervention business.

8

MAKING A PROPHET

Being Paid to Worship God Comes with a Heavy Price

BRKFST CLB. THAT was the name of the limited liability company I started in 2012 when I left Concord. I had the idea that I would produce statement T-shirts and teach at-risk youth about life skills and how to sell the shirts door to door so they could earn money for themselves and stay off the streets.

I went to a Muslim friend who owned a bakery and asked for some advice. He sent me to a white guy he said, "Advises startups." I knew from the start when I saw this man that nothing good was going to come from our meeting. When I walked in the café, he was sitting at a table sipping coffee like a mafia boss. He didn't even look me in my eye when I introduced myself. He had this snarky look on his face as I explained my idea. When I finished, he said, "First thing you need to do is file for nonprofit status. Then you can apply for grant money. You're not gonna get rich, but you might be able to convince some companies to donate to your cause."

I was fuming. I felt he was minimizing my idea and relegating it to "another useless nonprofit."

"I'm not going to start a nonprofit. I can earn a living doing this as a for-profit. And I believe this idea has no monetary ceiling. I don't beg people for money." I snapped back. Now I knew this was going nowhere.

"Okay well, suit yourself. I don't think it's possible for you to get this off the ground any other way." I thanked him for his time and left.

I met with a Muslim who was well-off financially. I was told that he had financed several other projects for people. He listened to my idea and then told me, "You're making a strategic mistake. You're an imam. You're not a businessman. Start an online school or something but I don't see this working for you."

I had been an imam for six years by then. I started giving Islamic sermons in 2003, but I wasn't officially given that title until 2006. It was 2012, and what that Arab brother didn't know is that I had washed half a dozen SAM dead bodies by then; brothers who had been shot, stabbed, killed in accidents, or overdosed. The world didn't need another Islamic online school, teaching Islamic sciences. Black and Brown boys needed something to help them live.

I washed my first dead body in 2001. Right after I had gotten married, brother Abdul Matin had been murdered; shot in the neck by his friend over an argument. His wife had just done my wife's hair for our wedding ceremony a few weeks prior, and now I was identifying his body with his widow.

When me and some of the brothers walked into the funeral home to wash him, I felt a sense of fear and dread. I had seen a dead body in the 'hood from a distance, but never touched one up close and personal, let alone someone I had eaten with, laughed with, and hung out with.

In Islam, the dead should be washed, prayed over, and buried within twenty-four hours of dying. We believe that rushing to send the body back to the earth from which it came is the natural way.

The Islamic narrative tells us that when Cain killed his brother Abel (known as Qabil and Habil in Arabic) no one had been killed before. He didn't know what to do with the body. He carried his brother on his back for several days until he saw two crows fighting. When one crow killed the other, he dug a hole in the earth and pushed the other bird in. Cain learned that this is the way a dead body should be buried.

Allah mentions this in Qur'an:

Then Allah sent a raven, scratching in the earth, so that he
might show him how he should bury the corpse of his brother.
He said, "Oh woe is me! I could not even be like this raven
and bury the corpse of my brother, then he became full of
regret."

Four of us removed the sheet covering our dead brother, Abdul
Matin. We put towels over his private areas and gently gave him *ghusl*
mayaat, or the final bath of the dead. Mixing water with scented oil,
we poured water over his head, washed his face, his arms, and his feet,
as his final ablution. Then we wrapped him in three white sheets with
no stitches: one for his bottom half, one for his top, and one for his
private parts.

When his body was fully washed and wrapped, he was brought
to the masjid where the congregation gathered, and the imam led us
in the ritual prayer for the dead, called *janazah*. After the prayer we all
drove in procession to the cemetery and removed his body from the
wooden coffin. I was one of those who jumped inside the grave and
took his body to place it on its right side, facing the direction of Mecca.

The Muslims present gently covered him with dirt, first with our
hands, and then, after sealing his tomb with a large block of cement,
the bulldozers brought in large amounts of sand. We also shoveled dirt
on his grave until it was completely covered. When he was buried, we
each sat quietly and made individual *dua*, or supplication for him as
the Prophet Muhammad had instructed.

Once, when the Prophet Muhammad buried one of his disciples,
he said, "Pray for forgiveness for your brother, and ask that he be made
steadfast, for he is being questioned now."

When a person, Muslim or non-Muslim, is placed in his or her
grave, two angels visit him. Their names are Munkar and Nakir and
they are the questioning angels. The Prophet Muhammad said that
these two angels are fierce and dreadful looking. They enter a person's
grave and sit them upright and ask them three questions: "Who is your

Lord?" the answer to which should be "Allah." Then they ask, "What is your *Deen*, or way of life?" The answer should be "Islam." "Who is your prophet?" The answer should be "The final messenger of Allah, Muhammad."

After the questions, if they were answered correctly, the grave opens as wide as the eyes can see, a light is placed in it and the deceased is able to see a window from *Jennah*, or Paradise. They remain in this condition until the Day of Resurrection.

However, if a person does not answer these questions correctly, then the angels slam him or her until the body disintegrates and then reforms. The grave is squeezed on them until their ribs touch, a window from *Jahannam* or Hell, is opened for them, and snakes and scorpions are made to torture them until the Day of Resurrection.

I believed it then and I believe it now, so as I crouched over Abdul Matin's grave I made fervent *dua* for him to be firm on answering the questions correctly.

The Prophet Muhammad said that when a dead body is placed in the grave, the earth welcomes it back by squeezing it because it was created from dirt. He said this is extremely uncomfortable. When a baby was being buried, he remarked, "If anyone were to be saved from the squeeze of the grave, this baby would have. But not even it can escape the initial squeeze."

That night, I went home and sat motionless for hours, just staring off into space. What had my life become? I thought by now I would be in Miami on a boat celebrating the spoils of my rap career, but instead I was washing and burying my dead friends with my own hands. I didn't know what to make of it, but I didn't feel good.

So, when the Muslim financier told me I was making a strategic mistake, he was speaking from a blind spot and from a place of privilege. After the fourth or fifth friend you've washed from an early death, your priorities shift.

I chose to take the approach of teaching business to kids because at-risk Black boys are always engaged by white nonprofits through music and sports. But after a certain age music and sports are consigned to hobbies, and guns and money still play a factor in destroying the lives of urban youth. Music and sports don't save young adult lives, they distract kids.

These smarty-pants young white executive directors with their MBA degrees win all the grant money from local and federal government. They come in the 'hood with their million-dollar grants and shave a quarter million off the top for themselves. They spend the rest of the money hiring Black and Brown staff at minimum wage, in order to recruit at-risk youth and make the numbers game work for them. The next time those "call for response" grants come down, they'll have all the right ingredients: Black and Brown staff, and at-risk youth shooting hoops and making rap beats, which ensures the grant renewal.

This process makes white liberals feel great about themselves. They've "dedicated" their lives to saving Black children from their miserable lives. But what they don't realize is that if you have something extra and the poor are in need, it's as if you've stolen from them.

Meanwhile, Black nonprofit founders work literally from their own savings. They drive Uber overnight and save young lives during the day. They sell plates of food to make ends meet and fund the entire cost of drug rehab out of their own pockets, for mothers strung out on drugs, trying to recover so they can save their children.

These Black nonprofit founders attend court hearings and sit for hours, just to support their clients. Sometimes they're on the defendant's side of the court, and sometimes the victim's side. Being a Black nonprofit executive is not a career choice like it is for white founders. It's a calling. Most Black nonprofit founders don't have health-care benefits for themselves. All their staff, if they have any, are volunteers who've lost children to the streets or been perpetrators of crime in the past and are now trying to pay it forward. They are people who have their hearts in the 'hood. They put in the grant bids, but almost never get the big grants.

And this position of being ostracized from power is the safest position, because our hearts and our work aren't tainted by a desire to be proximate to glory, fame, and wealth.

I would listen to podcasts about entrepreneurship and all those young white millionaires would make it sound so hard: "My uncle sold his vacation home and gave me the startup costs. We were down to our last two hundred thousand dollars in our account, and we had to pay all our staff! We had to eat Ramen noodles for two months in our 3,000 square foot office space! Those were hard times!"

I didn't have any rich uncles to loan me one hundred grand to start my business. I also knew no bank would give me a business loan with just a T-shirt idea. But as a Black person, I wasn't going to play myself by starting a nonprofit so I could be controlled by white donors and institutions with grant money.

History had shown me that whoever controls the money controls the narrative. Whenever religious figures coddle kings, clergy become the prostitutes. When the Christian church went from fish to crucifix with Constantine's endorsement, what started as a fringe group of peaceful rebels led by Jesus Christ himself became a state-sponsored religion. It became difficult to sustain Christian commitment to end poverty when the church was benefiting from the empire.

Likewise, when Islamic regimes beginning in the ninth century took initiative to sponsor Islamic scholarship, it was no longer easy for religious sheikhs to speak out against luxury and gluttony when their benefactors were Muslim leaders engaged in those very things.

Howard Thurman writes, "Hypocrisy from the weak is a sort of tribute, or tithe, paid to the dominant group. By withholding this tribute, by offering simple sincerity instead, the dominant group loses its advantage. Instead of relation between the weak and the strong there is merely a relationship between human beings. A man is a man, no more, no less. The awareness of this fact marks the supreme moment of human dignity."

The only ones to consistently speak truth to power are the desert dwellers. You have to be like *Yahya*, the Islamic name of John the Baptist: a wild man in the desert who answers to no one but God. A truly sincere imam, priest, pastor, or rabbi must remain aloof from the systems and structures that dictate who gets what wealth. I thought I was a desert dweller, I thought if I could generate wealth on my own, I'd have no need for anyone else. But I didn't consider that I might become like the kings and not the religious leaders.

I was raising a family of six children with another on the way; my wife was a stay-at-home mom homeschooling our children at the time, and my stepson had just been shot in his neck and chest due to the same youth violence I was trying to curtail. As he lay fighting for his life in the hospital, our family was trying to scrape by and make a new way for ourselves.

I was trying to start a business with no experience and only my personal savings. I would wake up at 5 a.m. and catch the Fung Wah bus for twenty-five dollars to New York to look for fabrics for my clothing line. After speeding on the highway for three hours in a cramped bus filled with college students, homeless people, and drug mules, I would walk around the fabric district for hours looking for the right material. After the sun set, I'd take a cab to the bus station with a duffle bag as big as me filled with fabrics, and head back home. I'd creep in the house at midnight and pass out until the next day. Sometimes I might go straight back to New York and do it all over again.

One Friday I decided to head to New York a little later in the day than usually because there was one particular Asian textile store I had to get to. When I arrived in the fabric district, the store manager was closing the gate. I begged him to let me just grab a few items after I had traveled all the way from Boston. New Yorkers don't budge. He told me they would be open first thing in the morning.

I couldn't afford to go home and come back, and I needed to get a very specific polo shirt material for a potential order I had from a PacSun store buyer. I decided I had to stay overnight. I walked twenty minutes to Manhattan and found a twenty-four-hour McDonald's restaurant to sit in all night. This was before smart phones, so I bought a few magazines and read them until I dozed off right at the table in McDonald's. I was in and out of consciousness until dawn. When the restaurant started to get busy with morning customers, I went in the restroom as soon as the janitor cleaned it, splashed some water on my face, and headed back to the fabric district.

I was desperate to make something creative happen, for my own self-worth, for my young family, for the SAMs, and for Allah. PacSun passed on my clothing.

Allah says:

> It is not righteousness that you turn your faces towards
> the East and the West, but righteousness is that you
> should believe in Allah and the last day and the angels
> and the Book and the prophets, and give away wealth
> out of love for Him, to the near of family and the
> orphans and the needy and the traveler and the beggars
> and for freeing the slaves and the ones who keep up
> prayer and pay the charity; and those who keep their
> oaths when they make a promise, and are patient in
> distress, and in time of conflicts—these are the ones who
> are sincere and these are the ones who have reverence
> for Allah.

I left Concord to honor that qur'anic verse. Music and sports don't teach Black youth how to access the goods and services that improve quality of life and Islamic sciences wasn't helping either.

I began to explore the idea of leadership in general. How was leadership defined by great men outside of Islam?

I read Dr. John C. Maxwell's books on leadership. I constantly listened to personal development guru Jim Rohn's lectures. I researched books and articles on Paul J. Meyer about success philosophy and studied Jim Collins's work as well. I had been so enveloped in my Islamic learning that I didn't realize that there was an entirely different set of information that I could utilize to get me where I wanted to be.

I took my life savings, $24,000, and bought an inventory of hundreds of T-shirts. I also bought a box truck and gutted it myself and redecorated it with my wife. We painted it, cut holes in it, installed a television monitor and a new floor to make it look like a store inside. I was determined to live on my own terms and not depend on Muslim community speaking events to pay me.

Local masjids never paid imams what they were worth. Most of the imams I knew had to take full-time jobs to feed their families. I was still doing lectures all over New England for $100 here and there, but that was essentially gas money.

Once, I was leading a group of pilgrims on a trip to Mecca. On the airplane home, I ran into a Muslim brother I knew who oversaw a small local Islamic school in a suburb of Massachusetts. He was trying to recruit me to be a full-time Islamic studies teacher for their high school. When I asked him the salary, he said it was $19,000 a year.

That would have been a great salary in 1945, but it was 2015 when he offered me that salary. It demonstrated several things to me. Everyone wants religious men to be pious enough to accept crumbs and religious men are often too shy to demand more.

I said to him, "But what about my children and family? We like vacations too. My children want to have new bikes and toys too. If I take your job, I can never save a penny for the rest of my life. You can't convince me that you care about my well-being if you offer me that kind of salary. It's an insult to my identity and to anyone who has an ounce of humanity. There's absolutely no future in $19,000 a year for me or my family. Its oppression."

Of course, I was told to calm down, as if I was going to kill him on the plane back from a holy pilgrimage of prayers and peace. Whenever you speak your truth as a Black person, you're considered angry and hostile. I made sure to keep a smile on my face and spoke in gentle tones, but he still told me to calm down. It was the meaning of my words not the sound of my voice that made him uncomfortable.

Allah says, "Oppression is worse than murder." Because people must live in oppression, death is final. This man was asking me to live in a perpetual state of poverty just so he could have his institution and say that he is the founder, or the chief, or the president, while me and my family suffer in piety. He would sacrifice me and my family at the altar of his ego just to continue his pet project.

If you can't afford real teacher salaries, then you can't afford to have a real school. Close it. But don't ask men to sacrifice themselves for your cause. You should quit your six-figure job and teach the children, since you love them so much.

Allah didn't pull me out of the gutter to be anyone's Black slave. I would make my own way or die trying.

I did, however, make the huge mistake of purchasing a 500 S Class Mercedes-Benz. To appear "cool," I compromised my own Islamic identity. A Mercedes-Benz is not *haraam*, meaning "forbidden," but at that time in my life it was *haraam* for me because of my own spiritual sickness. I had only been Muslim for twelve years. I had more work to do before I could expose my *nafs* to that kind of luxury. Nevertheless, I succumbed.

I removed my kufi and led with my secular identity. I put my Brkfst Clb baseball cap and T-shirt on and I headed to high schools to see if they would allow me to volunteer and teach their students life skills such as active listening, alternatives to violence, and entrepreneurship. I got a few schools to let me in and things were going well.

However, selling T-shirts from a truck as your main source of income when you are renting a five-bedroom home and you have a family to support is not smart. It wasn't long before my savings were used up and I was forced to move my family out of the large home we rented and into a small two-bedroom apartment, where one of my children had to put his bed in the shoe room and the other had to sleep in the attic. I was struggling financially. I had to sell my Mercedes, and my Brkfst Clb truck too. I was without a car, with no job and only minimal Islamic credentials that no serious secular institution cared about. I was depressed and feeling like a failure.

I took a job as a credit repair agent, but I didn't last long. My supervisor was one of those gung-ho thirty-something white sales guys who felt that he had the right to yell and scream at people like he was on Wall Street. He'd embarrass everyone. "Come on get your s--t together!" I didn't like that. I always told the men in Concord that you must take strategic losses living in *dunya*. You have to tolerate abuse, and sometimes even being taken advantage of. But no one has to tolerate humiliation.

During my second month working there, the scrawny, young white man started to berate me as soon as I walked in one Monday morning. Apparently, I hadn't checked the schedule because I was supposed to work that preceding Saturday. Instead of calling me into his office, shutting the door, and giving me a stern warning or even penalizing me, which I would have humbly accepted, he decided to yell at me in front of thirty other employees. "Tay! Tay! Really? You just stroll in here like nothing's wrong?" I was shocked. I really didn't know I had to work that weekend.

He had no idea about my Islamic background. I was always quiet and respectful, and I intended to continue that way, but I wasn't going to take being humiliated.

As a religious person, there's room for being disrespected; people calling you names, ridiculing you, harassing you or mistreating you.

But humiliation is different. It's debasing someone's humanity. At its core, it is someone pretending to wield ultimate power over another creature—could be a dog or a human—by treating them less than how they deserve to be treated, in an attempt to snatch away their dignity. I didn't mind being disrespected, but for me, it's always going to be death before dishonor when it comes to being humiliated. Allah knows best.

Islam teaches that, just as your body has rights over you—sleep, nourishment, amusement—likewise so does your personal honor. The Prophet Muhammad said, "Verily, your lives, your property, and your honor have been made sacred to you, just as the sanctity of this day of yours, in this month of yours, in this city of yours."

The key is to know the difference between being disrespected and remaining patient and resisting humiliation by any means necessary. I know now that, when that female police officer made me pull my pants down in the middle of the police station lobby, she was humiliating me. Islam had taught me this distinction and I try to live by it.

In the 'hood, we take disrespect as a carnal sin worthy of committing murder; someone stepping on your sneakers, being called a snitch, et cetera. Those are things to be patient with. Instead, we should rally around the laws and policies that humiliate us as a people: stop and frisk, three strikes, and life without parole for juveniles.

Before I lost my temper, I simply walked past him as he continued to berate me, went to my desk, gathered my things, and walked out. He screamed at me the entire time, "Oh yeah look at the big baby leaving because his supervisor made him sad!" He put on his best baby voice. He was a real character. Had it been a few years earlier, I might've tried to toss him out that fifth-floor window. But I was Muslim, an imam. If he didn't know, I sure did, and I was determined to remain poised. When I got home, I was proud of myself, but I still needed a job.

The local immigrant masjid interviewed me to be imam. And I got the job. They thought I would be good for the youth because I was young and had a knack for building rapport with teenagers. The masjid was a huge place. I was very excited.

Alas, I was only there a few months when the board told me after hearing one of my speeches, "Taymullah, you can't talk about hellfire, and criticize the people who come here. No one wants to be scorned and warned. If they stop coming, they don't donate. If they don't donate, the lights go off and your salary stops. Talk about good things, like Paradise." We were ideologically disconnected. That statement, along with several other factors, made it clear that I shouldn't waste anyone's time and we made a mutual decision to part ways.

Uber had just become popular, and my Turkish Muslim landlord hired me as a driver. I used his car to earn money to give right back to him for rent. He was a good man to help me in such a profound way. He used to say, "We are brothers. Just don't let all those children you have destroy my house." We would laugh, but his benevolence helped me hold on to the idea that Islam is real and not all immigrant Muslims are racist or classist.

I was approaching my thirty-seventh birthday and despair was written all over my life. Why was Allah humiliating me? I left prison to try and help save Black and Brown people. I didn't understand. I was a decent father and husband and here I was struggling again.

My Uber shift was 7 a.m. to 7 p.m., just like my crack-selling shift had been eighteen years prior. I'd ride around Boston looking for drunk partygoers to shuttle home at night, and sober millennials to take to the airport in the morning. But I was so bad at it. I'd lived in Boston my entire life, but I still had a horrible sense of direction. It got so bad—when the passengers would see me taking the long way to their destination, they'd interrupt the ride and ask, "Are you from out of town?"

One night I picked up four white girls at two o'clock in the morning. They were all drunk. Each one lived in a different place, so I was going to drop them off one by one. When I reached the first one's house, she told me to keep driving and drop the other girls off first. The other girls lived further away so I didn't understand why she wanted to be dropped off last. She just said, "It's late, I want you guys to get home safe." They agreed and I dropped the other three off.

When everyone else was gone, the girl who insisted she be dropped off last said to me, "Do you know where we can get some food? Let's hang out." That was it. I immediately got uncomfortable. Was she trying to set me up? Was she trying to have an impromptu encounter with me? I was shaken. I told her, "No, I'm taking you home according to the trip you requested on the app." I rushed her home and dropped her at her door.

When she got out, I went home and told my landlord I couldn't drive for him anymore. The stakes were too high. She could accuse me of sexual assault or something similar. It was better to retire from Uber and that's what I did.

In retrospect I know now that Allah would not allow me any type of success if I was trying to lead with a secular identity. I had left prison and, instead of committing crimes like some of the brothers had done, I had committed spiritual violations. In a strange way, it was just like Demani and many other brothers. I was still praying my five daily prayers, and I wasn't doing drugs or fornicating, but I was betraying my vertical self by not maintaining Islam as my first identity.

We all have several identities that we draw out or push in, depending on our environment. Some people call it code-switching. It's normal and can be very healthy. There are some parts of my identity that I know my mother just can't handle, and other parts I know my children can't handle. Every room we walk into, we're constantly recalibrating ourselves to fit in, which means we're always holding back 25 percent of who we really are.

I thought I had to be "cool" to appeal to the kids I was trying to save. In the process I had lost a piece of myself. My calibration was too much. I had more work to do. I had to stay vigilant over my governing energy, which was to be a Muslim servant, not a slick entrepreneur.

My wife warned me early in our marriage, after I had been tempted to enter the music business again as a Muslim when Desert Storm Records, a famous hip-hop label associated with Jay-Z's Roc-A-Fella records, offered me a job as a staff song writer. She said, "As long as you are Muslim, and Allah loves you, he won't allow you to find success in music. That's not your path to victory. You have to keep searching." She was right.

I learned my first lesson about governing energy when I was in my senior year of high school. I had been charged with assault and battery on a police officer after I had a melee with some guys who came up to confront me after school over something that had happened weeks earlier. While I was fighting one of the guys, the school police officer jumped on my back and I body slammed him and started to beat him up too. I had blacked out. He carried a gun and could've killed me.

We were arrested, booked, and bailed out. Sometime later, in court, the school police officer wrote the judge a letter on my behalf, unbeknownst to me. He testified that he didn't believe that I had intentionally meant to hurt him. He wrote that out of hundreds of students, I was one of the only ones who said "good morning" to him every day. That, to him, meant that I was considerate and thoughtful, and didn't deserve to be severely punished by the court for a mistake I made. Because of his letter, the judge continued my case without a finding for one year and I was released.

As we walked out of court, my mother told me, "You see? When you're a gentleman it pays off in ways you're not even aware of. That's who you really are, Tyrone."

She was right.

At the Academy Awards ceremony in 2022, Will Smith, after initially laughing at Chris Rock's joke, then tried to live up to some imaginary standard of masculinity that his wife apparently imposed on him. He smacked Chris and put himself outside of his governing energy, which is benign public goofball. And even though Chris took a public beating, he remained within his governing energy, which is sarcastic, public gadfly. And because of that, instead of Chris taking the embarrassment for being assaulted by another man and doing nothing, it was Will who was shamed.

That's how it works. Whenever I stepped outside of my governing energy, I always lost. Every man needs to know himself. If you're not a fighter and you're confronted, don't try to be something you're not just to save face in front of other people, because the situation will turn out worse.

As a man, you must defend yourself if you have no choice. I get that. But don't exaggerate and act like someone you're not, because it will backfire. I've seen it happen. If you know who you are then you must live in that energy until life is over. You will keep your dignity and integrity every time, even if it means being dragged in the dirt, because harmful actions against a man have nothing to do with who he is, if he stays true to himself.

I had violated my energy and broke my own rule. My hopes of starting my own business had faltered. But I learned valuable lessons that I would take into the future for a relaunch six years later.

When I put myself back into an Islamic headspace and temporarily gave up my entrepreneurial dreams, I was called to be Muslim spiritual advisor at Northeastern University. And once again, the experience shifted my Islamic lens.

During the first religious event I attended at the university, I met all the other chaplains and many students from different organizations, such as Hillel, Students for Justice in Palestine, Black Student Association, and more. But what really freaked me out was when they served the food. There was pizza, cold cuts, fruit, and cheese and crackers, but when I saw a Muslim student pick up a pig-in-a-blanket and eat it, I almost fainted. A pig-in-a-blanket is a tiny pork hot dog wrapped in bread. Eating pork is strictly prohibited in Islam. I had to stop myself from physically grabbing her arm so she wouldn't put it in her mouth. But it wasn't over. One of the Jewish students picked up a pig-in-a-blanket too! I was having an out-of-body experience.

How could this be? You're here because you acknowledge your religion and yet you're eating things outside of your religious code. I was a long way from Concord, where Muslims would rather die than eat a pepperoni. In fact, one time I visited a brother in his cell after he had just returned to prison from the street. He was very casual about his crimes. This time he was in for armed robbery, carjacking, and drug possession. He spoke to me from inside his cell, through the corner where the cell door had an opening. He said, "Yeah imam, I just can't leave that life alone. This guy was driving a Benz and I know he's not really a tough guy, so I jacked him for it." Then he paused and put his head down as if he were ashamed. When he lifted his head there were tears in the wells of his eyes. He said, "But I did do one thing I need to repent for. It got so bad that I ate a ham sandwich."

He was sincerely remorseful for violating the Islamic dietary law of abstaining from pork. He didn't care that he had just bashed a man in the side of the head with his gun until he bled, or that he was caught with several ounces of crack on him, he was concerned about his Islamic oath. I almost laughed at how cavalier he was about the other crimes, but I kept my cool.

But now I was surrounded by Muslims, Christians, and Jews who seemed to make their own rules about religion. They did what they wanted and said what they felt. I would hear Muslim students say things like, "Well, I don't really see myself in the traditional sense as a Muslim, I enjoy Eid, but that's it. It's more of a culture for me." I would hear Jewish students say, "Well, I think Mosha (the Hebrew name for Moses) is more of a construct than a real person." I was initially disgusted. I wanted to run away. But where was I going? I needed the job.

One day the chaplains had their biweekly gathering in the sacred room. We were all seated in a circle. There were about twenty chaplains from different faith practices: Catholic, Protestant, Hindu, Chabad, Buddhist, Sikh, Bahai, and others. Our supervisor, Alex Kern, a middle-aged free-spirited Quaker who was committed to social justice, asked us a question, "Please share with us one person who was a peace-maker in your faith during the twentieth century."

We were given a couple of minutes to reflect, and immediately names started popping up around the room: Mother Theresa, Dr. King, Gandhi, Thomas Merton, Howard Therman, among others. I was getting nervous. The only Muslim I could think of was Muhammad Ali, and although he is an American Muslim hero who spoke out against war and oppression, he was still a boxer who made his name being violent. It didn't feel appropriate for me to mention him. All I had left was Malcolm X. My personal favorite. Although he was a saint to me personally, and an archetype of peaceful courage, he wasn't known for spreading peace. I had no one. That hurt.

When the circle got to me, I said, "Pass. I need more time to think." My palms were sweating. I was a prison chaplain. I didn't know anyone outside of medieval Islam. I decided right there that I needed to go back to school.

Deacon Bruce was correct. I needed more religious education beyond my own context if I was going to function as a well-rounded and informed representative of my own faith. Dr. Celene Ibrahim, a white convert and scholar of Islam, got me some information on Andover Newton Theological Schools Master's program in Global Interreligious Leadership where she was a professor.

I soon left Northeastern as a spiritual advisor and joined Harvard University as the first paid Muslim chaplain. When Dean Dudley Rose invited me into his office and offered me the opportunity to teach a course on Islamic Polity at Harvard Divinity School it was surreal. When I left his office after having been given all the details of the course, I was overwhelmed with joy.

I sat on a bench outside the Divinity School and thought about how far I'd come and how humbling it was. Just a decade before, I was a discouraged, uneducated, young Muslim packing books in one of Harvard's warehouses. Now I was not only the first paid Muslim chaplain in Harvard's history, but I was going to teach at the prestigious

Harvard Divinity School. When I received the official offer letter from the Divinity School, I framed it. That was one of my most humbling moments. There are many masjids with imams all over the world, but there's only one Harvard University and I was the resident imam there. *Allah is great*, I thought.

Little did I know that Harvard University hated religion and tra-ditional values, but hid it behind the insidious mask of *tolerance and inclusion*. It was the worse place I've ever worked. They didn't really want to teach religion as much as they wanted to use religious space to dismantle traditional religious narratives, and allow free thought and philosophy as just as legitimate as religion.

The Islamic polity class that I taught was for graduate students. One evening before class, I prepared to pray in the mezzanine area and one of the Muslim students decided to join me. He lined up to pray next to me as Muslims do, but I could tell he didn't know where to stand. I asked him to call the *iqaama*, which is the short call to prayer which signals the people to line up in rows before the first *takbeer* He couldn't call it.

To put this in context, first-grade Muslim Sunday school stu-dents learn how to call the *athaan* and the *iqaama*. It is very basic and takes literally five seconds to say, but he had no clue. When I realized that he might've never even prayed in his life from the way he was behaving, I called the *iqaama* and told him where to stand. I also instructed him to follow my movements. He prayed with me in what seemed to be a total state of confusion the entire time. When I was going down to bend, he rushed to his knees. When I was raising my hands, he was folding them, all the while looking at me out of the corner of his eyes. This was a Muslim student in a Master's level Islamic class at Harvard.

I couldn't help but to think that when he graduates with a Mas-ter's in religion from Harvard University, he'll be the spokesperson for Islam on Fox News or CNN. But by then my critical conscience around Islam was becoming dampened by my tenure at the school.

At Northeastern, our chaplain meetings served pizza and blue-collar food, but here at Harvard when the chaplains met there were bagels, lox, yogurt, and exotic pastries. I felt so out of place and off-mission. It was intriguing to be privy to the halls of power in the Academy, albeit just as a chaplain, but there was a sense that I had betrayed the brothers in Concord.

While I smiled, made small talk, pretended to laugh, and piled lox on top of my bagel, I heard the same voice I heard in the nightclubs in California with Dr. Dre. *This is not who you are, or where you need to be.* But I knew I had to keep pushing forward because there was something in this experience that I would benefit from.

Then one day, as I sat in my car fiddling with my phone, it started to ring. A Washington DC number showed up, so I answered, and it was Sam from the Associated Press. He wanted my opinion about then-presidential candidate Donald Trump's immigration policy. Sam really viewed my opinion as Muslim chaplain at Harvard as newsworthy. He asked me, "How are the students handling his campaign? What are your thoughts?" I didn't know what to say. I was just a prison chaplain, I thought. "Ah, yes, well I see it as very polarizing, and the students are handling it as well as they could." I said something generic to that effect. He asked me a few more questions and thanked me.

When I hung up, I thought, *What the heck just happened?* It wasn't long before WGBH, NPR, and other national radio stations and television shows were calling my phone and sending me emails for interviews on topics ranging from my opinion about what Islam might look like under a Trump administration, to what I had been implementing to help students on campus.

Huffington Post gave me a private blog where I could randomly post my own essays to their digital audience of millions, WBUR's Cognoscenti newsletter began requesting me to write articles, and even the *Boston Globe* began to solicit my opinion quite often. I was being invited on local talk shows and even a few national ones. Harvard was paying off, so I thought.

When the masjids would call for a sermon, I started to demand $1,500 for an hour-long session. I was *the* Harvard chaplain, after all. I had a chip on my shoulder from the way I perceived their mistreatment of local imams. Besides, I knew some of the national Muslim leaders were receiving $5,000 a speech.

I had recently started a teaching position at Facing History and Ourselves, a global nonprofit that teaches students and high school faculty how to address difficult moments in history. I was finally making a six-figure salary doing what I loved to do, teaching justice and preaching about Islam.

But somewhere between the Harvard logo, and that biweekly direct deposit from Facing History and Ourselves, teaching justice became a job and not a calling, and preaching about Islam became managing my brand and not establishing the truth. I became so busy I started to delay my prayers. My beard, I rationalized was too messy to be standing in front of these civilized teachers, so I trimmed it shorter and shorter. I gave up eating only *zabeehah* meat, which is meat that is slaughtered according to Islamic law. I stopped eating *zabeehah* because it became too difficult to have a meal when I was hopping from school to school meeting teachers, I rationalized. And I needed my protein. Now I was eating a cheeseburger from anywhere.

I had lost my governing energy.

9

REBEL PREACHER

Becoming an Interreligious Student

ANDOVER NEWTON THEOLOGICAL School, or ANTS, was the first theological school in America, and was founded in 1807. It was affiliated with American Baptist churches and the United Church of Christ when it was founded. I say *was* because it has since merged with Yale Divinity School and moved to Connecticut.

ANTS is a bastion of liberal thought and social justice. I wanted to attend after a friend, Dr. Celene Ibrahim who was also a professor at ANTS, recommended that I apply. I knew about Islamic law enough to practice and teach it, but I felt as though I needed more interreligious knowledge, including a history of other religions and the personalities that pushed them forward. When I began as a student there, I wasn't prepared to be placed in an environment where Christian liberation theology and LGBTQ rights were placed on par with each other. Up to that point I had viewed the LGBTQ community as a pantheon of perversion.

I grew up in the 1980s in a culture where we didn't see many gay people. My only reference was seeing big Black men dressed in raggedy miniskirts with heroin needle tracks on their arms. They wore scary makeup and messy wigs, had big dirty hands and deep voices. They always seemed to be in a fit of chaos: three or four of them stumbling over one another in the street, fighting, running from someone else, screaming with one high heel on their foot and the other being used as a weapon. To a ten-year-old boy, they seemed like monsters.

I imagine now that these were people who had suffered a series of mental breakdowns after being abandoned by their families, kicked out on the street, using heroin, while in utter despair. They were often murdered or found overdosed in alleyways even back then.

Nevertheless, that was my reference point for the LGBTQ community, and I'm sure some version of that story is a reference for other Generation Xers. We were uninformed and had limited exposure to difference.

Every generation targets a group of people they think are going to ruin the country or the moral fabric of society. In the 1840s there was a movement called the Nativists, which preached that Catholicism was destroying America. They found a voice in a newly formed political party called the Know Nothing political party. They promised to purify America by getting rid of any Catholic influence. They ran Millard Fillmore for a presidential bid in 1856. In fact, Catholicism was illegal in Massachusetts in the seventeenth and eighteenth centuries. In the same vein, came the postslavery Dunning School, interwar anti-Semitism, post–9/11 Islamophobia, and now anti-LGBTQ sentiment.

The fragility of Western democracy lies in the tension between freedom and personal morality. The more we espouse the ideals of freedom, the more our collective morality dissolves into a melting pot of subjectivity.

I've come to accept that there are things in a Western democracy that are going to be legally necessary but incongruent with one's personal moral compass. Because the same laws and policies that protect my right to express my faith openly, to pray my ritual five prayers in shopping mall parking lots and in airports, must necessarily allow for LGBTQ rights.

America is not an Islamic caliphate. Although my religion dictates that acting on homosexuality is a moral transgression, I don't feel the sense of urgency to make that issue a foreboding pillar of destruction for America. I find it hypocritical for American Muslims to protest in the streets with anti-LGBTQ signs, shouting anti-LGBTQ slogans.

They always have a choice to travel and live somewhere else. Muslims can't pick and choose what to be outraged about.

For instance, in Islam *shirk*, or polytheism, that is, to associate a partner with Allah, is the greatest creedal transgression against God. It is unforgivable. Allah says to those who believe that Jesus shares in Allah's Divinity:

> *So believe in Allāh and His messengers. And do not say,*
> *"Three"; stop—it is better for you. Indeed, Allāh is but one*
> *God. Exalted is He above having a son.*

Muslims who live in America are in a country dominated by a Christian narrative. There is a Bible in every hotel, a church or two on every corner. Christian prayers are recited in our government meetings and yet where is the outrage from the Muslims?

There's no outrage because Muslims have more freedom to practice their religion in America than in their own so-called Muslim countries. If they start to rail against Christianity in America they know that they'll be overrun, intimidated, outlawed, harassed, kicked out, or possibly imprisoned for terrorist threats, so they remain silent and enjoy Christian-led democracy.

Likewise, the Prophet Muhammad said in a hadith about alcohol:

> *Allah has cursed alcohol, the one who drinks it, the one who*
> *pours it, the one who sells it, the one who buys it, the one who*
> *squeezes the grapes for it, the one for whom it is squeezed, the*
> *one who carries it and the one to whom it is carried.*

Allah says:

> *O you who believe! Alcohol and gambling, stone altars for*
> *sacrifices to idols, and seeking luck through cultural rituals*
> *are an abomination of Shaytaan's handiwork. So avoid all of*
> *that in order that you may be successful.*

According to Islam, alcohol is a transgression similar to acting on homosexuality. Where are all the Muslim Alcoholics Anonymous groups? Where are the Muslim boycotts and protests against liquor stores?

We won't see any outrage from Muslims because alcohol is a source of great pleasure for Americans and Muslims know it's a losing battle.

As a result, American Muslims have decided to pick a soft target: the LGBTQ community. In a post-Trump America, there are a large number of Christian conservatives who are anti-LGBTQ, so it makes it easier for the Muslims to join the lynch mob. This type of hypocritical selective outrage is the reason Muslims haven't been able to confront their true blind spots: racism, greed, misogyny, and rote practice without critical thinking, which, for me, are greater transgressions.

Even in the prison Muslim community, the hypocrisy persists. During my tenure in Concord prison, there was a young Muslim man who had been in prison on a murder charge since he was seventeen years old. Now he was thirty years old and had been caught tongue-kissing another man. As a result, he was banned from the masjid by the other inmates. The main ringleader in favor of banning was a young Black man who felt strongly opposed to homosexual behavior. I pulled him into my office, sat him down, and looked him in his eyes. I said, "*Akh* [brother], what the man did was wrong within the tenets of religion, but what about the Muslim brothers who gamble openly every day, and drink hooch [alcohol made in prison]? They are allowed to come and pray daily, and no one says anything to them." He listened attentively, then offered a rebuttal. "Yeah but imam, being gay is on another level!" "Is it on another level for you or for Allah?" I asked. "For both of us!" he answered back.

Certain moral transgressions and crimes are unconsciously accepted as noble in the regressive Black street-culture: murder, armed robbery, and narcotics distribution being among the noblest. I imagine the notion harkens back to the house and field slave. The house slave was docile and takes with gratitude whatever his master offers, be it food scraps from the worst part of the animal or even beatings. The field slave on the other hand was ferocious, ambitious, and dangerous: willing to fight back, commit murder, and fend for himself. The transgenerational trauma of constantly having to redefine Black masculinity and survival has left the collective Black psyche with deep, unhealed scars that compel us to celebrate backward morality.

And certainly, for Muslims on the ground, we have not thought enough about gayness to have any sophisticated ideas beyond acknowledging that it's *haraam* (forbidden). Realizing all of this in a moment of clarity, I dialed back my own frustration and smiled at him. "*Akh*," I said, "you're in prison for committing two murders. Worry about making amends for the two human souls you took." He thought about it and said, "Alright, that's fair."

The Muslim community in prison didn't totally acquiesce to allowing the banned brother complete access to the mosque, but I was able to negotiate with them and get him permission to come pray with us. Then he would have to leave right away. I told them, "Whatever the climate is against him, you can't prevent a Muslim from praying in the masjid." The brothers understood, but then explained to me that his act put everyone at risk, because if it got out that Muslims accepted gay behavior in that kind of dangerous environment, then other Muslims might be jumped, beaten, or otherwise victimized, and then a war would start in the prison. It was better for him to take his punishment and move on. I understood. Whether we civilians understand prison politics or not, they do exist.

The one caveat I will mention is that, because we live in a democracy, religious people should not be given a litmus test about their privately held views and then be ridiculed, canceled, or labeled a bigot if their views aren't in line with the emerging norms on LGBTQ issues. We make a mockery of democracy when we don't allow people to hold traditional religious ethics that, while not popular, do not infringe on anyone's rights.

Of course, my classmates were thoughtful, kind, and full of faith as they understood it. I was better off as a human being because of sharing space with them. It's easy to transform full human beings into one-dimensional caricatures when there's no proximity.

During preparation for a weekend retreat to a Benedictine priory where our graduate class would monitor the practices of the monks and nuns over the course of several days, we were asked if we had any requests which would make shared living space more comfortable. I mentioned that I would humbly appreciate it if people could be mindful of bathroom hygiene because fifteen or so people had to share just two bathrooms.

The day I arrived at the priory, I was a few hours behind the main group. When I entered the bathroom to check it out, I found that it was unusually spotless. My professor had followed behind me and, when I came out, she said, "When we got here Lisa [a lesbian classmate] took a look at the bathroom and how unkempt it was. She shook her head and said, 'Tay is not gonna be able to use this bathroom like this.'" Apparently, she gathered all the cleaning supplies and got on her hands and knees and scrubbed the bathroom floor, cleaned the toilet, and washed the sink. *For me.*

Even today, as I recall this story to write it here, I am overwhelmed with humility. The humanity. The goodwill that Lisa had displayed was almost unbelievable to me. I was humbled by her selfless act and learned yet again what it meant to carry out truly prophetic acts of kindness. Lisa never mentioned anything to me, and I didn't want to spoil her gift by mentioning it to her. But that moment brought me clarity. I finally saw Lisa because she saw me first.

Sometimes we must see someone else in totality first before they can really see us for who we are. She taught me a valuable lesson in faith and service that day. It didn't matter that she was lesbian. She was human and striving to please God through her own experience as I was. As we all were.

At Harvard, a small group of LGBTQ Muslim students approached me to set up a meeting about their status on campus. Apparently, there were enough closeted LGBTQ Muslims that it warranted a sit down.

We met at a small café in Harvard Square. Their leader was a tiny South Asian young woman who was pursuing a doctorate at Harvard. She had already memorized the entire Qur'an and was preparing to pursue another degree in Islamic scholarship somewhere else after Harvard. Although small in stature, she was very much a force.

She showed up with about fifteen or so other Muslim students in tow. They all found chairs and crowded around the small table. Natalia, the small leader, started first. "We wanted to meet with you because we're not represented on campus. We would like our own prayer space."

I said, "Wait, okay, tell me why you feel the need for a separate prayer space." Another young man chimed in, "Because we're not welcome in the Harvard Mosque." I said, "And how do you know you're not welcomed? You're welcomed if I'm there." They looked at each other. Natalia continued, "We know your conservative brand of Islam, Imam Tay. And we know the general sentiment in the mosques all around Boston too. We want to be able to bring our partners to any mosque without any problems."

I replied, "Well, you have to be patient with the general understanding of Muslims who have been trained to think one way for 1,400 years and now because of a lifestyle choice you've made. . ." Natalia interrupted me, "Excuse me! It's not a lifestyle choice. It's who we are! Do you think we want to be marginalized by choice?" I apologized and continued. "See? This is what I mean. You can't get offended because we don't understand. Your first objective should be to teach and inform Muslims if you really want to be understood and accepted. But if you want to just be antagonistic to prove how ignorant Muslims are then that's what will happen."

Our conversation lasted for two hours. I told them I would guarantee safe passage in the main Harvard Mosque, but I couldn't "admit" as they wanted me to, that Islam doesn't prohibit homosexuality. I also couldn't advocate for a separate prayer space. I told them, "Islam says that acting on homosexuality is a transgression, but that doesn't mean I would treat you any different or disallow you from coming to the mosque. We must teach people out of ignorance." I also couldn't endorse them opening a separate prayer space. I told them, "If separation was the answer, then Black Muslims aren't welcomed in the Harvard prayer space and there's been many conflicts about it, so they should separate and create their own prayer space. Pakistanis should separate from Arabs. *Hijabis* should separate from non-*hijabis*."

They disagreed with me respectfully and we agreed to continue the conversation later. Unfortunately, that date would never come for me because I decided to leave Harvard shortly after.

I had to leave. It had nothing to do with that meeting. I thought about when, seventeen years prior to my tenure at Harvard, I had been Muslim for about a year. I was recruited to act as security for the Eid prayer. Eid is the Islamic celebration the morning after the last night of Ramadan, the annual month-long fast. Eid would be equivalent in importance and sacredness to Easter. It's the Muslims' biggest holiday.

The prayer attracted seven to ten thousand Muslims in the early morning hours. There was always chaos and crowds. Families would lose their small children, old ladies would accidently be pushed to the ground because of the smash of the crowd, but generally it was a festive and joyous time.

However, that year there was an Arab man who was holding a charity box full of money and refused to give it to the head of our security team. For some reason he just refused. I later found out he had mental health challenges. However, at that time I had no idea. In my unrefined rationale I was security, and he needed to relinquish that box. I went over to him, grabbed him by the collar, shoved him to the ground, and took the box from him. *I was security*, I thought. It was my job. All the Muslim women sitting on the bleachers gasped when they saw what I had done.

Later that same morning, I got into another shoving match with someone else.

I had done security for my brother Mel a few times in 1998. He had a stable of several women who he would book to dance and strip for professional white men in hotels or for bachelor parties in the 'hood. I would put my gun on my hip, go to the party, and make sure no one touched the women too aggressively. There were times when things got heated, and me and Mel would both have to literally pull someone off a young woman. Now here I was at a Muslim gathering without a gun, but nevertheless treating this sacred family-friendly event like it was a stripper party. I was way out of line.

A Black American imam named Taalib Mahdi, who had become somewhat of a mentor to me, pulled me aside and told me, "Never take a job at the sacrifice of your own character. It's time for you to quit brother. You're going to ruin your reputation before you get one." He was right. I never did security again.

And now I felt I was confused and lost in the glamour of Harvard Islam. I found myself losing my own character. I was moving further away not just from my personal values, but from caring about anything other than promoting my personal brand. I decided to resign, and focus on my graduate degree and my work at Facing History and Ourselves.

At Facing History, I was being taught about the Holocaust in large doses by the likes of Professor Paul Bookbinder and others. I was also learning about post–Civil War Reconstruction from experts like Jeremy Nassoff. My mind was expanding rapidly. I had read Eli Wiesel's *Night* in high school, and it struck a chord, but I had long since forgotten about him and the book. Now I was reading about the horrors of the Holocaust and watching films that made me want to vomit. The sheer human suffering was unconscionable.

I found myself coming to the realization that everyone should learn this history. I'm no champion for Jewish people. However, it just so happened that they experienced one of the worst human tragedies that history has ever recorded on film and documented on paper, and if we can teach children and adults about how it happened, we might be able to prevent it from happening again.

Michael Berenbaum, a Jewish rabbi and scholar said, "To study evil is to strengthen decency and goodness." And I believe that. I was emotionally changed from learning about the Holocaust. If you've never studied the Holocaust beyond reading a superficial article, you're doing your own humanity a disservice.

Just before I left Harvard, I was being introduced at a benefit dinner full of alumni. In the introduction, the woman said, "He is a Holocaust educator and a board member of Kids 4 Peace, a nonprofit that brings Muslim, Christian, and Jewish children together to share fun experiences."

Later that evening a young Palestinian woman came to me and said, "You could never be my imam." I said, "Okay, so I guess this is where I'm supposed to ask why." She said, "Because you're allowing the Zionists to use you as a tool to justify their treatment of Palestinians."

She said, "By you working for Zionists, you are actually validating their position against Palestine." I nodded and listened. When she finished, I said, "Listen, I can appreciate your point of view. But frankly, I have seen too much death and bloodshed of young Black men whose lives were wasted before they were twenty years old. I'm in the business of prevention. Kids 4 Peace was founded by a retired teacher who is a liberal Christian. She's looking for help anywhere she can find it. And my teaching the Holocaust is about what led up to it, what allowed the world to sit and watch twelve million people, not just Jewish people—Black people, mentally challenged people, the Roma, the disabled, and Jehovah's Witnesses—be slaughtered for no reason. If

I can teach a little bit of this history to a child living under the Trump Administration, where dehumanization, which is one of the first steps of fascism, takes place daily in his speeches, then I will continue to warn as many humans as possible."

She responded, "Yes, but do you support Black Lives Matter?" I said "I support the sentiment of what they stand for but not everything they do. But for the sake of public solidarity, I refuse to criticize them openly." She said, "Well, they support Palestine in their charter. And demand for Israel to lift its occupation." I said, "I believe you're conflating two issues: one is teaching history and the other is holding a political position. Why can't I sit on the board of an organization that helps children create positive memories with other children from different faiths, teach the Holocaust, *and* support Palestine?" She said, "Because it's hypocrisy and disloyal."

I quoted Richard Rubenstein, who wrote in *The Cunning of History*, "Germans understood that no person has any rights unless they are guaranteed by an organized community with the power to defend such rights." I said to her, "Little Black and Brown boys and girls need to be warned that flipping over cars and burning buildings in St. Louis or in Palestine won't stop the Israeli or American police from killing them in the street, but organizing their power might."

She was a student at Yale University studying medicine. I asked her, "Do you have Jewish professors?" She said "Yes." I said, "Do you boycott them?" She said, "No, because I'm not a racist." I said, "Okay, but when you graduate where will you go and work? Probably at a hospital which has Jewish benefactors. You'll probably be interviewed by a panel of which some are Jewish people who support Israel. Will you boycott them if you find out their political leanings?"

Maybe I was being unfair at this point. But I wanted to point out that Zionism is alive and among us in the world. I wasn't telling her to submit to it and bow out, but to be more critical in how she approached her passion for Palestine, because there were better ways for her to channel her energy than to be angry with a Black imam who teaches about a horrible moment in history. If she insisted on being narrow-minded, then she'd eventually be accused of hypocrisy herself, if she were ever compelled to compromise her stance because of some career benefit.

I learned the hard way that life is more nuanced than we can imagine. Taking hard stances leads to hard falls. It's better to hold a firm position while honoring the subtlety of the opposition. Chivalry is emphasized in Islam, despite it rarely being utilized.

Allah says: "O you who believe! stand out firmly for Allah, as witnesses to fair dealing, and do not let your hatred for others or their hatred of you make you sway from justice. Be just: that is next to piety: and fear Allah. For Allah is well-acquainted with all that ye do."

We ended our conversation cordially. And I agreed I would be vigilant around issues that marginalized our Palestinian brothers and sisters.

I tried to understand her pain. But it's hard to get past my own when my people are also being slaughtered wholesale. After our conversation, one thing did become clear to me: I needed to take a closer look at my passive stance on Israel/Palestine.

After some thought, I concluded that you would have to have blinders on to not see the blatant oppression of the Palestinian people by the Israeli government.

No two human tragedies are the same and I don't want to conflate the Holocaust with the Palestinian issue, because they're not the same. The Holocaust was the systematic, intentional murder of Jewish people based on their race. The Israel–Palestine conflict is not that.

But from Ottoman rule in the sixteenth century, then the British Mandate, then Jordanian rule, to Israeli occupation—for five hundred years the Palestinians have been under the yoke of a foreign regime.

The Palestinians have tried to use nonviolent means, such as refusing to pay taxes on properties and businesses, organizing a national commercial strike, and discarding their labor cards, as a means of protest. Those are some of the same civic strategies Black Americans used during the civil rights movement. The only difference is that we received placation in the form of policy change and a slow crawl to equal access.

But imagine if there were no antidiscrimination laws passed? Imagine Medgar, Malcolm, and Martin all assassinated with no legislative reprieve for Black Americans. Who's to say we wouldn't have resorted to violence like the Palestinians eventually did. The violence we see from them is not from the nature of their people, it's the nature of desperation whenever human cries go unheard.

For me, the issue with Israel is not that it doesn't deserve to exist, it's that for a state which claims to be a democracy, its actions are not consistent with democratic standards when it comes to the rules of war and sanctions. It is allowed to use the language of democracy while perpetuating some of the worse crimes of usurpation and aggression against entire families the world has ever seen. You can't be both. Either you're a democracy or you're a right-wing regime that holds elections. Otherwise, it's not unfair to summon a democracy to a higher standard of principles.

Palestine and its people are under duress, and they are being oppressed. They deserve relief. And I say that not because Palestinians are my brethren in Islam, because many are Christian. I say it because if the world can rally around Ukraine and acknowledge it has the right to self-defense against Russian invasion, what makes Palestine different?

I often wondered why the Black Lives Matter movement mentioned the end of Israeli occupation in Palestine as one of their charter principles. Being entrenched in religious dogma, I didn't see the connection and considered it a strategic mistake for them. But I began to change my sentiment after my talk with the young Muslimah from Yale. She wasn't wrong in some of her assertions.

Black Lives Matter views Palestine as yet another instance of the world community overlooking Brown persecution. If the world's democratic nations recognized their errors in 1945 by remarking, "We didn't realize the terrors of the Holocaust," then how can they explain sitting back and watching modern-day Palestine, Cambodia, Myan-mar, Sudan, and Syria? These are places and people in need of human rights champions.

Despite my personal views on Israel/Palestine, I was on my way to becoming a pariah in my own Muslim community because I was an imam attending a Christian seminary while teaching the Holocaust. But I know what I was learning, and I know what Allah was teaching me. I wasn't raised to fall prey to groupthink. Just because Arabs and Jews didn't get along, that doesn't mean a Black man can't be in rela-tionship with both groups.

When I became Muslim, I would hear the Islamic sermons about Jewish deceit, and I felt that it was coming from a place of racial malice and not from the critique of religious disobedience. There was a differ-ence. Was I supposed to hate all Jews because some foreign sheikh insisted that the entire race was corrupt? I didn't buy it. Black Americans have been harmed by way too much racial violence for me to pay that forward.

The people I worked with at Facing History, Jewish and non, were the best colleagues and mentors I've had in my career. They were thoughtful, kind, and humble, even if there were some blind spots.

The work at Facing History was not rooted in the Holocaust only. They taught antiracism, and anti-immigration curricula more fre-quently than the Holocaust, actually.

So when, after years of studying Bedouin Islam, I found myself sitting in that chaplains' circle at Northeastern, and I had no reference of any religious figures in or out of Islam that advocated for peace, I felt ashamed and stripped of dignity. I wouldn't allow that to happen again. For the sake of my own edification, I needed to learn. If other Muslims disowned me, well they didn't make me Muslim in the first place. No one came to look for me in the ghetto. Allah saw fit to pull me out and give me direction. I must follow the pattern he set for me.

At ANTS, I was pushed to find contemporary heroes from my own worldview. And I did. They were hidden underneath the names of Islamic warriors and medieval scholars, which seem to be the only two identities that Muslims at large revere. Where are the Muslims politicians, activists, writers, scientists, explorers, and peacemakers?

I found Abdul Sattar Edhi, a Pakistani man who founded the world's largest ambulatory service from scratch. He is on record as being father to the most orphans in the world. He started by begging for change to open a small pharmacy to help the sick and, in fifty years, built a charity organization that picked the sick and dying off the street, gave them a place to sleep, to eat, and to be nurtured to health. He pulled babies out of the dumpster and took them home and raised them to full adulthood. And he never made a penny. He remained poor and lived with his family in the back of one of his organizational offices until his death in 2016. A real *mutaqqi,* or pious one, as Muslims would say.

There was Abdul Ghaffar Khan, an Afghan man who was a contemporary of Mahatma Gandhi. Khan was a pacifist and used peaceful tactics to disrupt Britain's rule over colonial India. He advocated for Hindu–Muslim unity and was arrested, tortured, and beaten many times for it throughout his long life. He died in his nineties in 1988. I would consider him a *wali,* or saint in Islam. And Allah is the final judge.

I've come to believe that there is a "big T" Truth, but it includes smaller truths based on lived experience. When we come to terms with our own human fragility and unawareness, we'll be able to accept that there are alternative human realities experienced by gays, Christians, Jews, Blacks, and even other Muslims. It doesn't make all those realities excusable or even valid Islamically, but it acknowledges them as part of the human experience.

Those Muslim scholars of the past who endorsed the inferiority of Black people, also wrote much of the religious commentary we hold sacred today. I'm almost positive that those public endorsements of racism harmed Black Muslims back then both physically and socially. If those scholars get a pass because they were nurtured upon a certain social construct and mindset or influenced by traumas of their era, then that pass must extend to those with whom we disagree today because they too are experiencing life as it unfolds for them, trauma and all.

Thomas Jefferson wrote that Blacks are inferior in mind and body, and he owned 125 Black bodies as his property, yet he was a great founder of the Constitution. No Black person in their right mind would look to him as a sage or to any of his writings for guidance. Likewise, SAMs must be vigilant around accepting blatantly bigoted or siloed Islamic commentaries and explanations from those scholars of the past. The same goes for accepting dogmatist opinions from any Muslim scholar of the present who's been sheltered from the strife of poverty, violence, racism, or something as simple as having to borrow food from your gay neighbor because scarcity makes that your only option.

For instance, Sultan, a seventy-plus year-old incarcerated Muslim serving a life sentence, came to me one day in prison and said, "I saved $5,000 over several years by selling homemade lollipops in prison so I can pay for my own *janazah* when I die in here. Can you ensure that if I die while you're serving in here, you'll make sure I'm buried properly?" I gave him an emphatic yes.

A year later, Sultan died from COVID-19 in prison. I was not allowed inside because of the quarantine, but I got the call from a former inmate who had spoken to an incarcerated Muslim who told him to call me.

I immediately contacted the prison to arrange for Sultan's burial, but the administration told me, "Taymullah, we can't release the body to you or the masjid. Only family members." I reminded them that Sultan had written a final will and testament, had it notarized, and they had a copy as well as me. "None of those things matter," they reiterated. "If no one claims the body in a month, he'll be buried in the prison grave." I was furious.

I began to panic. I knew Sultan had a brother somewhere in Boston, but I didn't know how to find him. I called around to anyone who I thought might know him, but I had no success.

Frustrated, and three weeks into my search, I reached out to Kathleen Patron, lead organizer for the Greater Boston Interfaith Organization or GBIO, a group that gathers people from different faiths for political advocacy around issues of housing, incarceration, and health care. I was part of the organization through my company, Spentem.

I told Kathleen what was happening, and she was just as upset as I was. She hung up and made a few calls. Within ten minutes she was back on the phone with me, but now she had Nommi and Jeremy from the Jewish Community Relations Council on the phone as well. They were also members of GBIO. They were sympathetic because, in the Jewish faith, they understood how important immediate burial is.

Nommi and Jeremy told me, "Tay, give us an hour." Within fifteen minutes of hanging up from them, the Massachusetts coroner's office called my cell phone to arrange burial for Sultan. Apparently Nommi and Jeremy reached out directly to the governor's office and the governor's office instructed the coroner to call me.

Sultan was given a proper Islamic burial using his money, within twenty-four hours of that conversation.

None of that would have happened, and his wish would not have been granted, had I not been in solidarity with the interreligious community. Some might say, "Oh well, let him get buried in the prison cemetery rather than allow Jews to help you." But that's ignorant. The Prophet Muhammad took assistance from Jewish tribes and Christian people. The point is not to be a religious supremacist. The point is to recognize how Allah uses people to help people. No one is above being helped. I remain grateful to all the people involved who helped me give Sultan the proper Islamic burial he worked hard for.

I believe that the Qur'an contains the ultimate "big T" Truth. But after I've declared my Islam along with my deal breakers and red lines, how someone chooses to comply with or reject certain values and beliefs speaks to the traumas and joys they've experienced in life. Another human being's experience with God is none of my business.

I realized that Allah had made me a Muslim who must carry the torch of Islam, but also an extra torch to make light for others during a visit from Dr. Terrence Roberts.

Dr. Roberts has the distinction of being one of the Little Rock Nine. He and a group of eight other high school students single-handedly desegregated Arkansas Central High School in 1957. Dr. Roberts is a civil rights icon; one of the last, I might add.

When I met him in 2015, he was a retired professor of psychology and would often take an annual trip to Boston from California to speak to middle school students on behalf of Facing History.

I had the blessing of being his chauffeur. I would pick him up from his hotel bright and early, and shuttle him from school to school, making sure all the arrangements were made and his speaking engagement went smoothly. It was an honor for me.

During a visit to one particularly rowdy middle school, the students were being unruly during Dr. Roberts's speech. They were laughing, throwing a few things across the auditorium, and some were moving around and getting out of their chairs. The teachers and administrators recognized the value of having Dr. Roberts, and tried their best to contain the chaos, but it was difficult.

Dr. Roberts just steamrolled through his speech, which was very spontaneous, energetic, and insightful. He had nothing prepared. He'd say something different about the importance of getting an education, civic engagement, and being a person of integrity at each school. He acted as if the children weren't misbehaving at all.

Later, at lunch I asked him, "Doc, I didn't like the way those students were behaving. How can you just continue to speak? Why didn't you ask them to settle down?" Without missing a beat, he said, "Tay, those kids have yet to realize the value of what I had to say, but some of it will stick. Ten, twenty years down the line, they'll remember me and my words, then it would've all been worth it. When they're shouting and cutting up, I must keep going. It's my necessary act. If you can find your necessary act, then you find your purpose."

Interreligious learning, fostering authentic relationships, and standing up for justice as I saw it, were my necessary acts. I felt as though I had no choice. Allah was calling me to it.

MISEDUCATION OF THE MUSLIM

Rote Memorizing versus Critical Thinking

A FEW YEARS back there was a Muslim scholar in the Middle East who issued a *fatwa* that a man can have sex with his dead wife up to twenty-four hours after her death. Obviously, the *fatwa* was condemned by the Muslim world and by other scholars, but the fact that he made it that far in his career is confounding.

Another one issued a *fatwa* that the digital game, *Pokemon Go*, was *haraam* (prohibited) to play because it endangered human lives. Men like this can trivialize Muslims being killed by other Muslims in countries all over the world—Somalia, Sudan, Yemen, and Syria—but, "Make sure you look both ways when you cross the street! And that's why you can't play *Pokemon Go*."

Pure insanity.

Jordan Peterson, the famous Canadian professor of psychology, speaks about people being born with an IQ they cannot change. Professor Peterson emphasizes that the only thing a person is capable of changing is their verbal IQ—essentially their vocabulary.

It's clear that either Allah gives you intelligence or he doesn't. And today many of the Muslim teachers and sheikhs that we revere as great thinkers are just memorizers who regurgitate rulings from books written seven hundred years ago. Nothing about the ideas of the past creates any tension for them.

Healthy tension is a necessary condition to embrace when jostling with new and old ideas. When our ideas create a problem for us, this is what instigates contextual analysis. When something is working, we don't question it. It's only when something stops working that we interrogate and research. I have felt and thought for the past decade that something is wrong with the practice of Islam, and all roads lead back to a toxic dogmatic interpretation exported by Islamic regimes bent on using their social position to set up a context that intimidates Muslims into adhering to a bastardized Islam which seeks to denigrate women, non-Arabs, and more liberal understandings of Islamic law.

One day, while teaching a group of eighth-grade Muslim students from a supposedly modern Islamic textbook which essentially repeated the same themes throughout the entire book—the Muslims have always had superior morals, they defeat whoever they battle, they are the most clever and brave, and they are always in the right—I was fed up. We had been doing this same type of lesson for months.

These were smart kids, bored out of their minds. They deserved to learn and be challenged, not to have half-truths deposited into their minds without the privilege of processing and discussing.

I immediately told them all, "Okay, close your books. We're gonna have a Socratic seminar today." I gave them a scenario. I said, "You're driving a very expensive sports car that doesn't have much room to fit more than two more adults in it. It's pouring rain outside. You see a Muslim walking in the rain with two grocery bags, and you see a Jewish man walking in the rain with two children. Who do you stop to pick up?" The class got silent. It was a tough call for them. They smiled nervously and looked at one another as if there was a glitch in today's daily lesson. *He wants us to think instead of listen?* I saw their eyes trying to justify different scenarios for their car ride.

Finally, after a sixty-second silence, one student started. "Does the car have a trunk? I would put the Muslim up front, the Jew and his kids in the back sitting on laps, and I would put the Muslim's groceries in the trunk." I paced the room with my hands in my pockets. "Okay. Not bad," I said. "But there's no trunk. And there's barely a back seat." They thought some more until finally another chimed in, "I would just take the Muslim!" A totally rational answer if you're a child surrounded by Muslims, learning how Muslims are the best people (despite evidence to the contrary), and learning a version of Islam that is exclusionary in its nature. I smiled and, before I could counter, another student shouted out, "I would take the Jew and his kids, but I wouldn't trust him."

This was the type of answer I wanted to draw out of them, not to demonize, but to question and dismantle this type of mentality. "Okay, why can't we trust Jews?" I asked. Again, before I could continue, another student spoke up: "That's not right to generalize people." It was a female student. The first student to push back.

Now we were having a meaningful discussion that included student voices and critical thinking. They were stuck between what they had been taught and what their guts were telling them was right. Where did this otherwise decent young man get the idea that he couldn't trust a Jewish father walking in the rain with his children? What was this Jewish man going to do in the car that was so sinister?

I asked, "Are you speaking from experience?" He smiled nervously. I could sense he knew what he said was morally bankrupt. He shrugged his shoulders as if to say he didn't know. "Okay—so we've established that this is a false premise: that you can't trust this Jewish man with two children, correct?" The class nodded enthusiastically in agreement. They were relieved.

Intuition told them they couldn't leave a father and his young children stuck on the side of road, but intellectually they were conflicted with what they had been reading. For me this was a moral question, but for them it was a question of loyalty to Islam.

And this continues to be a problem today. Many Muslims haven't been taught to think critically about anything; not false Islamic historical narratives, not their own circumstances, and not the political and social conditions that have placed Muslims at the bottom of the world's priorities.

While I was a teacher at the same Islamic day school, a female Muslim teacher insisted that all plastic baby stars be removed from the school's daycare because, "It was a symbol of Israel." Another father complained to the principal in full outrage because his toddler was being taught about the letter "P" using the word *pig*. Pigs are forbidden to consume in Islamic law. He held the small, colorful ABC book in his hand, waving it back and forth as he shouted to the principal, "Why would you use a pig to teach the letter 'P'?" You couldn't make this kind of comedy up on television.

I understand that all religions have adherents who take strange, cringe-worthy intellectual positions that make the entire faith look backward. But, for Islam, it's become institutionalized. Muslims are taught to be loyal to sheikhs' *fatwas* instead of loyal to justice. On the contrary, the original source of Islam, the Qur'an, teaches that to take the side of justice, even if it's against popular Muslim opinion, is to take the side of true Islam.

And for this reason and numerous others, I believe that all Islamic educational institutions that do not teach critical thinking need to shut down immediately. Unfortunately, that would essentially mean shutting down most Muslim educational institutions because they are simply using academic banking—making students memorize long texts written by medieval clerics who were no doubt influenced by the social and political constructs of their time: male chauvinism, racism, classism, and religious bigotry.

I've seen many Islamic syllabi, I've been privy to Muslim educational leaders' discussions, I've taught Islamic Sunday school. Muslims are not teaching hate. They're not teaching anti-Semitism. But when they don't give their students the tools to think objectively about everything, they're setting them up to hate in the future due to blind allegiance to false paradigms.

My evidence is empirical. In Islamic schools and universities there is no deconstructing of classical texts, no unpacking of narratives, no offering one's own opinion, no asking "Why?"

We've taken our learning model from the modality of the Prophet Muhammad, who was receiving unquestionable divine revelation from the heavens. Naturally, his companions shouldn't have and did not ever question the revealed Word of Allah. It was perfect. We've juxtaposed that learning model on our contemporary circumstance, so that if a Muslim student raises his or her hand in class and says, "Yes but . . .," it is as if they've cracked the sky open and blasphemed all that is holy and sacred. The throne of God will not shake because a human being has a question or two.

The true goal of Islam is to bring justice, welfare, and fairness to humanity. This is clearly stated in many verses of the Qur'an. It has never been fully realized because the Prophet Muhammad died before Islam had spread and it's been on a decline since his death.

The goal of Islam is not simply to pray and fast. If Allah were pleased with praying and fasting exclusively, then no group prays or fasts more than Muslims. With that understanding, Muslims should be in the upper echelons of humanity. And if sex outside of marriage and drinking alcohol were the most heinous of crimes in the sight of Allah, then there's no place that promotes this more than the West. With that understanding every Western secular country would be at the bottom of the barrel.

Most Muslims would insist that true justice is professing monotheism and true oppression is in practicing polytheism. That's true. But that's justice in the vertical context. Islam also considers horizontal circumstance.

For instance, there are two hadiths that demonstrate this.

The Prophet Muhammad said, "The first thing among their deeds for which the people will be brought to account on the Day of Resurrection will be prayer."

Likewise, he also said on another occasion, "The cases which will be decided first on the Day of Resurrection will be the cases of blood-shedding."

There's no contradiction. He was implying that, vertically, we owe Allah our obligation to monotheism, which is worship. But horizontally, we owe one another our obligation to justice, which is fair dealings.

This point was so important that one of the greatest scholars and pious men of Islamic history, Ibn Taymiyyah said, "Allah allows the just government to remain even if it is led by disbelievers. But Allah will not allow the oppressive government to remain, even if it is led by Muslims."

A right to fair trial, freedom to critique your political leaders and vote them in or out of office, free enterprise, human rights, job security, rights to education, equality of the sexes: all of these are spelled out in the Qur'an, but disregarded by many Muslim leaders. Instead, we see the West carrying out justice in leaps and bounds in comparison to Muslim countries.

One day, the principal of the Islamic day school I taught at called me to his office. He was an immigrant who had recently earned his PhD in international politics. He sat me down and said, "Taymullah, I'm graduating, and my university is inviting Condoleezza Rice as the commencement speaker. When they call me on stage to receive my diploma, she will be the one giving them out. I'm thinking of refusing to shake her hand as a protest against her treatment of Muslims all over the world. What is your opinion about this?"

I was dumbfounded. By now I had been exposed to a milieu of pluralism and high-level intellectualism as a graduate student and university chaplain. I thought he was joking, so I cracked a smile and waited for him to wink and do the same. He didn't. He was staring at me, waiting for an answer.

I shook myself out of shock and replied, "My brother, you spent four years as an undergraduate struggling to learn English and keep up with your studies. You were successful. You got your masters, and you were successful. You've just completed a PhD in international politics: the very subject that Condoleezza Rice specializes in, and after eleven years of study, you're going to do the same thing that an uneducated, unqualified person would do? Why wouldn't you seize the moment, slip her your business card, and say, 'I have some constructive ideas about Middle Eastern relations with the West that I would love to speak with you about.'"

His eyebrows raised. "I didn't consider that," he said. "I will take this into deep thought before I make any decision." I still didn't understand where he was conflicted, but it was none of my business.

The way many immigrants approach Islam is almost in jest of the true objectives of Islam. They think anyone who is curious about Islamic prayer or Ramadan wants to be Muslim. They think that any crime against Arabs is a crime against Allah himself. They don't concern themselves with anyone else's oppression but their own. And when it comes to disagreement with others, they assume either one of two extremes—total polemics, using Islam as a cudgel, or total apologetics, aiming to placate non-Muslim politics.

On the other hand, the Prophet Muhammad said, "When Allah wants good for a person, he gives them understanding of religion."

But when a Muslim comes with an enlightened idea—an idea that solves a problem, or makes something easier to accomplish, or offers an alternative, more critical, view of Islam—they're rejected completely.

There's enlightenment and then there's education. We need more enlightened thinkers. Fewer imams, more leaders. Most scholarly disciplines have almost no consensus. This is why situated knowledge is critically important. Muslims are looking for laws that apply for all time, but unfortunately *'ilm*, or knowledge, is far more nuanced and sophisticated than that.

Within theology there's the abstract and the practical. They vacillate to accommodate the human condition. True knowledge is defined as "useful ideas about the world and its creator that assist us in behaving in ways that bring benefit to ourselves and draw us closer to our objective." The accumulated knowledge of experience brings its branches, which we all share as experts.

What made Islam great in the past was that we were a faith of creators, but today we've been reduced to consumers. Is it possible that Allah gave all of us a living intellect to never come up with an original idea in religion? We're not allowed to broker our own thoughts, to ponder on an idea long enough that we come up with our own opinion about it.

Farid Esack, a Muslim scholar and activist who grew up in apartheid South Africa, writes about two kinds of religions—accommodationist and liberatory. He asserts that theology, across religious divisions, fulfills one of two tasks: it either supports and even blesses injustice, or it uses the process of praxis for comprehensive justice.

He argues that "The idea that the Quran can only be interpreted one way by a group of medieval super readers, linguists or historians is a false one. Rather this kind of approach underplays the temporal distance between text and interpreter and no one man or group can claim to have found the true meaning of what God intended in scripture."

I wholeheartedly agree with the idea that the Qur'an is a living document subject to reframing based on the social construct of a polity. If not, then the Qur'an as a guide and light is dimmed by archaic meanings and applications no longer relevant to any people striving to live with balance.

When Allah says he is the best of creators, he is emphasizing that his creation cannot be duplicated, but also this means there are more creators. He is also giving us license to make something! We weren't created as buckets to just be filled up; we were created to be springs that give life through our own experience. But everyone is afraid of questioning the popular Islamic narrative on YouTube and in books written seven hundred years ago; afraid of creating something of their own and being labeled a deviant, astray, or a reprehensible innovator.

Mainstream Islam suggests there is one way to understand God and it's cognitively based. Strangely this view is not based on the Qur'an. Allah is not A, B, C, D, E, et cetera. But all the books written about Allah are written in that fashion: "Memorize these 100 points and you've achieved salvation."

I agree with religious historian Jonathan Z. Smith's assertion in *Imagining Religion* where he essentially states that religion is the creation of the scholars' study.

We've made understanding Allah into a science project. Each group of theologians assert that they themselves have solved the great mystery of Allah's essence and all other Islamic sects outside of their narrow academic definition of Allah are at best astray. They answer theological questions with mundane statements that evoke more questions and require more clarification.

And when someone comes along and attempts to recenter the basic qur'anic description by insisting, "Hey, the Qur'an says, 'There's nothing like Allah.' Why isn't that sufficient? Why are we parsing and deconstructing Allah's description of himself? Who gave us license to do that?" Many Muslims will accuse this person of being an agent of Israel, a deviant, a liberal, and even an apostate.

The prophets of old came to break stale narratives and give justice to the vulnerable class. But today, religious institutions in the Middle East, where all religion originated, represent the "power class": that class of people removed from the oppressed masses and secluded in a world of isolation and profligacy. And it is our job to expose the ugly chain of capitalism, turned consumerism, turned atheism, turned idolatry, hidden behind the insidious mask of pretentious Islamic scholarship.

Many Islamic institutions outside of America are responsible for importing all the age-old theological controversies and distractions that keep Muslims in a perpetual state of theocide. *Theocide* is a term I coined to denote the perpetual doctrinal slaughtering of one Islamic group's theology over another, both groups condemning the other to hell forever because of a slight difference in creedal belief.

In the history of Islamic theological controversies, there was a moment in history called the *Mihna*, or the Inquisition. The great Islamic scholars of the Abbasid Caliphate in the ninth century were tortured and/or killed for insisting that the Qur'an was the true speech of Allah and not admitting (as the caliph wanted) that the Qur'an was in fact created.

This argument still rages today in certain Islamic circles, and it's still taught as if it matters and it's relevant today. Our children don't care if the Qur'an was created, or if it's the true speech of Allah. We're lucky if we can get them to believe that God even exists! We're blessed if they attend the masjid service with us! Why are we not addressing the issues that face our generation?

All these doctrinal disagreements have caused bloodshed, battles, war, poverty, and disunity and have subjected the entire Muslim world to the machinations of white supremacy and colonialism, which have led Muslims down the path of humiliation and deprivation in almost any way you can imagine.

All the while, no human being can prove or disprove any of the doctrinal claims made by these groups. It is all speculative knowledge using the same Qur'an to derive a million different conclusions, none of which are worth intrareligious fighting by Muslims.

Embracing Islam has become a succession of principles declared on the tongue, and a series of Arabic phrases pronounced perfectly, but it has almost no reality as it relates to morality and ethics.

This is why Islam is beginning to be rejected in the 'hood. The more that SAMs carry a toxic dogmatic version of Islam into the 'hood, the more other system-affected people are put off. People are exposed to world history on social media and the internet now. They may not know all of it, but they're realizing that Arabs were at one point the fulcrum of the African slave trade. They know Black and Brown people have suffered at the hands of Muslims. We don't need anyone outside of our context telling us how to worship God.

At one point, I was so busy defending the Middle Eastern man's version of Islam that I wasn't giving myself grace enough to live in my own experience and address my own traumas. I wasn't giving any of the other men grace enough to realize their own fragility.

This came to light one day when I was driving home after a long class inside Concord prison. I spent the day teaching the Names of Allah and how to use them according to the opinion of the scholars. I was listening to my Qur'an tape, trying to recite along, when suddenly a car came out of nowhere and cut me off as it entered the rotary. I swerved to avoid an accident, sped up next to the driver, and rolled down my window, "M@#$r F$%#r, are you out of your mind?!" I screamed at him, Muslim kufi cap on my head and all. I didn't even blink or hesitate to use that language or tone. There was no patience, no gratitude to Allah for avoiding an accident, and no grace for the other driver, only blue flames in front of my eyes.

A minute after I calmed down, I was embarrassed. I took stock of my entire day, spent telling the incarcerated Muslims I had just left, "Allah is *Al Ghafoor*—The Forgiving—and sheikh such and such says that we have to forgive others too!" They were easy principles to discuss, but very difficult to live out. I hadn't dug deep into my own triggers and fears. That would come later when I would use my own life as a scaffold for the ideas in Qur'an.

Sheikh Akram of Al-Salam Institute essentially teaches that Muslims think religion is what is seen by the people: praying, fasting, preaching, and reciting the Qur'an. But Islam is between an individual and her lord. It's what is seen by Allah: reverence, humbleness, sincerity, truthfulness and patience. No one can arrive at a sound belief without a sound intellectual understanding. You can believe and misunderstand too. Most people start with a sincere thought, "Islam is for me." But then they meet people that feed them branded ideas of Islamic supremacy and partisanship that reignite their egos until they persist in perpetuating the same behavior they had before Islam but just with an Islamic verbal IQ.

I've learned to be suspicious of absolutism. No one can speak about Allah's description or Islamic law with complete certainty. The seemingly benign labels Muslims use to identify our strain of practice— Hanafi, Maliki, Shafi'ee, and Hanbali—or our strain of theology— Ashari, Maturidi, or Athari—or our strain of methodology—Salafi, Tablighi, Ikhwaani, Sufi, Shia—they all are absolutist and contribute to normalizing partisanship.

Allah says, "And they did not become divided until after knowledge had come to them—out of jealousy and animosity between themselves."

Half of those labels are names of men. For a religion insistent on not idolizing human beings, you would think there'd be some critical thinking around naming your entire belief system after a man. You could go anywhere in the Muslim world and say you're Hanafi or Hanbali, the names of two founders of *fiqh* schools, but God forbid you say that you're Muhammadi, after the Prophet Muhammad, the founder of Islam. Muslims will vilify you, "We don't worship Muhammad," they'd say.

Allah says clearly, "He named you Muslims in the past and in this Revelation."

All names outside of labeling ourselves *Muslim* have been very harmful to the morale, safety, and unity of Muslims all over the world. And where there is disunity in Islam, women, Blacks, and non-Muslims are bound to become victims of that narrative.

11

SHIRLEY WORLD

Teaching Restorative Islamic Theology

AFTER SPENDING SIX years away from prison chaplaincy, learning, teaching, and growing, I decided I needed to return. I was one year into a doctoral program for leadership psychology at William James College. Although I benefited tremendously from learning the neuroscience behind leader and followership, I transferred to Boston University to pursue a more faith-based doctorate in transformational leadership.

With so much new information swelling my heart and mind, I felt it was a necessary act to go back inside the prison industrial complex to restore and repair the tainted Islamic framing I had ushered in twelve years prior. I knew this was what Allah wanted from me because when I called the Department of Correction just to inquire if there was a position open, it was as if they were waiting for me. "Tay! So happy to hear from you! There's a position open in Shirley Correctional Facility! We'd love to have you back!"

When I told my wife I wanted to go back into prison chaplaincy, she was reticent. "Are you sure you want to put yourself through that pain again? You were always occupied with those brothers' problems. And it literally got you sick." She saw how much anguish I felt when I couldn't solve their problems and she was the one who would have to coach me out of that sunken place.

I told her I felt that I had to go back, but this time I had a different plan. I would teach Restorative Theology, and I would base it on my audience and not on centuries-old books. She knew I was a different Muslim by then and told me she would support my decision no matter what. That's all I needed to hear.

Once I had her support, within a month I bid farewell to Facing History, took a huge salary cut, and headed back into prison with a new identity and mission: to teach Restorative Islamic Theology.

This time, gone were the long Islamic thobes that characterized my previous stint. Now I wore a white button-down shirt, Timberland boots, and chinos every day. My demeanor was much more friendly and relaxed. I smiled at the correctional officers and offered greetings to the administrators. I felt like the Islam I was carrying today was the Islam of the Prophet Muhammad. I also knew that, once the incarcerated brothers saw me and understood how much I'd changed both in my disposition and religious philosophy, I would receive some pushback and there would be some unhappy campers.

Ironically, the land that Shirley prison is located on was purchased by the Commonwealth of Massachusetts from a Shaker community in 1903. The Shakers were an offshoot of the Quakers. They were pacifist, egalitarian, celibate, and welcoming to the orphan, the homeless, and the hungry. Because of that legacy, twisted on its head by a high-security paramilitary prison environment currently occupying the same physical space, there's a conflicted spirit of religion, reform, penitence, and oppression that permeates the camp and has an indelible influence on the hearts of all who walk the grounds.

My first week there I was greeted by some old faces who had been transferred from Concord prison. It was good to see the brothers. There were also some new men who were just as remarkable as the ones I knew in Concord.

There was Zakariyah, a guy who was well respected in the prison and the *de facto* leader of the Muslims. Zak was very knowledgeable about Islam, but as a rugged intellectual. He was dark-skinned, good looking, and stout, with a thick black beard peppered with gray. His smile could light up a room, although he was mostly serious all the time. He was my clerk and would help me keep my office clean, run prison errands for me, and file my paperwork. He was paid $1 a day. Zak was twenty-six years into a natural life sentence.

There was also Sheikh Jaffar, an older Cape Verdean gentleman, who had already done twenty-five years in the federal system and had just been recently transferred back to Massachusetts where he was from, to finish the final ten years of his sentence. He was brown-skinned, handsome, and reminded me of my uncles. He was my second clerk. He and I would spend hours chatting about life, politics, and society.

The rest of the men were also very happy to see me. They had heard about my first time in Concord and were looking forward to learning more Islamic sciences from me, even though they had already spent the previous ten years learning Islamic sciences from a very knowledgeable imam and close friend of mine, Abdul-Latif, who was the Muslim chaplain in Walpole, another state prison.

Little did they know I had no intention of teaching any more Islamic sciences.

When I had my first few sessions with the men, I was focused on building rapport. We laughed, joked, and carried on without one word of Islam. I didn't want to come in like a "Know-it-all, Mr. Imam Dr. Harvard chaplain," who had come to save everyone from themselves. It was important for me to melt into the culture of fraternity they had already established.

While at Facing History, I had spent some time with Elizabeth Dopazo. She was forced to become a Hitler Youth during the Holocaust. She was eighty-eight when I met her in 2017. Small in stature with a huge, bright, charming personality, she managed to take such a dark subject and make it palatable for young people during the speeches she would give at high schools. Her parents had been killed in concentration camps by the Nazis for being Jehovah's Witnesses and refusing to pledge allegiance to Hitler. She somehow survived to tell her story.

She was a genuinely funny woman. She would invite me into her home whenever I dropped her off and pack me a bag full of knitted winter hats she'd made by hand for all my children. She loved people and people loved her. You would never know what she had endured from the way she carried herself.

Dark knowledge, that is, the witnessing of bloodshed, violence, and suffering with the naked eye, is a type of sacred trust that not everyone can handle. I decided after meeting her that the best way to approach heavy topics is with a light heart. That's how I attempted to present myself at Shirley.

She reminded me of a hadith of the Prophet Muhammad, who went to some of his companions who were laughing and told them, "Indeed, if you knew what I know you would laugh less and weep more." At that moment, the angel Gabriel came to him and said, "Indeed, God says to you, 'Why do you put despair in his servants?'"

The gist is that Muhammad had been privy to visions of the dead in their graves, and the destruction on the Day of Resurrection, but those companions did not know what he knew and were therefore excused from constant contemplativeness. I understood that what I had to offer the brothers in Shirley was going to be very different from the usual flavor, and although I knew how much the process of self-reflection and restorative theology had benefited my own identity, I didn't want to pretend to be profound. So, we laughed together for a few weeks.

When I finally started my first intensive session with the men, they brought their pens and pads and dressed in their best prison attire to receive what they thought was going to be something along the lines of *mustalah hadith*, hadith terminology, or perhaps *Usool al-fiqh*, the foundational sciences of jurisprudence. Instead, I spoke about the need to be personally accountable for yourself and not for the Islamic caliphate that so many Muslims emphasized.

I said, "So when anyone says, 'We need an Islamic government,' when you look at the lives of the prophets, none of them lived in an Islamic government and yet they were righteous. Because if you're good, you're good, wherever you are: in the bathroom, at the grocery store, in the desert, the jungle, or in prison."

I continued, "That's why we're not impressed with bad people who do good things. If you say, 'Well, he killed thousands of people, but he did give charity,' we don't measure him on the good things he did, we measure him on the bad things he did. Because both good and bad people do good things. You can only look at the extent of a person's transgressions if you're going to decide if he or she is truly a decent human being or not."

This seems simple, but they were looking for technical bullet points and precise rulings to be written on the board, not philosophy about moral relativism. I ended with, "It's not about establishing Islamic governments all over the world. That's not even in Qur'an. What's mentioned in Qur'an is to establish the government of your heart."

I saw them squirming. Most didn't move their pens one time. What was this new mystic speech I was giving? Some brothers voiced dissension. But that was fine too. I gave them a spiritual pass.

Everyone needs a pass sometimes. I was empowered by two things: I understood their mentality (because they were me fifteen years prior) and I understood what I was capable of in terms of my knowledge-base and experience. There was no reason for me to be upset or offended. This was new territory for all of us.

Back in my hustling days, one of my big homies, Lefty, had given me about eight ounces of crack cocaine to hold for him. Shortly thereafter an indictment came down and several of his associates were swept off the street by police. I didn't see Lefty for over a month. I usually saw him once or twice a week. I didn't know what to do with the drugs, so I asked another big homie and he said, "Lefty is on the run. Sell it and keep the money for yourself. He won't be back for a while."

It's not like I could donate the drugs to charity or give them to Lefty's family. I didn't know his family. Besides that, altruism was the furthest from my mind. I was in shark mode. So, I broke the eight ounces down into dime bags and made about fourteen thousand dollars.

Lo and behold, about two years passed. The money had long since been spent. I was at a New Year's Eve celebration in a nightclub when I spotted none other than Lefty sitting at the bar decked out in a winter fur coat, big gold chain, and diamond rings. I froze. Lefty was six feet three inches and two-hundred-and-forty pounds of hulk, and not someone to play with. I had seen him punch a man down a flight of stairs and knock him out cold. I was nervous, but running wasn't in my DNA. I decided I would address the problem head on and deal with the consequences. I made my way to the bar until we both made eye contact. He gave me a sly smile. His eyes said, *Don't you owe me eight ounces of crack cocaine?*

He bent down to yell in my ear over the loud music, "What up Ty Ty?" I yelled back to him in his ear, "Ain't nothing big dog. I know you left me with your stuff. I looked for you, and I waited, but I couldn't find you." I stopped talking directly in his ear and backed up so we could make eye contact again. I wanted to check his temperature. He looked intoxicated, but there was no trace of anger. I leaned back in, "I got rid of it. But if you still need it, let's talk about how I can get it back to you."

Lefty smiled and patted me on the shoulder. He was satisfied with my explanation. "That's nothing. I hope you ate!" He gave me that sly eye again. I laughed out loud and nodded in the affirmative. I was relieved.

Lefty let me go that night and I was grateful. I never saw him again. God bless him. We were all tangled together in a web of flashy poverty.

Lefty understood the same two things I understood about the brothers who expressed some hesitancy about my class: my mentality and his capability. One, I was a young kid desperate for cash, and two, he could've beaten me up in that club if he wanted to.

I had to pay that energy forward with some of the young guys in Shirley. Of course, my context wasn't about violence, but I would give many of them spiritual passes when they would fuss or act out of character about my lessons, because I knew they were sincere and in search of a life-giving message.

Meanwhile, I was up late most nights, sitting at my computer crafting a deeply personal approach to faith for system-affected Muslims in the form of Restorative Islamic Theology.

These men needed to learn *imaan*, or true faith. True faith couldn't be found in books and true faith couldn't be achieved without first addressing the hidden damage that had been done to their hearts and minds. Restorative Islamic Theology is my way of centering system-affected lives within the canon of Islam. The lessons would focus on healing and repairing the harm done by childhood trauma and corrosive Islamic rulings which combined to create a double-conscious Muslim.

My first course of action was to address what I called "legacy self." I began to ask about their family histories. I introduced them to the concept of dark mentors: people who love you but are fundamentally bad. I told them to begin journaling about their dark mentors: What was redeeming about them? What did they learn from them? And finally, could these men forgive their dark mentors for leading them astray?

I told them to find out how many generations they could go back into their family history. What occupations did their great-great grandparents hold? Were they factory workers? Landowners? They started to understand what I was trying to elicit in them: a sense of attached purpose from the before to the now. The seeds were beginning to be planted and I saw the spark in their eyes.

Ali, a young, good-looking Haitian man who always managed to keep a clean haircut and new sneakers after seventeen years in prison, found out by questioning his extended family over the phone that he was related to a man who fought alongside Toussaint Louverture in the slave rebellion of 1803. He stood at the whiteboard and brought names, dates, and places, to the surprise of the entire class. His ancestors were a family of successful farmers. Ali said this made him feel as though his family had a legacy of producing and giving life and not taking and destroying. After Ali, they all wanted to find out more of what made them who they were now.

After several weeks of "legacy self," we dove into "self-management," which included a step-by-step analysis of their individual lives from early childhood to the present day, using verses of the Qur'an and hadith of the Prophet Muhammad as the backdrop.

The trust that grew from these exercises was like none I had ever experienced in prison chaplaincy. I told them, "To learn as adults we must be comfortable not knowing, not being right, asking for help, admitting mistakes. Then we must teach ourselves what to care about, which would mean moving from *law* to *spirit*."

I embraced this notion as a life-giving concept for myself after a friend of mine, Rabbi Or Rose, and I began to discuss the burden of being clergy who are expected to absorb everyone's pain and suffering, but not allowed to experience it ourselves. We've both faced debilitating anxiety and continue to look for ways to ease that mental illness.

One gratifying way I've found to be helpful is to just admit that I need a break: to embrace my own powerlessness and know that Allah is the only Perfect and Powerful One.

I wanted the men to know that I too was trying to do my own mental/emotional work.

Many of the men were beginning to see the benefit. It wasn't hadith they needed to master, it was their feelings. It wasn't *fiqh* rules they should be concerned about bending, it was mending relationships they had broken.

I understood from my doctoral work in leadership psychology that through cognitive behavioral therapy all actions are governed by a combination of thought and feeling. And our beliefs about events influence our feelings and in turn influence our actions. The most effective way to change maladaptive behaviors is to address cognitive distortions or maladaptive thoughts. If you ask a man, "Why did you shoot such and such?" He may answer, "Because of my gang rules." That's his answer, but not necessarily his *reason*.

Cognitive behavioral therapy assumes that, if someone is repeating maladaptive behaviors, you don't intervene around the behaviors or feelings, you go to the thoughts. You can control or change thoughts. This was how I used the Qur'an and hadith to teach Restorative Islamic Theology.

You can change anyone temporarily with power and force, but when they reach saturation they'll stop changing because they've become immune to the power and force. Prison life breeds immunity. However, Restorative Islamic Theology says while you can't unkill someone, you can produce new meaning from the experience, and save another's life through mentorship. As Allah says, "And whoever saves a life it is as if they have saved all of mankind."

When it came to the very controversial but popular topic of *aqeedah*, I would ask, "What is your network of creedal ideas? Not theirs, yours?" I wanted to know in a very rudimentary way, without dogma, how they believed in God.

I was trying to move them away from the paradoxical language of traditional Islamic *aqeedah* and into the universality of Abrahamic creed. I did this through something a Christian colleague of mine calls "apocalyptic theology"—if the world were overrun by zombies or a nuclear holocaust—may Allah protect us—what would be important about being Muslim if we had to start over?

The men would journal a list of twenty things, but we had to agree on the top five.

The list would inevitably come down to the most germane things:

- unity
- formal prayer
- gathering strong people

- gathering smart people
- structure and organization

When the men began to realize that names, labels, and the minutiae of worship wouldn't matter, I saw their dogmatic stances begin to loosen. One brother commented, "If these values are the only principles necessary during an apocalypse, then they must be the only important principles that matter, period."

I implemented a program called "Experiments with the Truth." Each week we would take one objective to practice: not using curse words for twenty-four hours every day for seven days; not telling even a small lie for the same period; finding someone outside of their worldview to share a meal with; calling home and asking someone to forgive them; writing a letter of gratitude to someone who nurtured them as children.

The chivalry that began to emerge was remarkable.

There was a correctional officer named Tommy who oversaw the building where both my office and the prison masjid were located. He was known as a wise guy to the incarcerated men, Muslim and non. Department of Correction officers were generally always polite and professional. I liked many of them. Tommy always treated me with respect. He would come see me in the morning and ask if I needed anything. He was a comical guy and he and I always greeted each other with enthusiasm and smiles. He had been in prison corrections for over twenty years. He was Sicilian and always game to tell a good story. I'd walk down the hallway and find him holding court surrounded by ten staff members. "So I told the guy kiss my @#$!" he'd be wrapping up a long story to the laughter and amusement of everyone.

When I first started working in Shirley, Tommy would come into the masjid space while all of us were there. He would step on the prayer rugs with his boots and disregard any reverence we had for our sacred space because he was in charge. Some of the men would always start to chastise him with anger, but I would give them a silent headshake and an indication to let him have his way.

Tommy couldn't help himself. He loved a good racial joke and, being in a prison environment, I had to respect the code of conduct. No one was off limits. Tommy told jokes about all races, including his own.

One day while we were in my office engaged in a somewhat serious conversation about Italy and colonization, Tommy says, "Yeah, the Blacks raped our women so that's why I'm Sicilian dark." I was stunned. He was telling me that Black people had raped all the nice white Italian women and thus made him somewhat Black. Of course, Tommy had to throw in a joke with it, "And that's why the ladies say I'm hung so good!" I ignored those kinds of jokes, but he always got a kick out of himself. He was a simple-minded man.

When Tommy made the remark about Blacks raping Italian women, I didn't offer a rebuttal. My instinct was to correct him with an emotional response. But my experience had taught me that, as a Muslim and Black religious leader, I needed to learn tolerance for people and their lived experience.

This was something I called taking "strategic losses"; that is, when you understand that reacting to an adverse situation would cause more harm than not. I always stressed to the brothers that life for a responsible Black or Brown man comes with many strategic losses. It has nothing to do with bravery or cowardice. There was no American man more courageous in the twentieth century than Dr. Martin Luther King Jr., and he mastered the art of taking strategic losses.

I was learning the difference between racism and ignorance. Tommy was just ignorant and no amount of my righteous anger or correction about true history was going to change that. I had to pick my battles.

But after being encroached upon by Tommy and his cocky demeanor time and time again, we were growing uncomfortable. Some of the brothers and I decided we were going to try a different approach with him. We were going to use the restorative theology we were learning.

We made sure to intentionally treat him with respect. Zak began taking a few seconds to say good morning to him, which for incarcerated men was a big no-no. *Never speak to cops*, was the motto. But Zak had proven his street credibility for decades and now was a mature leader who set the tone for other incarcerated Muslim men to follow. It was important that he participated as a responsible party. He was deeply committed to being a restorative Muslim. Sheikh Jaffar, being a seasoned prison veteran himself, began making small talk with Tommy daily, and both he and Zak would immediately honor any request he made.

A strange thing began to happen. After a few months of our new approach, when Tommy would come into the masjid, he no longer stepped on our prayer rugs, but would instead actively avoid them. He even began to ask permission before he entered!

After a year of giving him deference and showing him the respect he thought his position warranted, he began to let us do whatever we wanted. He even fought the administration to get us an air conditioner inside the masjid space. I overheard him arguing with the captain, saying, "Those guys are in there trying to worship God, and you got them in the hell fire already, it's so damn hot in there!"

Allah confirmed our restorative approach when, during the COVID-19 pandemic, Sheikh Jaffar got deathly ill. I wasn't allowed in the prison at the time, as all civilian employees were working from home during quarantine. But as Sheikh Jaffar told it, "I was laying in the infirmary taking my last breaths of air. I couldn't breathe at all, and the nurses were ignoring me. I didn't have the energy or breath to call out, so I laid there and prepared myself to meet Allah."

He continued, "But as I lay there, I saw a face at the window, it was Tommy. He opened my cell door and said, 'Hey, are you okay, Jaffar?' When I didn't answer, he yelled a Code Red into his walkie talkie. The hospital staff rushed in, and an ambulance sped me to the local hospital where the doctor told me had I not gotten there when I did, I would've been dead in an hour. Tommy saved my life."

Allah had showed us the power in restorative theology: to act with intention to repair instead of reproach. By practicing true Islamic chivalry on him, Tommy's heart had softened for incarcerated Black and Brown Muslim men until he worked to save one's life.

When he was initially on his power trip, we could've told him about himself, but instead we showed him about himself and the goodness he was capable of. All the Muslims were very grateful to Tommy for helping Sheikh Jaffar.

After addressing our personal lives and our belief system, I taught the men that Restorative Islamic Theology understands that power is a central concept in analyzing social structure. Power is always relative. When we say *power* we mean *authority*, which is power that is socially legitimate on some level.

The prophets were always rhetorically asking, "What are the metrics of equality under the circumstances I am in?" And they would respond accordingly. They understood that the modalities of solutions must evolve.

Therefore, I exhorted the men, for us to change our collective social condition we needed to recalibrate the stories and identities in the Qur'an to fit our context. Jesus needed to become an unhoused man of color terrorized by law enforcement. His mother, Mary, needed to become a teen mother rejected by her community. Moses needed to become a community activist. His mother, Jocabed, needed to become a single Black mother who fears for her son's life. The stories need to make sense for us if we were to draw on their lessons.

I used Islamic texts as a foundation and then I began to build a framework of leadership based on the diverse collection of authors and leaders I had become familiar with.

We read books like *Grit* by Angela Duckworth, and discussed what that meant for our emerging identities as restorative Muslim citizens.

This method served me and the men to the purpose. I admonished them for not branching out in their reading interests: "We all want to be Muslim leaders, but it's impossible to consider yourself a leader in this contemporary world of information without being intimately familiar with its vices, virtues, types of peoples, varying philosophies, ever-transforming politics, and social ramifications."

Concerning the history and legacy of criminal justice in America, this system, which is the unholy offspring of chattel slavery, is so violent and pernicious in its nature, so insidious in its implementation, that it can only be successfully countered by emphasizing the same tools utilized through restorative theology: public acts of patience, wisdom, and compassionate truth.

This concept is embodied in Dorothy Day's words: "And the works of war are the exact opposite of the works of peace, feeding the hungry when we are destroying crops, and sheltering the homeless when we are destroying villages, wiping out cities. It's all the way through right down the line, the opposite."

This is a remarkable way to counter evil; classify it and do its exact opposite. As we witnessed with Tommy, when we approach darkness with micro acts of public love, we help to stamp out the mutuality of enmity. It's very empowering and, while pacifist in nature, it is aggressive in scope.

Allah says: "We bring forward the Truth to crush and destroy falsehood; it is doomed to be banished. Woe to you for your way of thinking about God!"

There's always tension around which one of my two identities should deserve the most advocacy, my Islamic identity or my identity as a Black man in America? Frankly speaking, the intersectionality of both is undeniable, but being a Black man in America contains far more historical risk and a greater sense of urgency for me.

And because of that, in Shirley I was ready to teach that the first line of order is for Black and Brown people to learn about themselves and then work from there. You can't be spiritual without first addressing who you are physically, mentally, and emotionally.

Just as Howard Thurman suggests that we define our enemy, we must also define ourselves, our allies, our heroes, and our own legends to find contentment and happiness in the approval of our own people because, as Thurman emphasizes, to capitulate to oppression "may involve a repudiation of one's heritage, one's custom and one's faith."

This time around as a prison chaplain, I understood what had been totally lost during my first tenure: that when we begin to establish a construct of what it means to be Black, Muslim, positive, and participatory we can then begin to search for systemic solutions.

After four years of extensive restorative work, I felt I had somewhat redeemed my former missteps and established a new precedent. Some of the so-called "unsalvageables" I counseled and taught became Boston College students in prison because of the restorative identity work we had been doing together. Many had mended broken family relationships, and many had come to terms with their trauma. They were ready to serve Allah with a clean heart.

The praise was for Allah. My job was done.

By 2022, I wanted to get back to establishing my own business. I knew I couldn't speak the truth about prison abolition and my new restorative lens of Islam until I had my own independent source of income. But I was afraid to leave the security of my job. I was afraid of falling on my face again and losing everything I had built in the last ten years. My wife sensed I was itching to move on. She told me, "You can't count on anyone to make your dreams come true. You have to do it yourself. I believe Allah loves you. So go and bring your dreams to life with his help. And if it doesn't work, we'll just start over until it does, insha'Allah."

That was what I needed to hear. I left Shirley and founded Spentem.

12

GRATITUDE

People Are at the Heart of the Matter

PRISON ABOLITION IS not about getting rid of all prisons, it's about getting rid of the conditions that make prison necessary. We believe that American poverty is manufactured, which in turn creates an exploited class of people—people who are mentally and emotionally affected by severe deprivation, which causes maladaptive behavior.

Prison abolition imagines a world where the "breadbasket of goods"—proper health care, education equity, and adequate housing—is available to this exploited class. And it also imagines a society where people who violate the public social contract are treated with mental and emotional rehabilitation that restores fractured hearts and minds back to health.

But for that to happen, American policymakers must not only see value in Black and Brown lives but, believe it or not, they must find gratitude for the rich cultural contribution they've made to the fabric of American society.

Ibn Qayyim wrote that the foundation of worship is love. He didn't mean a sentimental love but instead love as an internal variant of gratitude. I believe that teaching and counseling is also connected with love, and so is healing. That's why it's so difficult for the prison population to truly become rehabilitated. They've been shown no love because few see their value. You can only love someone when you understand their value, which in essence, is being grateful for their existence. When you're grateful for other identities you make them feel a sense of belonging. Black people are always made to feel like orphans, both in America and in Islam.

I really came to appreciate how much belonging mattered after a friend of mine from Facing History, Jody Snider, a producer on a 2023 Oscar-nominated documentary called *Stranger at the Gate*, invited me to the premiere. I initially thought it was just another film about inter-religious relations. Nevertheless, I attended because I was honored that she would think enough to invite me. As the half-hour film unfolded, I found myself wiping tears away from my face in the dark. I don't like to cry in front of white people.

The true story is about Richard McKinney, a trauma-affected American war veteran who, because of his hatred for the Muslims he fought in Iraq and Afghanistan, decides he's going to blow up a masjid in America, "his" country. He surveils one particular masjid and then enters as a stranger "interested" in Islam, to assess the logistics of where to put his bomb. Eventually, he returns a few times and is so over-whelmed by the compassion and hospitality he receives, he converts to Islam.

In this author's humble opinion, Mr. McKinney's conversion wasn't because he discovered how great Islam was. He converted because those immigrant Muslims in the masjid loved on him. He was desperately in need of public tenderness.

If he'd entered a golf club and they made him feel loved, he would've become a golfer. I don't want to insult his faith. I have met Mr. McKinney, and I do consider him a true Muslim. But the point I'm trying to make is that helping people through their personal struggles of isolation, depression, and self-hate with a gentle smile or small gesture of public love can be far more effective than the dissemination of dogma about religion.

I cried involuntarily because I thought about my incarcerated brothers. Prison is the only place they feel truly accepted. In retro-spect, it is the only place I feel truly accepted. In fact, I would say that I've never felt as safe in my entire life—not even tucked away in my own bed—as I have when sitting in a circle of incarcerated Muslim brothers.

There is something so meaningful about feeling loved and accepted by your peers that surpasses any value that intellectual principles bring. I miss prison. Because I miss being loved in that way by those men.

I disagree that the popular correct religious methodology should be *believe, behave, then belong.* I believe it should be *belong, behave, then believe.*

Kindness is not overrated. People want space to be made for them, so they can feel warmly owned by something greater than themselves, before you can assume they will behave according to your expectations and then believe as you believe. We are a human race in reckless need of being adored.

Names, divisions, and categories of people *do* matter. This is not a dismissal of our individual beliefs and identities. While I don't mean to trivialize our differences, I want to highlight how our lives and views are shaped by our experiences.

My story is about being touched by so many different hands along the way, until I could no longer see who touched me first, or for the longest. But it's also about those who haven't been touched by others and how that shapes their worldview and actions, whether bigoted religious types or criminals who have never had anyone lift them up as children.

For me—whatever Paradise looks like, I hope that I might be in the company of my brothers who were incarcerated in Concord and Shirley. Those were the safest moments of my life. The greatest moments. The most profound and spiritual.

In the early 1990s, Notorious B.I.G. rapped in one of his songs that, "Being broke at thirty, give a n$#$a the chills." I remember sitting in the passenger seat of my friend Cheddar's Volvo and listening attentively. It was profound. We were trapped by the trappings of the Trap. At the time we heard it we were barely twenty years old. But we took that quote, and later drank Mad Dog 20/20 to it, and plotted how we would avoid having the chills by thirty years old. It was the type of vulgar hope we needed.

But today, after living longer than many of my childhood friends, I know differently. I watched my buddies be killed off in rapid succession: first Jeff, then Joel, then Ronni, then Twon, then Booga, then Tommy, then my cousin Rizz, then Mike, then Boo, and I could go on . . .

As I write this, I'm a forty-seven-year-old father of nine children. I've got almost five decades of stress, pressure, responsibility, and Black anxiety on my dead friends. They weren't privy to what forty-seven years of life experience brings. I know now that it's not the absence of money at thirty years old that gives a man the chills, it's the absence of a sense of purpose that does.

Allah says:

> We have commanded people to honor their parents. Their mothers bore them in hardship and delivered them in hardship. Their period of bearing and weaning is thirty months. In time, when the child reaches their prime at the age of forty, they pray, "My Lord! Inspire me to always be thankful for Your favors which You blessed me and my parents with, and to do good deeds that please You. And instill righteousness in my offspring. I truly repent to You, and I truly submit to Your Will."

A person at forty no longer prioritizes the horizontal plain. Priorities begin to shift to the legacy self—that piece of your existence to be left behind and inherited by your progeny and embraced by the world. What color shirt matches with what shoes starts to matter less than the mistakes you've made in raising your children, and the grace you've given others.

I've welcomed this period. My life is not how I imagined "better" would look. I pictured yachts in Miami, not snow in Massachusetts.

But my life is even better than yachts in Miami. Allah has given me everything I ever wanted, but he's also held me accountable along the way. Which makes me think he loves me. I pray that he does.

This story is not about me at all, but about the goodness of people. *People* are at the heart of all our successes. They lift us up and some even carry us until we can find the strength to carry ourselves. They are the superheroes I dreamed of becoming as a child.

The words of my mother encouraging me to work hard to become a superhero still linger. She was right. There *is* a mystery I could unlock if I worked hard enough. There *are* real superheroes. And there *is* someone who chooses others to become super. Those sentiments have stayed with me, tucked away in my heart even as I write these words. I'm still working hard, waiting to be chosen.

My life has not been a particularly pious one, nor has it been distinguished by scholarship. However, if read with an open heart, I believe this book will inspire some to see the subtle signs of God working to save a wretch like me. And in this, perhaps they could find true faith in him and compassion for the people he uses to rescue others.

And if I could have any part in inspiring another to find hope in God, then I conclude with the words of my brother Malcolm X, El-Hajj Malik El-Shabazz, who said, "The glory and praise is for Allah—only the mistakes have been mine."

Taymullah Abdur-Rahman
March 24, 2023/Ramadan 2, 1444 H

NOTES

Introduction

As guests of the state: *Masjid al-Haram* literally means "the place where everything not considered as worship is prohibited." It is the holiest site in Islam.

as well as access to the Kaabah: The Kaabah is the black cube-shaped edifice in the center of Mecca that serves as a primary focal point for Muslims all over the world to face during prayer. It was built by the prophet Abraham and his son Ismael as the first house of worship dedicated to Allah.

Chapter 1

We had Big Daddy Kane, Slick Rick: The term "Black and Brown," as used in this book, refers to those who descend from African, Latin, or Caribbean roots and were raised in Western society.

Studies link the adverse effect that parental incarceration has: Jeremy Travis and Michelle Waul, *Prisoners Once Removed* (Washington, DC: The Urban Institute Press, 2003), 204.

In sixth grade I dropped out of school completely: Travis and Waul, *Prisoners Once Removed,* 158.

Beyond the inner doors a guard is seated: Jonathan Kozol, *Savage Inequalities: Children in America's Schools* (New York: Broadway Books, 1991), 104, 105.

Paul Tillich, the twentieth-century Lutheran philosopher wrote: Paul Tillich, *Dynamics of Faith* (New York: Harper Perennial, 2001), 4.

Religious exhortation of people to raise their minds: Marie Augusta Neal, *A Sociotheology of Letting Go* (New York: Paulist Press, 1977), 20.

Black slaves were being taught: This label has its origins in an ad bought in the *New York Times*, "'Black Power' Statement by National Committee of Negro Churchmen," *New York Times*, July 31, 1966. The article reframed the Black struggle for freedom by contextualizing Christianity as the religion of the oppressed and using the Bible as a framework to justify this position.

Black slaves found hope in gathering secretly: John Boles, *Masters and Slaves in the House of the Lord: Race and Religion in the American South 1740–1870* (Lexington: University Press of Kentucky, 1988), 66–71.

"When de niggers go round singin'": Portraits of African American ex-slaves from the US Works Progress Administration, Federal Writers' Project slave narratives collections, 1970.

"Take him and mold and make": Big Daddy Kane, "Ain't No Half Steppin,'" composition and lyrics by Antonio Hardy, produced by Marley Marl. Cold Chillin Records, 1988.

"Too often the price exacted by": Howard Thurman, *Jesus and the Disinherited* (Boston: Beacon Press, 2012), 2.

But when their lead rapper Brother J rapped: "Funkin' Lesson," lyrics by Barbarella Bishop, Garry Marshall Shider, George Iii Clinton, George Jr. Clinton, Jason Richard Hunter, Linda Shider, Philippe Wynn, Ronald Ford, and Walter Morrison. © Universal Music Publishing Group.

"You ain't ready yet": "T.O.N.Y. (Top of New York)," lyrics by Carlos Broady, Kiam Holley, Nashiem Myrick, Percy Lee Chapman, and Victor Santiago. © The Administration MP Inc., Warner Chappell Music, Inc.

"In essence Rome was the enemy": Thurman, *Jesus and the Disinherited*, 12.

"I worship a Negro God": Henry Louis Gates Jr., *The Black Church* (New York: Penguin, 2021), 97.

"I paid my way through": Kendrick Lamar, "Untitled 2 (Blue Faces)," Top Dawg, Aftermath 2016. Kendrick Duckworth.

"Aiming high, passed the idea of slanging": Kid Cudi, "Mojo So Dope," lyrics by Anders Rhedin, Emile Haynie, Fridolin Nordsoe, Jannis Noya Makrigiannis, and Scott Mescudi. © Kobalt Music Publishing Ltd, Sony/ATV Music Publishing LLC.

"I guess we just pray like the minister say": Kanye West, "Heard 'Em Say," lyrics by Michael Masser, Gerald Goffin, Adam Noah Levine, and Kanye Omari West. © Universal Music/MGB Songs, Universal Music/Careers, Emi Blackwood Music Inc., Screen Gems/EMI Music Inc., Prince Street Music, Sudgee Music, and Please Gimme My Publishing Inc.

"Mirror mirror on the ceiling": Drake, "Diplomatic Immunity," lyrics by Matthew Samuels, Aubrey Graham, Nicholas Brongers, and Maneesh Bidaye. © Sony/ATV Tunes LLC, Sony/ATV Songs LLC, Stellar Songs Ltd, Sandra Gale, 1damentional Publishing, and LW Music GMR.

"Made in the image of God, that's a selfie": Jay-Z, "Jail," lyrics by Charles M. Njapa, Dwayne Jr. Abernathy, John Peter Moylett, Kanye Omari West, Malik Yusef, Mark Williams, Michael Dean, Raul Ignacio Cubina, Sean Solymar, Shawn Carter, and Warryn Jr. Campbell. © Kobalt Music Publishing Ltd, Songtrust Ave, Sony/ATV Music Publishing LLC, Universal Music Publishing Group, and Warner Chappell Music, Inc.

Chapter 2

"In terms of parenting however": Libra R. Hilde, *Slavery, Fatherhood and Paternal Duty* (Chapel Hill: The University of North Carolina Press, 2020), 13.

"Young black n---a trapped": "Dedication," written by Alexandria Denise Dopson, Axel Albert Morgan, Ermias Joseph Asghedom, J. Lewis, John Wesley Groover, Kendrick Lamar Duckworth, Lamar Daunte Edwards, Larrance Levar Dopson, and Malik Cox. © Concord Music Publishing LLC, Peermusic Publishing, Sony/ATV Music Publishing LLC, and Warner Chappell Music, Inc.

Chapter 4

In his final statement in the murder trial: The Legal Papers of John Adams, Case 64, Rex v. Wemms, pp. 260–70, The Soldiers Trial.

"self-fulfilling prophecy": When an original false social belief leads people to act in ways that objectively confirm that belief.

When Tupac rapped: "Fuck the World," written by Gregory E. Jacobs and Tupac Amaru Shakur. © O/B/O Capasso, Universal Music Publishing Group.

"Little Latasha": Latasha Harlins was a fifteen year-old Black girl murdered in Los Angeles in 1992 by Soon Ja Du, a female Korean store owner. Du shot Latasah in the back of her head after accusing her of stealing a bottle of orange juice. Ju was never given prison time, but instead was fined $500, and made to perform community service.

"As for the poets—the deviant people follow them": Qur'an, The Poets 26:224–26.

"Except for those who truly believe": Qur'an, The Poets 26:227.

"And do not trade Allah's covenant": Qur'an, The Bees 16:95.

"everything boils down to": The Bag is a euphemism for a big payday or final payoff, regardless of its origin, moral or otherwise.

"Toward the end of time music": Sahih Bukhari 5590, part of a longer hadith narrated by Abu Malik al-Ashari.

Chapter 5

"Do not prostrate to the sun or the moon": Qur'an, Surah Fussilat 41:37.

"And jinn we created before from smokeless fire": Qur'an, Surah Hijr 15:27.

"And no soul knows what joy": Qur'an 32:17.

In one of the Islamic books of fiqh: *Fiqh* is an Arabic word that literally means "understanding," but in this context loosely holds the meaning of "applying daily Islamic rulings to your life": how to wash for prayer, where to place your hands during prayer, what to say during prayer, what was permissible to eat and what wasn't, etc.

facing away from the qiblah: *Qiblah* is the Arabic word for the direction all Muslims face when we pray.

The next day we traveled to Mecca: Umrah is the lesser holy pilgrimage performed in Mecca. It lasts several hours and consists of certain actions and prayers.

Council of Senior Scholars: The Saudi Arabian Council of Senior Scholars is the governing body of religious law in Saudi. Its members advise the king and act as Saudi Arabia's version of the United States Supreme Court.

Chapter 6

historian Kambiz GhaneaBassiri writes: Kambiz GhaneaBassiri, *A History of Islam in America* (Cambridge: Cambridge University Press, 2010).

Built by Muslim migrants for use as a place of worship: Sally Howell, "Laying the Groundwork for American Muslim Histories 1865–1965," in *The Cambridge Companion to American Islam*, ed. Juliane Hammer and Omid Safi (Cambridge: Cambridge University Press, 2013), 45.

This is because the census currently: Institute for Social Policy and Understanding, "Who Are White Muslims?" April 30, 2021, https://www.ispu.org/who-are-white-muslims/; Pew Research Center, "Demographic Portrait of Muslim Americans," July 26, 2017, https://www.pewresearch.org/religion/2017/07/26/demographic-portrait-of-muslim-americans/.

"Virginia law defined a Black person": Race – The Power of an Illusion, PBS, accessed May 17, 2023, https://www.pbs.org/race/000_General/000_00-Home.htm.

According to a 2017 Pew research study: Institute for Social Policy and Understanding, "Who Are White Muslims?"

After the Egyptian and the Indian: W. E. B. Du Bois, *The Souls of Black Folk* (Oxford: Oxford University Press, 1903), 8.

the ninth-century hadith: Hadith are the recorded sayings and actions of the Arabian prophet Muhammad. They are considered a second source of guidance for all Muslims, after the Qur'an.

l-Bukhari: His full name was Muhammad ibn Isma'il al-Bukhari (d. 870). He is widely regarded as one of the most important scholars in the history of Islam as it relates to collecting the sayings and actions of the Arabian prophet Muhammad.

Negroes—that particular race: Edward William Lane, *Lane's Arabic–English Lexicon* (London: Williams and Norgate, 1863–93), vol. 4, #1463.

Ibn Qutayba: Muhammad 'Abd Allah ibn Muslim ibn Qutaybah al-Dinawari (d. 889). He was a prolific author of theology, philology, and literary criticism.

wrote that Wahb Ibn Munabbih: Wahb Ibn Munabbih was an early convert to Islam who was originally a Yemeni Jew. He was known for his narrations of *Israeliyyat,* or religious stories from the Jewish tradition.

Ninth-century Persian historian, al-Tabari: Abu Ja'far Muhammad
ibn Jarir ibn Yazid al-Tabari (d. 923) was a prominent Islamic
historian who also had expertise in qur'anic exegesis (*tafsir*).

Ibn Khaldun: Abu Zayd 'Abd ar-Rahman ibn Muhammad ibn Khaldun al-Hadrami (d. 1406) was an Arab traveler, philosopher, and
historian.

***dumb animals in his* Muqaddamah:** Often recognized as one of the
first writings on social science, *Muqaddamah* (Introduction) was
a look into the politics, demographics, and cultural history of
different peoples.

"*O mankind, indeed, We have created you*": Qur'an, Surah Hujurat
49:13.

Chapter 7

Shakir had successfully commissioned the Innocence Project: The
Innocence Project is a nonprofit organization founded by Barry
C. Scheck and Peter J. Neufield that helps to free men who are
falsely accused of crimes.

***she was a* kaafir:** *Kaafir* is the name Muslims use to designate non-
Muslims. Although sometimes used in a derogatory manner to
mean *infidel*, it is not an inherently antagonistic label. It derives
from the root Arabic word, *kufr*, which means "to cover," as
in "covering the truth of God." This label doesn't mean that a
Muslim should hate a *kaafir*, but there is simply no other Arabic
word for someone who does not believe in Islam.

"*Whoever puts their trust in Allah*": Qur'an, Surah Talaq 65:3.

Allah says: "The Bedouins say": Qur'an, Surah Hujurat 49:15.

There is nothing for man except what he strives for: Qur'an, Surah
Najm 53:39.

Some say he even allowed them: This claim comes from a very
respected book of qur'anic exegesis called *Tafseer ibn Katheer*,
reported from a scholar named ibn Ishaaq.

"*Go to Abyssinia*": A nomenclature for modern-day Ethiopia.

Among the people of the Book: "The people of the Book" is a general
designation for both Jewish people and Christians who follow
"the Book," meaning the Torah and the Gospel.

"*for Allah knows well the righteous*": Qur'an, Surah Al-Imran 3:113–15.

"Among the people of Moses": "The people of Moses" is a reference to those Jewish tribes who follow the Torah revealed to Moses.

"and by it establishes justice": Qur'an, Surah Araf 7:159.

"Bear witness that we have submitted ourselves": Qur'an 3:64.

"Fight in the way of Allah": Qur'an, Surah Baqarah 2:190–91.

"Allah does not forbid that you be kind": Qur'an, Surah Mumtahina 60:8–9.

"All Israel has transgressed thy law": Bible, Daniel 9:11.

"Jerusalem, Jerusalem, you who kill the prophets": Bible, Matthew 23:37.

"They [The followers of Moses] were stricken": Qur'an, Surah Baqarah 2:61.

"The Jews who join us as clients": Having "clients," or *Tabi ana* in Arabic, is a social practice where outsiders join a tribe to live alongside them.

"A man will not act unjustly": Muhammad Hamidullah, *The First Written Constitution in the World*, 3rd ed. (Lahore: Sh. Muhammad Ashraf Publishers, 1975).

"You will certainly find that the closest": Qur'an, Surah Maidah 5:82.

be allowed to give **dawah:** *Dawah* is the Arabic word for proselytizing.

"He placed the basin": Exodus 40:30.

"O you who have believed": Qur'an, Surah Maidah 5:6.

In a 2017 poll: Institute for Social Policy and Understanding, "Across Faiths, Black Americans Equally Likely to Experience Racism in Own Faith Community," accessed April 18, 2023, https://www.ispu.org/wp-content/uploads/2018/09/AMP-2017-23_Logo.png?x46312.

Chapter 8

"Then Allah sent a raven": Qur'an, Surah Maidah 5:31.

"Pray for forgiveness for your brother": Sahih Abu Dawood 3221.

"But not even it can escape": Reported from Abu Ayub al-Ansari in Sahih Bukhari.

"Hypocrisy from the weak is a sort of tribute": Thurman, *Jesus and the Disinherited*, 73.

"It is not righteousness that you turn your faces": Qur'an, Surah Baqarah 2:177.

"Oppression is worse than murder": Qur'an, Surah Baqarah 2:191.

I had more work to do: Nafs is the Arabic word for *ego* or *self*. It denotes the unseen soul of a human that desires attention, comfort, vengeance, passion, and satisfaction. It is the lowest part of the soul.

"you must take strategic losses": Dunya is the Arabic word for "the world," but, more specifically, the *stuff* in the world: our jobs, our bills, our possessions, all the things we covet. *Dunya* literally means "that which is low."

"Verily, your lives, your property": The day was Islam's holiest day, the Day of Arafah, when Muslims complete the final rituals of the Hajj. The month was Dhul Hijja, one of Islam's holiest months. The city was Mecca, Islam's holiest city. This hadith was reported by Abu Sulaiman in Hassan Tirmidhi.

stop and frisk: Stop and frisk is a law implemented in some inner cities, specifically in New York, that allows police to briefly stop anyone they have a reasonable suspicion of committing a crime or attempting to commit a crime. Obviously, police stopped any and every Black and Brown youth they wanted to. This makes walking down the street a subversive criminal act for people of color, and to randomly be stopped and patted down causes distress, anxiety, and humiliation.

three strikes: California's Three Strikes sentencing law was originally enacted in 1994. If a person convicted of any new felony had one prior conviction of a felony, they would be sentenced to state prison for twice the penalty of the crime. If the person was convicted of any felony with two or more prior strikes, the law mandated a state prison term of at least twenty-five years to life. Obviously, Black men were convicted and sentenced to life in prison over the pettiest of offenses. In 1997, Norman Williams was sentenced to twenty-five years to life for stealing a car jack from the back of an open tow truck. He had two previous nonviolent crimes on his record. Williams was released in 2009 with the help of the Three Strikes Project at Stanford Law School.

life without parole for juveniles: How can someone who is seventeen be sentenced to life with no chance of parole, but they can't buy alcohol or cigarettes in a convenience store because they're too young, they can't vote because they're too young, and they can't rent a car because they're too young?

I don't really see myself in the traditional sense: Eid is the annual celebration of Muslims all over the world, equivalent to Christmas, Easter, or Passover. It's a time to have dinner, visit family, exchange gifts, and rejoice. There are two Eids in Islam: Eid al-Fitrah, which happens after the last day of Ramadan, and Eid al-Adha, which happens after Hajj to commemorate the prophet Abraham's willingness to sacrifice his son for Allah.

I asked him to call the **iqaama:** *Takbeer* literally means to say *Allahu akbar* ("God is the greatest"). When a Muslim raises his or her hands with palms facing out and utters *Allahu akbar*, he or she has entered the formal prayer and is considered in a sacred state until the prayer is finished.

I gave up eating only **zabeehah** *meat:* Slaughtering an animal according to Islamic law means the animal is killed swiftly with a sharp knife that slits its throat, while the name of Allah is mentioned over the slaughter. The blood is drained out completely and sold in *halal* meat markets all over the country.

Chapter 9

"So believe in Allāh and His messengers": Qur'an 4:171.

"Allah has cursed alcohol": Sahih Abu Dawood.

"O you who believe!": Qur'an 5:90.

Hijabis: A *hijabi* is a Muslim woman who wears the head scarf, called a *hijab*.

"To study evil is to strengthen": Michael Berenbaum, Foreword to *The Holocaust Chronicle: A History in Words and Pictures*, by John Roth and Marilyn J. Harran (Lincolnwood, IL: Publications International, 2000), 11.

"Germans understood that no person": Richard Rubenstein, *The Cunning of History* (New York: Harper & Row, 1975), 33.

"O you who believe!": Qur'an, Surah Maidah 5:7.

Chapter 10

"The first thing among their deeds": Part of a longer hadith narrated by Abu Dawood, 864; classed as *sahih* by al-Albaani in Sahih Abu Dawood, 770.

"The cases which will be decided first": Al-Bukhari, al-Sahih, Hadith 6533, 6864.

Ibn Taymiyyah: Taqi ad-Din 'Ahmad ibn 'Abd al-Halim al-Harrani, who lived in the thirteenth and fourteenth centuries and was a Sunni Muslim scholar of jurisprudence, hadith, and law. He was also an ascetic, a warrior, and a traditionalist who was both hated and loved by multitudes of Muslims.

"Allah allows the just government": Al-Amir bil Maruf 1/29.

my university is inviting Condoleezza Rice: Former secretary of state under the George W. Bush Administration, who was instrumental in the war in Iraq and in the decimation of entire Muslim populations.

"When Allah wants good for a person": Sahih Bukhari 71.

"The idea that the Quran can only be interpreted one way": Farid Esack, *Quran Liberation and Pluralism* (Oxford: One World, 1998), 73.

"And they did not become divided": Qur'an 42:14.

"He named you Muslims in the past": Qur'an 22:78.

Chapter 11

There was also Sheikh: The term "Sheikh" can have several different meanings depending on context. It can mean "One who is learned in Islamic sciences or Qur'an" and in that case, even a young person can be considered a sheikh or sheikha (f.). In the case of Sheikh Jaffar, as it is with many older Muslims who have signs of gray hair, it is a title of honor meaning "one who is an elder and experienced."

"Indeed, God says to you": *Kitab al-'ilm.* Ibn Hibban narrates it in *Kitab al-Birr*, *hassan sahih* grade.

These men needed to learn **imaan:** *Imaan* (true faith) is not to be confused with *imam* (a Muslim leader).

"And whoever saves a life": Qur'an 5:32.

"And the works of war are": *Christopher Closeup* show, 1971.

"We bring forward the Truth": Qur'an 21:18.

"may involve a repudiation of one's heritage": Thurman, *Jesus and the Disinherited*, 13.

insha'Allah: *Insha'Allah* means "if God wills" in Arabic.

Chapter 12

Ibn Qayyim: Shams al-Din bin Abi Bakr al-Hanbali, a major fourteenth-century Sunni expert on Islamic law, theology, and spirituality. He was the foremost student of Ibn Taymiyyah and an author of major works that added value spiritually and jurisprudentially to the canon of Islam.

"Being broke at thirty": "Real Niggaz," written by Deric Michael Angelettie, Todd Eric Gaither, Kimberly Jones, and Christopher Wallace. Lyrics © Universal Music Publishing Group, Sony/ATV Music Publishing LLC.

We were trapped by the trappings of the Trap: Slang for "drug house or impoverished neighborhood."

We have commanded people to honor their parents: Qur'an 46:15.